Queen and Philosophy

Pop Culture and Philosophy®

General Editor: George A. Reisch

VOLUME 1 *Dave Chappelle and Philosophy: When Keeping It Wrong Gets Real* (2021) Edited by Mark Ralkowski

VOLUME 2 *Neon Genesis Evangelion and Philosophy: That Syncing Feeling* (2022) Edited by Christian Cotton and Andrew M. Winters

VOLUME 3 *The Ultimate Supernatural and Philosophy: Saving People, Killing Things, the Family Business* (2022) Edited by Richard Greene

VOLUME 4 *Dark Souls and Philosophy* (2023) Edited by Nicolas Michaud

VOLUME 5 *Pokémon and Philosophy* (2023) Edited by Nicolas Michaud

VOLUME 6 *Queen and Philosophy: Guaranteed to Blow Your Mind* (2023) Edited by Jared Kemling and Randall E. Auxier

VOLUME 7 *Punk Rock and Philosophy: Research and Destroy* (2022) Edited by Richard Greene and Joshua Heter

VOLUME 8 *Better Call Saul and Philosophy: I Think Therefore I Scam* (2022) Edited by Joshua Heter and Brett Coppenger

VOLUME 9 *Asimov's Foundation and Philosophy: Psychohistory and Its Discontents* (2023) Edited by Joshua Heter and Josef Simpson

VOLUME 10 *Warren Zevon and Philosophy* (2023) Edited by John E. MacKinnon

VOLUME 11 *The Godfather and Philosophy* (2023) Edited by Joshua Heter and Richard Greene

VOLUME 12 *Anthony Bourdain and Philosophy* (2023) Edited by Scott Calef

VOLUME 13 *Post-Punk and Philosophy* (2024) Edited by Joshua Heter and Richard Greene

For full details of all Pop Culture and Philosophy® books, and all Open Universe® books, visit www.carusbooks.com

Pop Culture and Philosophy®

Queen and Philosophy

Guaranteed to Blow Your Mind

Edited by

Jared Kemling and

Randall E. Auxier

OPEN UNIVERSE
Chicago

Volume 6 in the series, Pop Culture and Philosophy®, edited by George A. Reisch

To find out more about Open Universe and Carus Books, visit our website at www.carusboooks.com.

Printed and bound in the United States of America. Printed on acid-free paper.

Queen and Philosophy: Guaranteed to Blow Your Mind

ISBN: 978-1-63770-032-7

This book is also available as an e-book (978-1-63770-033-4).

Library of Congress Control Number: 2022951891

Contents
(We Will Rock You)

A Kind of Magic ix

I Some Body to Love 1

1. Love of My Life?
ANDREW KAPLAN 3

2. Good Old-Fashioned Lover Boy
DARCI DOLL 15

II Stone Cold Crazy 27

3. I'm Going Slightly Mad
SNITA AHIR-KNIGHT 29

4. Hitting Rock Bottom
ROBERT S. VUCKOVICH 39

5. Creatures of the Dark and the Light
RANDALL E. AUXIER 53

III A Night at the Concert 67

6. Be Free with Your Tempo
DOUGLAS RASMUSSEN 69

7. Performance as a Tour de Force
JULIE KUHLKEN 79

8. The Quintessence of Queen
RANDALL E. AUXIER 91

9. Vulgar Romanticism and Prog Rock
JAN OLOF BENGTSSON 105

IV The Show Must Go On 121

10. Is Adam Lambert a Killer of Queen or Somebody to Love?
MEGAN VOLPERT 123

11. Is Red Special a Member of Queen?
STEVEN GIMBEL 133

V Made in the Heavens 147

12. Hot Spacetime
KRISTINA ŠEKRST 149

13. The Mystic Art of Music
RANDALL E. AUXIER 159

VI Supersonic Men 171

14. He Will Rock You
MICHAEL F. PATTON 173

15. My Uncle's Delicacy of Taste and Passion
CHRISTOPHER M. INNES 183

VII Sheer Head Attack 193

16. Don't Lose Your Head
KEVIN TAYLOR 195

17. Hammer to Fall in the Shadow of Death
ROBERT DEVALL 207

18. We Want to Love Forever, Forever Is Ours Today
JOHN SHOOK 217

VIII My Fairy Kings 229

19. Master Stroke of a Fairy Feller
JARED KEMLING 231

20. Worshiping the White Queen (As It Began)
JARED KEMLING 245

Bibliography (I Want It All) 259

Bohemian Biographies 263

Index (Now I'm Here) 267

A Kind of Magic

Magic. That's what they called it . . . and we have to believe them, don't we? What other word is there? Four paths, four unique voices—lovingly harmonized into "one dream, one soul." A dream that exploded out from West London, calling people by the millions to gather and share in that "golden" vision. This book wouldn't exist without those four voices. So . . . To Freddie, Brian, Roger, and John—thanks for all the *music*. Thanks for all the *magic*.

From Jared: I would like to express my gratitude to the team at Carus Books for their vision and professionalism. I'd especially like to thank Randy, my co-editor, for the faith and goodwill he showed by inviting me to join him on this project. A big thanks also to the excellent contributors to this volume. Creating this book has been its own kind of magic, one built out of the efforts and energy of many talented and hardworking people. Finally, I'd like to thank Larissa and Florence for always inspiring me . . . and for keeping philosophy, music, and magic alive in my life!

From Randy: I want to thank Jared, of course, for doing the hardest part of the work. Also there were eager audiences who were happy to let me test out my ideas about Queen and talk and drink and mull both our brains and our wine while we tried to put into words what our bodies and ears already knew. Specifically, there were great people at Charles University in Prague and the City University of České Budějovice in Czech Republic, and colleagues at the University of Warsaw in Poland who were willing to listen and add to my thinking. The contributors to this volume have made the journey a great pleasure, and it was really wonderful to spend the last two years remembering and thinking about Queen. As always, my efforts are dedicated to my spouse of several decades, Gaye.

I

Some Body to Love

1
Love of My Life?

ANDREW KAPLAN

Although the word 'love' is imprecise, a common interpretation is that it's an irrational emotion. You don't 'fall' in love the same way you 'fall' asleep. But the shared analogy of an overwhelming force which takes control of your self applies, and although we may choose, to some extent, when we sleep, we have even less control over whom we love.

And when we do, by some cosmic force, fall in love with someone, the 'love' becomes even more imprecise. Surely love is at least to some extent physical, as evidenced by the likewise common analogy of describing another individual as 'alluring' or 'attractive'.

At the same time though: surely there must be something more to love than this. In addition to physical attraction, love likewise entails at least some degree of emotional connection between the parties. A connection that transcends, or is at least concurrent with, love's physical side. So, love is a term describing two interlinked, but independent, concepts.

Born Farrokh Bulsara in 1946, Freddie Mercury moved to the United Kingdom when he was eighteen. A few years after arriving, he befriended Brian May and Roger Taylor, joined their band Smile, and renamed it Queen. This was also the period of his life when he was involved with Mary Austin.

Freddie asked her out on September 5th 1970, and three weeks later they had their first date. Matt Richards and Mark Langthorne note in their biography of Mercury that their relationship was "beyond question; those around them identified the love and passion they had for each other."

Despite this, their relationship was far from typical, especially for the time period. Sometime in the mid-1970s, Freddie began an affair with David Minns, a record executive at Elektra.

At the same time, Mary was becoming suspicious of Freddie, and the two began to avoid each other (despite sharing a one-bedroom apartment). Eventually, Freddie would tell Mary he was bisexual. Although Mary and Freddie would remain close friends for the rest of his life, their romantic relationship ended.

It would be easy at this point to dismiss Freddie as someone who used Mary as a 'beard' to hide his non-heterosexuality. After all, he had entered into a relationship with Mary only to begin cheating on her with David. However, two factors suggest this surface-level interpretation is incorrect.

The first is that Freddie and Mary remained close until Freddie's death. The second, and more interesting, are two songs Freddie wrote as his relationships rose and fell, "Bohemian Rhapsody" and "Love of My Life." These tracks were written and released in the early to mid-1970s, which understandably was a period of transformation for Freddie.

Self-Discovery and (Self) Love

The opening of "Bohemian Rhapsody" is almost ethereal, with all four band members multi-tracked to create the sound of a full-member tenor choir. For the first two lines in the classic music video, the four are in silhouette, coming into focus as we open our eyes, "look up to the skies and see."

The song is a masterstroke not just because of its range of styles or musical acumen, but also the variety of themes it takes on—especially if we can read into it the story of Freddie's inner conflict and coming out.

Even if Mary had provided affection and partnership, that relationship was founded, at the time, on false premises; a happy heterosexual Freddie was not, and without that basis of being comfortable with who he was, that affection which did exist would have been, to some degree, stunted—as Freddie was not a friend to himself.

The opening and first verse of the song mirror the final two stages of grief: depression and acceptance. At first, Freddie is a poor boy, helpless and passive against the onrushing landslide of the reality that he could not live the lifestyle expected of him by society—or, perhaps more importantly, by himself and his parents.

The verses of the first part are washed in self-pity; our protagonist has shot and killed a man, and now weeps for his own fate. In a sense, he has committed suicide by killing this man; it is our singer's time to go and face judgment for his crimes. But, can we not read this as presaging a rebirth of the same man? And more importantly: who is our protagonist, and whom has he killed?

Although Freddie himself never said as much, Sir Tim Rice argues that our shooter is Freddie himself, and the man he shot was the pre-1975 Freddie. The third verse opens with the appearance of "a little silhouetto of a man"; the vague outline of this new character (perhaps signally the uncertainty of what this future will bring), while the light behind him perhaps signals that whatever that future is will be bright.

All this is despite the calls "Bismillah," ("in the name of God") and "Beelzebub has a devil put aside for me" which will surely reveal the silhouette for what it is and spare his life from that monstrosity.

Penned in 1975, "Love of My Life" is undeniably a song of longing for someone. Although the recipient of this sentiment is never clarified in the song, at this point his relationship with David had cost him his relationship with Mary—making either a probable recipient. The song opens with Freddie's proclamation that his "love" has hurt him, has broken his heart, and has now left him.

He then begs the subject to come back, not to leave him, asking his love to "bring it back, . . . because you don't know what it means to me." The second verse repeats the address to his love before asking them not to take that love away from him "because you don't know what it means to me."

Although it was John Deacon who wrote "You're My Best Friend," it serves as a useful foil to "Love of My Life." The tones are entirely different: the first is almost jaunty, especially with Freddie's vocals. Having that friend makes our protagonist live; "I've been with you such a long time. You're my sunshine." He wants us to know that his feelings are true, he really loves that friend. We might even go so far as to say that the two complete each other. Now, it isn't out of the question to suggest that, were that friend to leave him, our vocalist could pivot into "Love of My Life," begging them to return.

Freddie and Mary were, at the bare minimum, friends: though this seems a bit shallow given how widely we can use the term "friend." The more basic forms of friendship are those founded on the utility or pleasure that relationship brings to each party: such as business partners who advance each other's careers and bank accounts.

If we assume (justifiably, I think) that Freddie felt something deeper than mere utility with Mary, then their friendship was instead founded in some manner of deep interpersonal connection. Founded on an appreciation of Mary herself. Even after he came out—and despite all the partying and other good-natured fun and experiences—they simply enjoyed each other's company. He most definitely saw something in her.

Isn't Love Just a Really Good Friendship?

Let's assume that "Love of My Life" *is* about Mary. Can we say that Freddie 'loved' her? How exactly do we go from a close friendship to love? 1976 would see Mary leave Freddie, albeit temporarily, with David departing shortly thereafter.

The year after would see Queen's 1977 US tour, which freed him from the ever-present eyes of the UK press. New York and Los Angeles in particular stood out to Brian May for the series of gay one-night stands and male followers Freddie attracted (and on whom he spent extravagantly).

Despite this, at least early on, before the US tour, there remained a seed of doubt: he works hard and does as God wants, and yet he still cannot find somebody to love. According to Mary, Freddie had "convinced himself he was having a good time" with the sex, partying, drugs, and alcohol, although she would express some doubt that that was really who he was.

The issue was that Freddie had two sides to him—the former the quiet and reserved individual, and the latter a frequenter of various clubs and bathhouses. In learning to express the latter (between 1975 and 1977), Freddie had undoubtedly gained a tremendous amount of knowledge about himself. He would eventually strike a balance.

Freddie would end up referring to Mary as his only friend, the only person no other person could replace. It seems only fair to say that despite the collapse of his relationship with Mary, Freddie still felt a deep affection for her. He would likewise eventually give up the club scene (following this period of self-discovery) and have a series of long-term sexual and romantic partners.

Mary's response is entirely understandable. On a perhaps narrow, though admittedly commonplace, interpretation of what it means to be in an intimate relationship, he had violated its conventions. Perhaps she felt used: either as a girlfriend useful to dispel any unwanted accusations regarding his own sexuality, or simply for his own fulfillment. With a more expansive view of intimacy, however, the inner turmoil of "Bohemian Rhapsody" comes back into play.

Whatever the nature of their early relationship, it was tainted, perhaps, by the issue that Freddie was not really Freddie. His ultimate form was the person who would emerge from that little silhouetto—even as God, and perhaps his desire for Mary, called him back. Freddie's self-realization came into conflict with contemporary social mores. On the one hand, the inner conflict had been resolved (as Freddie had learned to love himself). On the other, non-heterosexual sexual deviation still made him a target of hostility. This issue was further compounded by Freddie's own religious upbringing. His transition likewise could not have been helped by the growing distance between him and Mary at this point.

Lurking in the background of this discussion is the crotchety old Greek Aristotle, who raises a pretty important question for Freddie: how is it that love, which contains within itself desire for both pleasure and affection, is capable of bringing about such good—yet also such bad—outcomes?

Himself silent on an answer, Aristotle's ancient contemporaries (including Plato), suggest that the solution is to think of love as being directed towards someone's character or moral worth. That is, I love someone for their personality, the content of their soul, or some other non-tactile element—rather than how they might be of use to sexually satisfying me. We might even describe each other as soul-mates.

And, importantly, this view of love aligns with the interpersonal elements we've been tracking between Freddie and Mary. The two completed each other as moral entities, and to Aristotle this would have made them friends—in the strongest sense of the term.

Can Sex Ruin Love?

This still leaves the matter of sex itself unresolved, however, and this metaphysical interpretation opens the door for Aristotle to throw a metaphorical wrench into the works. Even if we accept that love, using the soul-mate view from above, enjoys a special moral status (whereas sexual desire is a base appetite akin to hunger or thirst), how do we square the circle of that appreciation of another's moral beauty bringing about such an appetite in us? Or: won't we eventually want to have sex with the people we love?

Now, it would be easy to dismiss Freddie's period of clubbing, drugs, and anonymous sex as one of unabashed hedonism. Indeed, Mary did just that. If we're a bit more charitable though, we might view the late 1970s and early 1980s as a period of searching for something to satisfy that desire for affection (absent Mary) while also satisfying the more physical side of sexual desire.

Five or six years on from our other songs, "Body Language" points in the right direction. If nothing else, the tone is more assertive. Freddie is no longer pleading but rather demanding "give me your body, . . . just give me your body. Don't talk." Likewise gone are the operatics and complex story-telling, replaced by an emphasis on our subject's "red lips, . . . long legs, great thighs," and "the cutest ass I've ever seen."

Even the style of the music video had likewise changed, with the soft lighting and blurred edges around the band replaced by a much harder Freddie either lording over the band or leading a group of scantily-clad women. The emotion-laden ballad is replaced by a stripped down, though admittedly catchy, listing of conventionally physically attractive traits.

The confidence-filled Freddie we meet in "Body Language" is a far cry from the wavering character of "Bohemian Rhapsody"—having fully accepted and taken command of his own direction in life. Is this Freddie in his ultimate form? Well, no, but it is certainly an aspect of him, here the contrasting aspect.

Both "Bohemian Rhapsody" and "Body Language" represent the same person—the difference is in what side of himself he's showing. In a way, he's come into his own. Perhaps we can indeed write off any indiscretions as self-discovery and exploration—after which he needn't repress this aspect of himself anymore.

What Even Is Love?

The Greeks had several words to describe different forms of love. Among others: love between friends or equals was *philia*; love of one's self was *philautia*; and sexual love was *eros.* For us today, what counts as love is often muddled—we just call love love, and add qualifiers later. And this is to say nothing of our differences from the ancient Greeks in morality and customs governing inter-personal relationships.

But, were the Greeks wrong in this division? Pre-1975, it isn't beyond the realm of possibility to describe Freddie as lacking *philautia*; a crucial aspect of himself had to be denied. *Philautia* is just a reflexive form of *philia*, meaning that the journey we went on in "Bohemian Rhapsody" was Freddie learning to be a friend to himself.

For Freddie though, being a friend to himself is exactly what ran him up against the sexual mores of the times. New York was a breath of fresh air—not just because the British paparazzi couldn't hound him, but also because the Big Apple lent him the space for self-exploration. Of course, he had this with David at least to some extent, but sneaking around isn't exactly comparable to New York.

Freddie's developing *philautia* opens the door for Aristotle to raise another issue; the paradox of erotic love. He divides this sort of love into two halves: the want for the other person's affection in appreciation of their inner beauty, and (to put it bluntly) the desire to have sex with someone because they're hot. The issue is that they're (potentially, at least) inseparable—feeling one side of these erotic feelings will eventually make you feel the other.

For Freddie and Mary, whether they explored the physical side of *eros* at all is between them. But after 1975 even the affectionate side was, at least for a few years, cut off. Does this signal that one or the other had lost their inner beauty, or that either had ceased to recognize it in the other? Not in the slightest.

Rather, it is more a transformation of the nature of that love. *Eros* can appear at first to be synonymous with sexual appetite, but more than anything else it is simply an intense, passionate longing for something. Can that be sex? Yes.

But it is also that intense, passionate longing for affection, or even just companionship. And what makes the dual nature of *eros* important for us is Freddie's dual life. On the one hand, he was Freddie Mercury, a quiet and reserved man struggling with his own identity. On the other, he was Freddie Mercury, the flamboyant leader of Queen.

Mary was one of the few who knew both sides of Freddie, and this is what gives "Love of My Life" its punch. Her leaving removed from Freddie the object of that longing, but also removed a key figure from his life: someone who understood him. Aristotle's paradox raises the question of whether this could have been sustainable; could Freddie and Mary satisfy each other's desires for affection and sex? The short answer is no, but the long answer requires a clarification of Aristotle.

This is because it isn't entirely truthful to say that one will eventually lead to the other (but you knew that, right?). That's because the two are not two distinct elements but are more two aspects of the same thing. *Eros* might very well begin from mere physicality, but that perception of physical beauty evolves into a perception of more abstract or intangible qualities; the person's inner beauty.

Even if we describe *philia* as friendship, viewing it as its own form of love isn't wrong. What makes this sort of relationship is the fondness or attachment felt between people—not for the pleasure or usefulness the relationship brings, but instead an appreciation of the other person's character.

Now, doesn't this sound not too dissimilar to the erotic desire for affection? That *eros* involves personal desire means it creates, to Aristotle at least, a lesser friendship, but a friendship it does still create. But the appreciation of the other person's intangible qualities, if reciprocated, is similar to a friendship based on mutual virtue. And this is even more true where the personal desire for sex in itself is cast aside.

It's exactly this sort of relationship we saw between Freddie and Mary. Far stronger than a mere *philia*, but only having one half of the two supposedly inseparable elements of *eros*—what they had defies classification.

Even if he didn't know it at first, Mary did complete Freddie. The turmoil expressed in "Bohemian Rhapsody" swirled around, the fallout took place in "Love of My Life," and Freddie experimented in "Body Language." What exactly it was they saw in each other is between them. But even as Freddie became Freddie, and both went off into relationships with others, they still ended up incredibly close. They were close all the way until Freddie's passing.

So, did he love her? Absolutely.

2
Good Old-Fashioned Lover Boy

DARCI DOLL

The fame and popularity of Queen have spanned decades. Known for their musical abilities—and frontman Freddie Mercury's impressive vocal octave range and flamboyant stage presence—they also presented themselves in such a way as to challenge certain social norms.

Such challenges were not always well received (for example, the backlash to Queen dressing in drag for the music video "I Want to Break Free.") One of the lingering criticisms comes from the way in which gay culture influenced Freddie's style. Throughout the band's career there was speculation about Freddie's sexual orientation, though he deftly skirted the issue in the rare instances when he consented to an interview. Asked about his sexual orientation, Freddie would reply that the messages were in his songs or would comment that he's content.

In an attempt to keep his private life private, in public he presented Mary Austin as his partner and companion. Despite these public appearances, the speculation about Freddie's sexual orientation would not subside. Amongst his close circle it was known that Freddie was gay (or bisexual, as he had had sexual relationships with women, though not as frequently as men). His friends, by and large, respected his privacy and did not betray his trust (the exception being Paul Prenter, who tremendously betrayed Freddie near the end of his life). Since Freddie's death in 1991, details of his personal life came to the surface and are now common knowledge.

It's known that Freddie liked to live a big life. In *Somebody to Love: The Life, Death, and Legacy of Freddie Mercury*, Richards and Langthorne describe Freddie's life as hedonistic and quote him as saying, "excess is part of my nature," and asserting that his life was not made for sitting home watching TV (p. 197). Throughout his career there were lots of parties, drugs, and sex. Towards the end of his life, during his time with Jim Hutton, this would change considerably—but living large was a significant part of Freddie's life. This larger-than-life attitude positioned Freddie as a significant influence on the world around him. For example, Freddie's pushing against gender roles was inspirational to the LGBTQ+ community during his career and has left a lasting impression since his death.

While his sexual orientation was not confirmed on a broad public scale during his lifetime, he has become a gay icon and represents, amongst other things, the struggles associated with being gay in the twentieth century. There's no doubt that members of the LGBTQ+ community have benefited from Freddie's life. Aside from being a gay musical icon, Freddie's death from AIDS helped bring awareness to the disease. This awareness paved the way for funding, a search for a cure or vaccine, and the beginning of the de-stigmatization of HIV/AIDS. While this endeavor still has a long way to go, Freddie's death (and in retrospect his life) made a huge impact on that movement.

While a role model to many (whether it be musically or for his significance to marginalized communities), Freddie was not without his critics. During his career the media would speculate that he was gay and, in that speculation, would bring with it the (unwarranted) vilification of being gay in the twentieth century. Freddie's choice to stay relatively closeted and use Mary as a frequent date was in large part a strategic response to this (and potentially worse) vilification. People in Freddie's close circle were aware of his sexual orientation, but with the exception of Prenter, they all respected Freddie's desire to stay closeted.

The speculation regarding Freddie and his willingness to bend gender norms was (in part) why Queen's popularity in the United States waned in the 1990s. In the music video for "I Want to Break Free," the band dressed in drag. This had mixed reviews in other countries, but was censored and condemned in the US. The band never recovered from that negative reaction. Haunted by the tabloids and newspapers, Freddie had to walk a tightrope over how to be his authentic self without jeopardizing his (or his partners') safety. While we've made many strides in the advancement of the rights and acceptance of LGBTQ+ individuals, in Freddie's lifetime being publicly gay was dangerous (and not only because of the risk of HIV/AIDS). Hate crimes against gay people were rampant.

Even today, the courts have ruled that it is acceptable for a straight person to kill a gay person "in self defense" if the former felt the latter was hitting on them. This was the reality of Freddie's existence. Since his death, there are still anti-gay responses to Freddie and to Queen. Their work has been boycotted; Freddie has been condemned. Whether you loved or hated Freddie, the reaction is typically a strong one. What we can learn from Freddie (and his relationships) can help us have a better understanding of virtue—specifically within the LGBTQ+ community.

The anti-gay rhetoric and actions against Freddie are based in unfounded biases and prejudices. Built into this worldview is the idea that there is something deviant or unnatural about same-sex relationships. However, scientifically speaking, same-sex relationships happen across species and occur naturally. Other anti-gay approaches look at religious justification for the vilification of the LGBTQ+ community.

This, however, tends to require a combination of selective translations, selective interpretations, and the cherry-picking of religious texts. In addition to these claims being unfounded, they miss the point of what it means to be in a morally acceptable erotic, or sexual, relationship.

Who Needs You

Aristotle was a Greek philosopher who studied under Plato and died in 322 B.C. Aristotle employs an approach we now call 'virtue ethics'. According to Aristotle, we ought to develop virtuous characters through practical wisdom, intellectual contemplation, and habituation of moral virtues. Aristotle believes that all people desire *eudaimonia*, or flourishing. This flourishing is only possible, for Aristotle, through the development of excellent character and excellent intellect.

One contributing factor in the development of these virtues is the relationships we form with the people in our lives. Aristotle speaks at length about the ways in which a friend can contribute to the cultivation of these virtues. Friends, for Aristotle, present us with opportunities to see ourselves; they act as a mirror. These mirrors help us confirm our virtues, as well as areas in need of more development. Additionally, true friends will be virtuous and will provide examples for us to follow as we develop our own virtues. The most important friendships are these true, or perfect, friendships.

In these relationships, the friends have a reciprocal feeling of well-wishing that is founded on the recognition of virtuous character. This is in contrast to friendships based only on usefulness or pleasure. These friendships are weak and dissolve when the relationship stops being useful or pleasant. We have a moral obligation, then, to surround ourselves with true, or morally virtuous, friends. For Aristotle, moral virtue does not require a sense of moral perfection. Rather, a virtuous person is one who has the practical wisdom to know the balanced way to act in a situation. Courage, for example, is the appropriate amount of fear. It's knowing that despite some fear, the action is still worth pursuing and fighting for.

The approach Aristotle took to friendship can be extended to erotic relationships. The important question about erotic or sexual relationships is then not limited by a heterosexual norm. We can see thing more broadly, allowing for a variety of sexual relationships so long as the relationships are fully informed and voluntary. Just like friendship, these true erotic relationships have the ability to help us attain *eudaimonia*. The criticism of Freddie's sexual activities, then, ought not be about whether he is gay or straight. Rather, we should ask whether his nonsexual and sexual partners are contributing to his flourishing.

Under Pressure

Freddie Mercury seldom spoke about his childhood and remained a fairly private person when it came to his family. In one rare instance, he said that spending his formative years in boarding school taught him to fend for himself and to take responsibility. This period was, according to Freddie in another interview, marvelous (*Somebody to Love*, p. 17). Freddie was remembered as being shy during his boarding school years, but he excelled in sports and was developing his love of music. In these formative years there is little to be found about the friends he may have had at that time. This means that we can't tell whether his friendships helped contribute to his developing good character traits. To get a glimpse into the quality of his relationships we have to look at his adult relationships, both platonic and sexual.

When Freddie arrived to the United Kingdom in 1964, there were no gay role models and the world was wildly homophobic (even more so than today). The religion that Freddie grew up with, Zoroastrianism, forbade homosexuality. However, a maths teacher at the boarding school Freddie attended said that his homosexuality was known then (p. 18). The juxtaposition of being gay, wanting to have (and then having) fame, but living in a homophobic world undoubtedly made Freddie feel pressure.

As evidence of this pressure, Freddie's companion Mary was his public image partner—even after they broke up and Freddie maintained a predominately gay lifestyle. In the 1970s, Freddie turned to Glam Rock as a way to simultaneously express and conceal his homosexuality. Like Bowie, he was able to hint at being bisexual without confirming, which would have left him vulnerable. But this showmanship gave Freddie the protection of being perceived as an act for shock value, not an actual declaration of his real self.

Play the Game

As his fame grew, the questions about his sex life grew, as did the pressure to have people believe he was straight. While maintaining this façade of heterosexuality, Freddie did not live a heterosexual life. While he did spend a significant amount of time dating Mary, and even considered her a common-law wife, he eventually told her he thought he was bisexual. Her response was "I think you're gay" (p. 95). Despite their sexual relationship ending, their friendship seemed to have strengthened. Mary said that after his "confession" he seemed truer to himself and happier.

A virtuous, true friend for Freddie had to be one with whom he could be his authentic self without fear of being outed. Fortunately for Freddie, most of the people he surrounded himself with respected (and when needed, protected), his privacy. They allowed Freddie to be his authentic self without jeopardizing his career or safety. In an Aristotelian sense, Freddie's friends had an obligation to exhibit character traits that prioritized Freddie's autonomy, authenticity, and safety. The press's inability to conclusively prove private aspects of Freddie's life demonstrates that his friends were willing and able to live up to that charge.

What's important for a true friend, according to Aristotle, is that friends care about the wellbeing of each other for their own sakes, and that both have good character. In the case of Freddie's entourage there's likely a mixed bag. There are some people who hung around Freddie for personal gain, for pleasure, or for some other form of gain. Despite this, they still protected his privacy and respected the 'rules' of being in his life. On the other hand, there were true friends. These are friends who remained close to Freddie because they wanted what was best for him and sincerely cared for him. Roger, John, and Brian are the most obvious examples of such friends.

Throughout their decades together, the members of Queen supported Freddie and protected his privacy and safety. By surrounding himself with people with whom he could be safe, Freddie created an environment that was conducive to finding his authentic self. His true friends reinforced his strengths and provided guidance when needed. While there were some outliers (such as Prenter), Freddie seems to have cultivated people who could be trusted and would contribute to his flourishing.

The fidelity of his entourage is an important part of Freddie's development, but it's not the part that is most controversial. The more controversial question would be whether there was anything wrong with Freddie living a hedonistic life involving having sex with multiple partners, mostly men, sometimes more than one person at a time. This is the crux of most of the criticism of Freddie's lifestyle. It wasn't just the drugs, the partying, or the extravagant expense.

Many people who condemned Freddie did so because he was gay and, as an icon, that sent the message that being gay was okay. This message was received by the LGBTQ+ community, who felt his support even without him coming out. If nothing else, many identified him as an ally who allowed them to feel more comfortable experimenting with self-expression. Perhaps more than his being gay, his influence—sending the message that it was okay to not be straight-conforming—was a bigger cause of criticism.

What matters ethically is not the sexual orientation or even the number of partners, but rather, in what way relationships contributed to, or interfered with, flourishing. In Freddie's case, he *did* die from a sexually transmitted disease, AIDS. This, however, was not inherent in sexual activity. At the time, the transmission of the disease was not generally known and it was believed it could infect anyone.

If the involved parties are consenting adults and the sex is safe—or the partners are fully informed and voluntarily take a risk (like a person who openly discloses they're HIV+ but tells their partner and engages in safe sex)—then the sex is morally acceptable. The places where the sex act becomes unacceptable are: minors; non-consenting adults; knowingly exposing someone to a disease without their consent; psychological or physical damage, and so on.

In Freddie's case, he had multiple lovers. Some were short term, some long term, some on and off. As far as we know, none of these relationships fell into the category of unethical sex acts. Those involved were knowingly entering into an adult relationship without deceit or coercion. So at face value, Freddie's promiscuity, whether gay or straight, is not inherently harmful, or a sign of a lack of virtue. The majority of these relationships were for utility or pleasure, so they aren't the true relationships we want to see under Aristotle's theory of friendship. However, these lesser relationships are still useful, and not to be condemned by default.

Love of My Life

The most important turn for Freddie (as far as sexual partners is concerned) is when Freddie met Jim Hutton. Freddie saw Jim in a bar and approached him—only to be rebuffed with a "Fuck off" (p. 228). Over time Freddie was able to win over Jim, and they became sexual partners. This partnership grew and evolved over time. At times, Freddie was unfaithful, which on my model does not count as virtuous sex (because Jim didn't consent to an open relationship). They fought, they made up, they went through the ebbs and flows of love.

Eventually they exchanged rings, though Freddie didn't wear his publicly, and still used Mary as a facade in the public eye. What Jim had (that others didn't) was a close, lasting connection. Jim brought out some stability and happiness that Freddie hadn't found previously. Roger Taylor reportedly asked, "Freddie's been different this year. What have you done to him" (p. 286). The Freddie that Roger saw was less anxious, happier, calmer (though others still noted a general anxiety, unrelated to the relationship with Jim). Jim seemed to have a calming and soothing effect on Freddie, without stifling his creativity.

Freddie and Jim were not without their difficulties. Freddie had a problem with fidelity, and Jim sometimes struggled with Freddie's hedonistic life. But eventually they fell into a routine and an agreement about their relationship. Not long before his death, Freddie kicked Jim out of Farden Ledge, but then asked him not to leave—Jim stayed until Freddie died. In these years with Jim, Freddie was engaged in an erotic, or sexual, relationship with someone who wanted what was best for him for his own sake. Jim was not a partner of utility or mere pleasure.

Jim sincerely cared for Freddie and wanted to see Freddie flourish. Likewise, though it took a longer route, Freddie seemed to sincerely want what was best for Jim for Jim's sake. Jim helped Freddie, not through restriction, but through a stability where Freddie could explore what mattered (and then decide how that affected who he was becoming). With Jim, Freddie had a supportive partner he hadn't had before, outside of Mary. On an Aristotelian account, Jim was a person of good character who was helping Freddie direct and form his own character.

The important thing about Freddie and Jim isn't whether they were straight (or even whether they were monogamous, if Jim had agreed to it). The real question is whether Jim helped Freddie become the best version of himself. The love that Freddie and Jim had was strong, based in an appreciation for each other's character. They had a reciprocal well-wishing for one another.

In so far as they were in a true erotic relationship (according to my definition), they were an ideal couple. Jim's dedication to helping Freddie flourish transcended Freddie's death. Even after Freddie died, Jim used his resources to help carry on Freddie's memory. In many ways, Jim and Freddie were meant to love each other. That is what we should retain from Freddie's sexual legacy. In the end, he spent his days with a partner whom he loved and who loved him in return. In doing this, Freddie no longer had to live solely as the great pretender.

II

Stone Cold Crazy

3
I'm Going Slightly Mad

SNITA AHIR-KNIGHT

Stomp, stomp—clap! Stomp, stomp—clap! Stomp, stomp—clap! Stomp, Stomp—clap! When immersed in the energetic beat and repetitive lines of "We Will Rock You," there is a familiar and well-known collective response, be that at live Queen performances or sporting events. And even in therapy rooms. The world's greatest rock band has provided us with an anthem that not only connects us, but also connects us with a path to manage mental distress and other kinds of suffering.

Queen has illuminated mental disorder: if you look hard enough in their awesome songs. Mental disorder—or mental illness, or disease, or condition, or psychiatric disability, or psychiatric disorder, or madness, or psychopathology, or behavioral disorder, or cognitive disorder, or . . . you get the idea—is hotly debated. We haven't even decided what to name this phenomenon that has something to do with our thoughts, feelings, beliefs, desires, and actions. And when it comes to figuring out *what mental disorder is* as a concept, well there is much more work to be done.

To establish what something is—in this case, mental disorder—philosophers identify its *necessary* conditions.

I'll put that another way: philosophers try to find the "must-have" features of mental disorder. Queen helpfully gives us two necessary conditions of mental disorder to explore: irrationality and distress.

Irrationality

Have a listen to the lyrics and watch the music video of "I'm Going Slightly Mad." Like me, have you spotted the illustrations that irrationality may be a "necessary" feature of mental disorder?

Here is what I have spotted. Near the opening, Freddie Mercury is seen among daffodils—one of which he smells. This scene links to the belief that yellow daffodils are dancing, and if this is true then perhaps "you're missing that one final screw." During the song, Mercury also sings about thinking he's a banana tree while he wears a bunch of bananas on his head. Of course, Mercury is playing a character, so it's the character I am talking about. I would never suggest that Mercury or the other members of Queen had or have a mental disorder.

The daffodil and banana examples show that irrationality may be about (at least) beliefs, thoughts, and actions. The belief that daffodils are dancing. The thought that he's a banana tree. And the act of wearing a bunch of bananas.

There is also something here about irrationality relating to false perceptions. In the music video there is a scene where Mercury's band members are on a sofa—and Freddie perceives being dismissed by one, strangled by another and ignored by the final one. The sign that Mercury is irrationally perceiving these reactions is that Brian May—the final band member who ignores Mercury—is admiring his long metal-like fingernails. And it's doubtful that he would actually have these fingernails.

Two Perplexing Puzzles

There are some puzzles, however, to work out before saying for sure that irrationality is a "necessary" feature of mental disorder.

The philosopher Lisa Bortolotti works on the topic of delusions and irrational beliefs. In her article "Rationality and Sanity," she claims that most of us hold and act on beliefs that are not logical and empirically supported. There are many examples of beliefs that are not rational—and yet are not a feature of mental disorder. For example, beliefs that are not responsive to the available evidence—racist beliefs that a certain ethnic group is violent; the belief that the government is spying on us; beliefs about alien abductions; and the superstitious belief that accidents are caused by full moons. These beliefs may cause someone to fail to engage in reality, such as refusing to drive when there is a full moon because of the fear of having an accident. According to Bortolotti, all these beliefs are false, unsupported by evidence, and often the holder of the belief is resistant to evidence or arguments that disprove their belief.

Another puzzle when considering irrationality to be a necessary feature of mental disorder, is that in some cases being irrational may be beneficial for human flourishing. Imagine societies that have the privileged role of a healer or shaman. This healer does their work effectively due to losing touch with reality—they may ask their community to take irrational leaps of faith with them as they experience hallucinations in a healing ritual. This society wouldn't agree with being told that their healer (and their practices) are disordered.

Thus, our two puzzles are: 1. there are many commonly held irrational beliefs that are not signs of mental disorder, and 2. some kinds of irrationality may even be beneficial. Considering these puzzles is important because it's clinically thought that irrationality *does* play a part in mental disorders. So we must be careful to understand what, exactly, the relationship is between irrationality and mental disorder.

Clinical Frameworks

There are two widely used classification frameworks that are often referred to in the clinical practice of mental health. They're the World Health Organization's "International Classification of Diseases" (ICD) and the American Psychiatric Association's "Diagnostic and Statistical Manual" (DSM). These frameworks list symptoms, mental states, or behaviors that (when added up together, usually over a period of time, or having occurred a certain number of times), results in a diagnosis. They're used by clinicians, researchers, policy makers, and insurance companies—among others.

Both frameworks describe many mental disorders as involving variations from rationality.

But as the above puzzles show, being irrational is not enough to *guarantee* that someone has a mental disorder (even if irrational beliefs may be an important component of many mental disorders). A philosopher would put it this way: irrationality is not a *sufficient* condition of mental disorder. Let's take a practical example. Having gas in a car's tank (assuming a traditional combustion engine vehicle, of course) is *necessary* for the car to start and run. Without gas, you're not going anywhere. But gas in the tank is not alone *sufficient* for the car to run: you also need spark plugs, working pistons, and so on. So, to return to our example: irrationality may be *necessary* for mental illness (or for many cases, at least), but it is not *sufficient* to determine mental disorder.

There is more to the story, and "I'm Going Slightly Mad" gives us some things to think about.

Queen Illuminating Ways Forward

Throughout "I'm Going Slightly Mad," there is a sense from Mercury that he and those around him recognize that his mental state is on the decline, or disordered. Of course, this is demonstrated with the repeating of the song title. However, there are other lines in the song, such as "unraveling fast," and not being at the top of one's billing. Plus, those close to Mercury all agree (by nodding yes when he sings) that he has finally become "slightly mad." The point to take away is that, when considering whether a particular person has a mental disorder, it's important to ask them (and those close to them) their views.

The irrationality depicted in the song is a large collection of irrational beliefs, thoughts, and actions, which is having a significant negative influence on Mercury's flourishing. Mercury's irrationality is resulting in the negative perception of his friendships, and I suspect that many would agree that having friends is good for one's flourishing. The point to take away from this illustration is that, in our attempt to find the necessary conditions of mental disorder, we should not abandon considering irrationality. Irrationality on its own does not count as disordered. There is more to say. And this includes thinking more about the large collection of irrationality and its negative influence on one's flourishing.

Distress

Another potential necessary feature of mental disorder that Queen can teach us about is distress. This is through their song "Under Pressure." In the latest edition of the "Diagnostic and Statistical Manual," commonly referred to as the DSM-5, there is a definition of a mental disorder. The DSM-5 says that mental disorders are usually associated with significant distress, or disability in important activities.

But there is a trickiness about saying that distress is a feature of mental disorder. A difficulty for the distress feature is that it may risk classifying justified human feelings with being disordered. It's justified to feel sorrow after a loss; however, there is a question about when—if ever—this grief slips into a disorder, such as depression. There are also other examples: it's justified to feel anxious after a traumatic event, such as an earthquake, pandemic, or assault. However, again, there is a question about when—if ever—this feeling becomes disordered. The line between justified feelings and disorder is a tricky one to be clear on. And correctly balancing that line is important.

The Double-Edged Sword

It's important to make the right decision when deciding when something—in this case, distress—is a mental disorder.

The philosopher Serife Tekin has worked on the topic of diagnosis and self-concept. She claims that the mental disorder diagnosis functions as a narrative that influences how one understands their self and the distress one is experiencing (Tekin 2011). She gives the example of how being diagnosed with a major depressive disorder may allow someone to redefine and reevaluate past experiences and events as being earlier symptoms of having a mental disorder. So, a failed relationship and failure in a job may now be understood as a result of someone's depression. According to Tekin, receiving a mental disorder diagnosis (or a change in diagnosis) affects how one may perceive such things as: their mental states, coping abilities, relationships, and performance at work. This may lead to changes in, for example: their plans, desires, and habits. And eventually, this shapes their possibilities and self-perception. Or misperception. As, after all, someone may misinterpret their experiences as being linked to a diagnosed mental disorder.

According to Tekin, a mental disorder diagnosis is a double-edged sword for someone's self-concept. On one hand, the diagnosis may give someone insight into their situation and experiences, which helps enable self-understanding. (Also, someone receiving a diagnosis may have a more helpful direction to treatment.) However, on the other hand, there is the worry that someone may understand the distress they're experiencing separately from other parts of their life, and instead focus on framing their experience as a result of the mental disorder.

Illuminating the Difficulty, and a Way Forward

Queen and David Bowie—not Vanilla Ice—illuminate the difficulty with distinguishing the line between justified and disordered feelings when it comes to distress. On the one hand, the "Under Pressure" video shows examples of times when feeling mental distress is justified—in other words, feeling (as the title of the song puts it so well) under pressure. The video depicts the daily grind of: work, unemployment, poverty, and injustice (resulting in rioting). But, as the sharp tone of Bowie's words reminds us, "insanity laughs under pressure we're breaking." There is a line between disorder (insanity) and justified distress (pressure). But there are no easy answers to where that line is—because the two can be intertwined.

The song has more to teach us. In the second half, a solution is offered to address the distress we experience. Love. The cynical Bowie is not convinced at first—after all, love is "so slashed and torn." There is some pleading about giving love "one more chance" from the more hopeful Mercury. And Bowie is persuaded (in the end) that love is the solution. Not the romantic love that is depicted by the smoochy black and white movie scenes in the video—that is "old fashioned." It's the love of human connection that may help manage distress—whether justified or disordered. I have listened hard enough to the song to hear Bowie start the song by singing about the pressure on us as individuals—if you listen closely, you'll hear *me* and *you*. But at the end of the song, it becomes *ourselves*.

Stomp, Stomp—Clap!

Connection as a means to manage mental distress is not new to Queen, which brings us back to "We Will Rock You."

The song takes us through three stages of someone's life. In boyhood, he has dreams of being a man; then as an adult he dreams of taking on the world; and finally as an old man he pleads for some peace. But, during all three stages he's a "disgrace." In between each of the three life stages, there is the repetitive chorus that rings out the title of the song, and throughout the song is that familiar collective beat. This cleverly acts as an anthem to cheer him along: to help him manage the distress.

This great anthem is used in therapy for all kinds of suffering—mental and physical. According to Chroma, an arts therapy provider in the UK, it's the number one song used by their music therapists. (Music therapists are an official profession with strong evidence for their effectiveness. They use music to help people with a wide range of issues including: motor skills, cognitive function, and emotional development. You may find them in such places as schools, hospitals, or hospices.) Chroma reports that "We Will Rock You" is the ideal song for circumstances ranging from rehabilitation following a stroke to working through conflict.

More generally, there are a variety of potential benefits from incorporating music into health care. Music can act as a way to process and regulate anxiety and emotions related to trauma. Research shows its benefit for mental disorders such as depression and schizophrenia. Researchers have found that playing and listening to music increases the body's production of an antibody that improves the effectiveness of the immune system. And a study of pediatric patients found that children who listened to relaxing music reported significantly less pain when having an IV inserted.

In my work as a child and adolescent therapist, "We Will Rock You" is a song I have often used. (I am not a fully-fledged music therapist, but I use music in my toolbox of creative-based support.) Before I go on—take a moment to belt out the words, stamp your feet and clap your hands. Do you instantly feel uplifted and united? Pure genius! I have found it to help when working individually with children and youth, when doing group work, and when working with families. I've used the song with those experiencing conflict, grief, addiction, and depression. I have used it both in the UK and Aotearoa New Zealand—the song has been effective with the different cultures I have worked alongside.

One major way to use music therapeutically is to actively listen to music with the person, group, or family. When I provided therapy for someone with depression, some of the sessions involved playing music to match their mood. Although there are benefits to mood matching music, it can lead to the person remaining stuck—in this situation—in the depressive state. To change their mood, I slowly shifted the music over sessions. We slowly moved to listen to "We Will Rock You," which breathed life into them. The song provided a representation of understanding, and a means of connecting with them about their suffering.

The Power of Human Connection

Over the years my appreciation for Queen has grown. Of course, it's difficult not to fall in love with Queen's music. I am sure their experimental brilliance will keep entertaining generations to come, and inspiring future musicians. However, my personal appreciation has grown due to my clinical work, where I have seen their anthemic music help people heal. And also from my philosophical research on mental disorder and health care, where I have seen that their songs have important things to teach us—about irrationality, and distress, and the power of human connection.[1]

[1] I would like to thank Lydia Wevers, whom I deeply miss, and Simon Keller for their much-appreciated comments.

4
Hitting Rock Bottom

ROBERT S. VUCKOVICH

Fans, inquisitive fans, might not know that Roger Taylor's 1977 single, "I Wanna Testify," is not a glam rock rendition of the song by the R&B funk band, The Parliament. To set the record straight, Taylor, being the first member of Queen to put forth a solo effort, actually covered the R&B a capella group The Persuasions' 1977 song, "Women and Drinkin'," (off their album *Chirpin'*) which incidentally incorporates part of the chorus from The Parliament's song into theirs.

Taylor recorded the cover during the July and August 1977 *News of the World* sessions, released it August 26th, and performed the single live on Marc Bolan's (of the band T. Rex) TV show on September 14th 1977. I mention this bit of trivia for the sake of historical interest. The Persuasions' song advances an interesting moral lesson that Taylor preserves.

Standing out philosophically in both versions of the song is the domestic dilemma expressed in the lyrics (note that there is some confusion online around Taylor's lyrics; I will assume that Taylor is faithfully repeating The Persuasions' lyrics, unless otherwise noted). A personalized issue develops when a young man finds solace in things and persons that worsen his life. These preoccupations led him to neglect those close to him, including himself. Both "Women and Drinkin'" and Taylor's "I Wanna Testify" warn about individual vices contributing to the collapse of the family unit before it has time to establish itself.

"I Wanna Testify" presents a cynical outlook for those men who intend on forming long-term relationships without first being able to control the course of their lives. Such an individual, frustrated with their situation, becomes ignorant of how indulging in carefree sexual relations with women and alcohol consumption can bring about the decline of a once upbeat soul. Since Roger Taylor performs the song solo, the vibe he gives serves as a relatable testimony about working on a loving relationship and unfortunately ruining it—but there is a bit of a thought-provoking twist.

Several philosophers from ancient times have made it their business to advise others on how to conduct themselves in various social situations. In particular, the Cynic philosopher, Diogenes of Sinope (404–323 B.C.E.), famously castigates persons for behaviors that harm (or display insensitivities to) others. Or even for harming themselves. Sometimes that harm is of a psychological nature, as opposed to a physical one. Of course, we have to be cautious before blindly following a stranger's advice—a point made by the Roman Stoic philosopher Seneca (4 B.C.E.–65 C.E.).

In his moral letters, Seneca outlines several considerations that should be carefully considered before taking anyone's advice to heart. Seneca's insights parallel much of what Taylor is relaying in his song. The drummer's message may seem simple (cautioning others with one's own downfall), but there are personal complexities, sometimes unseen, worth addressing.

It Don't Come Easy

"I Wanna Testify" begins with a tale of a quick romance between a man and a woman that leads them to becoming *husband and wife*. Family and friends doubt their compatibility, but the lovebirds share an optimistic view that any hardship they encounter will be bested. Taylor, strangely, distorts the Persuasions' line that "love conquers all" to "love counts for life." Perhaps Taylor is being cynically realistic with that line: implying that love may be ineffective. Regardless of the change, optimism blinds the couple in their thinking that love is always binding. Nope, nothing can go wrong when two people are so in love.

Since the observations and concerns of family and friends are ignored, it is unlikely that the character in Taylor's song would have heeded Diogenes's cynical reproach for those who choose to marry. Diogenes Laertius (180–240 C.E.)—a biographer of eminent philosophers who shared a name with the ancient Cynic— relates Diogenes of Sinope's views on marriage. The Cynic claims that marriage should not be pursued by young men, because they are not ripe enough—and old men should abstain from it, because their time for such a commitment has expired. Saying that marriage is out of the question is not quite what the Cynic has in mind, even though the specifics about when that appropriate matrimonial moment should occur have not been presented. The point is that some thought must go into when that blessed bond should be formed. The romance that motivates Taylor's "soon to be husband and wife" couple alerts us that the relationship is at a premature stage. Also, the line from the chorus about "not enough thinking" serves as an admission that there is a lack of planning to ensure that this life-long relationship will work.

Getting down and making love seems to be what initially counts for them. But procreative responsibilities soon become a notable hardship that this couple must endure. Finding joy in having a son may have transformed the husband to a parent, but maintaining that joy also means that his finding work (to support a growing family for the long haul) marks an advanced commitment to preserving the relationship. What follows is a shift in personal priorities—working on the relationship becomes labor intensive. As Taylor testifies, despite good intentions and a willingness to work, the man assumes responsibilities that become too much to handle.

Out of Work and Down . . . All Inside It's so Frustrating

Taking "a job day and night" will wear anyone down. Taylor warns of this excessive preoccupation, for it creates conflict between your need for rest with your inability to do so. Plus, supporting your family consists of being separated from them. Adopting such an extended routine disorientates an individual mentally—with a commitment to your work instead of the relationship that drove you to work. Simply put, the man has become married to his job. Even such a marriage, generating its own hardships, isn't meant to last.

Developing a wiry frame of mind places your standing at risk, for an individual's inability to properly focus on work will result in dismissal. Unemployment takes a person (who hopes to benefit from being productive) to a different level of down. Taylor declares that "with time on his hands, a man ain't a man / and all he loves he starts to neglect." Being deemed a failure as a provider undoubtedly hurts him, and affects his relationship with his wife and son in a troubling way. So instead of finding work elsewhere, this character finds solace down at the bar, a place where "women and drinking" might surely raise his spirits—but inadvertently add to his problems, as opposed to solving them.

When work is over, it's usually time for an individual to play. Yet socializing at the bar where there isn't any work to go back to demonstrates that "not enough thinking" has gone into that life changing decision. Neglecting his family—whom he once deeply cared for—with new entertaining preoccupations has transformed this individual. Abandoning his "pride and joy" for the sake of bodily and inebrious gratifications justifies Taylor's remark that such a figure has ceased to be *a man*.

Diogenes of Sinope expresses concern for the well-being of the family unit in a scene where he scolds an upscale prostitute's child for throwing stones into a crowd. Telling the child that his carefree actions might hit his unsuspecting father, the Cynic philosopher indirectly targets the neglectful parent (the unknown man, who could be among the crowd), for neither directing nor disciplining the child's conduct. Shirking this responsibility makes that man well-deserving of Diogenes's scorn, for Diogenes Laertius never reports the Cynic as picking on well-behaved persons. If you meet your domestic obligations, then there's no need for a philosophical family intervention.

Tempted by the Fruit of Another

Let me get on back to my story now. Taylor testifies that it is at the bar where this so-called man drinks up all his "self-respect." His new-found dependency on substances (and women) brings him further down. No job leads, no sources of income to support his wife and his son, are found when he's busy roaming from "bar room to bedroom." Allowing himself to be caught up in this pattern contributes to further isolating him from his family: those who once inspired and gave him purpose. Taylor is rather vague about these convenient liaisons, perhaps because these indulgences offer nothing beneficial. Partaking in fleeting relations and alcohol consumption serve as a substitute for that initial relationship that generated self-worth.

Obviously the initial romance has died when you seem content with getting liquored up (and then shacking up) with a like-minded stranger encountered at a bar. This changing of partners furthers, as Taylor repeats in the chorus, the spiral downwards. Enjoyment from frequenting bars means not having a need to put forth effort into any other lifelong endeavor. It is as though our protagonist has ventured into a cave—similar to the one in Plato's cave allegory from the *Republic*—and instead of heading out of its dark depths, prefers to remain trapped within, not interested in seeking any greater fulfillment. Being able to think about matters beyond these confines is only for individuals who realize that a certain amount of hardship is required to break free from the disparaging world that you find yourself in.

Having lost that sense of belonging and comfort sparked some contempt in Taylor for "what the women done" to him. To anyone listening, that message is a bit odd to take, as the one testifying directs blame at the "women and drinking" for his situation. Yet the part about "not enough thinking" is solely attributable to the guilty party. Sexy women and fine wine act as definite distractions to his cognitive limitations; still, they're not responsible for the break-up of his family. So when Taylor pleads to those listening to "please pay attention to the words" he mentions, the onus is on the listener to figure out which words reflect the moral problem of the song: and to start thinking a lot more.

The Heart's Filthy Lesson

What has been learned from "the moral of the song" is not to follow the path that this lone man has taken. Mistakes are only beneficial as long as there are others who heed them. For Seneca, in his piece *On the Value of Advice*, "the persons who take the greatest pains to proffer such advice are themselves unable to put it into practice" (*Ad Lucilium*, p. 17). Taylor's "I Wanna Testify" functions as a beacon for others to stay clear of similar pitfalls. There isn't any hope for this lone person, operating as a case study, to reconnect with those whom he has disappointed.

Taylor's line "finding yourself going down, down, down," stresses a slippery slope based on an individual's lack of reasoning and determination to overcome those particular difficulties in one's domestic duties. The "great pains" that Seneca mentions present such an individual as reaching a state of personal uselessness, in which he seems to know better, but does nothing to rectify his decline. A hapless soul's realization of this situation might be the single saving grace for such misfortunes—especially when Taylor's rendition of the song fades out without suggesting that life will take a turn for the better. All he can do is *just* testify.

It's a Sad, Sad Situation . . . and It's Getting More and More Absurd

Disparaging domestic themes resurface in another one of Taylor's solo efforts from *Strange Frontier*. The lead single, "Man on Fire," bears a close resemblance to "I Wanna Testify," for it too gives an account of a man's difficulty in landing decent employment to support someone close to him. Unlike the 1977 cover, this original track has nothing to do with boozing and womanizing; rather, Taylor reveals how a despondent man's mindset develops hostility towards the world, after he puts more thought into his quandary. Seneca, too, notes that "when a man finds that some of his plans have turned out contrary to his expectations, he becomes impatient with men and things, and on the slightest provocation becomes angry" (*Moral Essays*, p. 271). Being unemployed over a period of time wears down an individual's stamina and hopes. Again, the idea of uselessness really takes hold of a person, for many attempts at improving their circumstances "don't work and it's not that fine." This last part indicates that there's more to this man's obvious problems.

What comes across as the main factor contributing to the man's downfall in "I Wanna Testify," namely *not enough thinking*, is the opposite in "Man on Fire." Wondering why he is in such a predicament is stressed in the lead-up to the chorus. Taylor's emphasis on calling this personal matter into question demonstrates that the mind is active, probing into his misfortunes. More thinking is involved in this composition. No particular reason, though, is given. It may be the sign of the times that an ordinary man spends so much of his free time "to find some work."

Philosophically, the man with good intentions (even in a mundane sense) discovers that those intentions aimed at benefiting others as well as himself do not amount to anything when he cannot act on them. In such a case, Taylor provides an introspective point of view of what develops when you frequently stop to wonder why.

The chorus establishes that some inner turmoil has been building (as one walks the streets to no avail). He returns home with nothing positive to show for his efforts. In the second verse, expressing that his "role fits too tight" is an admission that the pressure from these repeated unsuccessful attempts agitates him.

We should wonder why Taylor spares the loving partner from the man's hostility. Perhaps restraint prevents him from worsening his situation by burdening that one love (who incidentally keeps him focused on his daily unproductive undertaking). His plans remain intact—but alternate plans, more spiteful in nature, are brewing as well. There is even the realization that a tough dignified individual must "be made of sterner stuff" to face this particular hardship. Not blaming the one close to him does not mean that the man on fire has not directed blame elsewhere.

I Don't Care if It Takes All Night . . . Gonna Set This Town Alight

Taylor doesn't indicate (at least precisely) where blame should be directed, but in the last line of the chorus, burning "down this crazy town" suggests that it may well be everyone *else* (definitely not him). Carrying out such destruction shows how an unfortunate situation escalates, producing additional misfortune for others. There seems to be a decline in his mental state should his temperament reach a certain level. Taylor isn't promoting dance moves in the pre-chorus where the Man on Fire acknowledges that he's "smoking, burning, twisting and turning." Instead, he testifies that these pressures from within are becoming quite unbearable. We can only imagine what might happen should they flare up.

Near the end of the second part of his essay "On Anger," Seneca questions the state of your soul when it directs contempt at others. The stoic's description of a man's indignant soul as "inflamed, distorted and swollen" matches Taylor's visceral account of the man on fire (*Moral Essays*, p. 249). Even contemplating such a destructive course of action definitely makes others wonder what would finally set someone off for real. Perhaps, as a hint, Taylor does not mention "sometimes" in the final line of the song, announcing that this time "I wanna burn down this crazy town." It's likely that so much wondering, maybe even too much wondering, has led this man to pursue a pyrotechnic response to his lack of employment.

Misguided thinking characterizes this man: seeking revenge on a town for failing to notice his desperation. This unfortunate soul teaches us that when a man seeks assistance and doesn't receive it, he can come to believe that he's justified in harming all who have ignored his pleas. Equating anger with an illness of the mind, Seneca would deduce that Taylor's song displays an individual's ascent—not descent—to "madness." The music video for *Man on Fire* ends with an assortment of explosions and pyrotechnics—as though to show us how the fire within the song's anti-hero (first seen as sympathetic, and then pathetic), externalizes itself and destroys as much as possible. No one can expect a happy ending to come from the Man on Fire—especially anyone near him as he finally erupts.

Where Do We Go from Here?

The morbidity surrounding this tune might leave listeners wondering what message anyone is supposed to gather from it: especially when it comes from a guy who composed "Tenement Funster." There is the relatable situation of a person trying to earn a livelihood through employment (regardless of whether it is for survival or career-oriented), but who is unable to obtain such employment.

It is a practical tale about anyone who has ever struggled for a considerable time at finding a job—but up to a point. Since this rather ordinary objective is presented as unattainable, a spiteful reaction emerges from someone who tries to cope with being disadvantaged, but ultimately becomes fed up. Plus, the questioning of rationality draws attention to how the mind formulates (and possibly carries out) a violent act.

Similar to Taylor's first single—testifying about miscalculations and sinking into a life of indulgences and misery—*Man on Fire* is testifying about a man's struggles. His thinking finally takes an odd turn, leading to the ominous plan to lash out at just about everyone. This focusing on whom to blame gives the impression that such thinking ceases to be constructive and favors a destructive response. Taylor may very well be alluding to an individual's development of flawed reasoning—or even mental illness—because of how he assesses his predicament, almost obsessively, without a fitting resolution.

An attempt at redirecting such thinking does not appear in Taylor's song, which thus presents itself merely as a warning about individuals with a deep-seated contempt for others. So, is there any chance of remedying this problem? Seneca offers some hope for weak-minded individuals, for such "are disturbed but not hopelessly gone" (*Ad Lucilium*, p. 35). His whole spiel on giving advice is not entirely "effective in overthrowing the mind's mistaken beliefs" unless "they accompany other measures also" (p. 25). Without articulating what specifically those measures are, Seneca admits that keeping good company—similar to that which Brian May sings of in *A Night at the Opera*—will help "in straightening out the wavering spirit" (p. 37).

Despite advice from such venerable souls, the solution still requires someone to work at it. Consider how Diogenes sought to find good men among puzzled onlookers, as he carried a lit lantern during the day. His method might seem completely out of whack, but from a cynical standpoint, his findings are quite possibly realistic—good men are not easy to find. Keeping good company may be just as difficult as finding decent employment.

Could Be Better, Should Be Better . . . Lessons in love

Queen may be responsible for composing an anthem about being champions; but the lyrics illustrate that there have been hardships for even those striving to succeed. Queen's drummer has a knack, in his solo outings, for presenting the worst-case scenario when singing about individual losers.

Perhaps "I Wanna Testify" and "Man on Fire" provide us a clue to the mindset of those who have given up after being unable to accomplish some reasonable goal. Classifying the men in those songs as quitters might seem harsh—when misfortune hampers someone's attempts to live adequately, not everyone will become a champion (or even accept a disappointing outcome). Failing at any common task, large or small, doesn't automatically make a person a complete failure. Failing should never exclude the possibility of becoming wiser.

These two songs should serve as practical lessons learned: from the standpoint of someone who has lost in love in "I Wanna Testify," and someone who has lost focus by becoming too focused in "Man on Fire." Taylor issues warnings not to venture into the psychological quagmire of those who have failed to fully rationalize their situations. In one case, "not enough thinking" has contributed to one man's downfall. While the burning thoughts of another frustrated man intensify to the point where thinking clearly just doesn't work (which may include the unnecessary downfall of others). Establishing the appropriate amount of thought, or directing our concentration to sensible objectives, involves a great deal of work and effort so as to prevent some individual from failing—or failing even more.

Taylor is neither celebrating nor berating those who have failed. He merely relays what is needed to understand the troubles of certain individuals, and how they have gotten worse. Is it possible that life will get better for such individuals? Taylor is not providing answers, because these are issues, though very domestic in nature, for philosophers to ponder. Some ancient ones (philosophers, that is) have given such practical matters some thought, and provided some insight.

As Seneca claims, "We should . . . have a guardian, as it were, to pluck us continually by the ear" (*Ad Lucilium*, p. 47). The testimonies in Taylor's songs *do* perform that task. In the end, Taylor is quite content to think that—as long as people are not only just trying to get by, but put forth a little more thought and work into improving their lives—then it is possible that things will start looking up.

5
Creatures of the Dark and the Light

RANDALL E. AUXIER

A band is a lot like a marriage, often same-sex, plural marriage, so San Francisco meets Salt Lake City. A band that does *not* take pleasure from the mutual presence of the group won't work, and the pleasure must be complemented with utility—there has to be work, or it won't work.

When these two combine, pleasure and utility, you have the necessities for success. But sometimes the friendship moves beyond these transient considerations and develops toward what Aristotle calls "true friendship." A true friend, he says, is like a "second self," and it works only when the true friends are "alike in virtue"—they strive for what's right and good and just and courageous and wise and yes, moderate, *together*. If one is more morally developed than another, there can be no true friendship. At least, that's what the old philosopher claims.

It's pretty clear that the members of Queen were friends in a pretty tight way. Yes, they quarreled, but people now want to see their bond as going deeper than the usual bandmates. There's something unusual in it, and like Fox Mulder, we want to believe. I don't know whether it's true, of course, and maybe Brian and Roger and John don't really know either. It is hard enough to know our own deepest motives, let alone somebody else's. Everyone wants to find a way to excuse the behavior of our d'Artagnan, while our Athos and Porthos and Aramis try to carry on without him. The comparison is tempting, no?

But our d'Artagnan seems a tragicomic rather than merely comic character, and his pathos leads us to see him as the mix of a Musketeer and a Hamlet-esque prince. So let's see if we can understand the darkness in and of this person, who is increasingly becoming a caricature of himself, as history tosses his story about like, well, like a character from a Dumas adventure novel: The Count of Monte Zanzibar. He called himself a Persian Popinjay. If you look at the standard depiction of Zarathustra, he looks like a blue popinjay with a tambourine. If you look *very* closely you might see the shadow of a ragged clown behind, chasing. I wouldn't pay it any mind.

Pain Is So Close to Pleasure

What was all that hullabaloo in the Seventies and Eighties (and just a bit of the Nineties) anyway? I was there but I didn't get an invitation to that long party, not that I can remember. Everyone remembers the music and the gay old times as being such fun. It didn't seem so back then, to me at least. The music was great.

Queen was really different, unclassifiable. Refusing to be defined by the trends. There were plenty of virtuoso rock bands, the prog bunch in the vanguard, and Queen had its prog side. But even commercial bands, like Styx and Kansas, were playing music that required serious chops. You don't just plop down and chord these tunes out for a campfire with friends. Well, maybe the Dylan tunes, but the era was for serious talent only. Even Dylan's muse took a vacation in the Eighties.

It's clear that, among the classical virtues (wisdom, justice, courage, and the rest) *moderation* certainly wasn't a virtue the Queen's musketeers shared, especially one of them, and we know which one. Also, it is clear that in spite of their unusual virtue of having four hit songwriters (even the Beatles didn't have that), some members of the quartet were "more equal than others." And we know which one. And, eventually one member seems to have put his own talent/ego/importance ahead of the others for a while, only to discover he needed the rest of his friends to do what he did at a level of excellence that the public would notice.

We know who that was. We resist calling it "dark." But he had a darkness, didn't he? It took all four to hold chaos at bay, to make a yasna, as my Zoroastrian friends like to say. But pain is so close to pleasure.

Death (on Two Legs) and the Darkness

The departure of one member from this life, was effectively the end of the line for the 'real' Queen, although they've dug up some lost tapes recently and put out some 'new' material. But we all know *The Game* was up. John knew it and simply went away. All this suggests that maybe this wasn't a "true friendship," in the classical sense, just one helluva useful pleasure trip. But the fire went out. Without that one dude, the band was a somewhat bland bunch of musical blokes beating and bellowing. Talented, yes, but not edgy or interesting, to be honest. It wouldn't have helped if John had stayed.

Why no fire? Maybe it wasn't so much fire as a feeling of the edge of darkness. That place around the fire where one begins to lose the light, the warmth, the safety of the circle, that red fire light of home. We go to that edge when we want to see without being seen. We sat in the darkness and watched the popinjay command the light. But without him there was no, well, tantalizing forbiddenness about the music and their shows. And so, we learned that there need to be a few dark dabblings in the otherwise drab and dreary dealings of the otherwise ordinary men about town. And indeed, Queen had its dark side. Lusty, edgy, maybe dangerous? The man was a paradox. As he said himself "I seem to have created a monster. When I'm performing I'm an extravert, yet inside I'm a completely different man" (Blake, *Is This the Real Life?*, p. 182) We all know that, ironically, it was off-stage that he got himself in trouble.

Let's also admit this: in some sense, he had to die. He seems to have known that, he cultivated it, wrote about it, and in the end made a performance of it. David Bowie's "Lazarus" is copycat stuff compared to the way Freddie left us. There, I said his name. May he be conjured thereby. One thing to know about the kind of darkness that we find alluring is that it needs to *seem* not so very dark. Bowie is on and on about his impending death (some critics were brave enough to say "enough already"). Freddie never complained, he just *performed* it brilliantly. And his path was always unexpected, even by his friends.

So I began thinking: I wonder if the reason Freddie surprises us may have some relation to the fact that most of us know he was raised in a very "religious" household, but we know nothing about this religion. The movie presented the sternness, but not the religion itself. But many articles say that Freddie was quite proud of his connection to Zoroastrianism.

The Devil Put Aside

What little do we know? One thing many of us do know about this religion is that Friedrich Nietzsche (1844–1900) sort of re-worked Zoroastrianism for our modern ears. We know there was a prophet of some sort, named Zarathustra, and that he wandered around, eventually becoming disgusted with us. He taught us of the Overman, whatever that is. The Overman was beyond good and evil, whatever that means. Definitely not the real Zoroaster's view. Nietzsche's prophet seems to have thought not much of God or of the traditions that uphold that figure. The real Zoroaster apparently *invented* monotheism. Nietzsche's hero doesn't like women, or much of anything else, and couldn't be bothered with the details of ordinary human struggle. The real Zoroaster called humans to the forces of light to stave off the forces of chaos. Nietzsche did condemn "nihilism," but as far as I can tell, that includes rising above such struggles and seeing the ridiculousness of daily life. So Nietzsche isn't much help.

We know that Richard Strauss wrote a nice piece of music in recognition of Nietzsche's prophet, which then became a hit song when Stanley Kubrick put it in a movie. Some of us are aware that as *Game of Thrones* reached its climax, the writers went in a Zoroastrian direction. For most of us, that's about the extent of what we know that we can associate with Zoroastrianism.

How much Nietzsche knew about Zoroastrianism isn't clear. He wasn't interested in teaching us the historical religion. That religion had been under serious discussion in Europe (especially among the French) for a hundred years before Nietzsche showed up. See especially Montesquieu's *Persian Letters*, and don't miss Mozart's *The Magic Flute*. Indeed, when Nietzsche was a lad, a physicist who studied light, Gustav Fechner, had re-written the *Zend Avesta* (the holy scriptures of Zoroastrianism) as a philosophy for the modern humans. This figure of Zarathustra hovers above, behind, our culture. So Nietzsche had reason to think he was writing for future people who might understand what he was doing better than his contemporaries.

Made Up in Heaven (and Elsewhere)

What Nietzsche seems to have admired in Zarathustra was that he took stock of the traditional Persian religious ways and wasn't impressed. So he (apparently) made up a new way. He said that the universe is a struggle between the forces of light (order) and the forces of darkness (chaos). Every person must choose which side to serve. The forces of the light are led by Ahura Mazda (yes, the car company named itself after this deity). The forces of darkness are led by Angra Mainyu or "Ahriman" in Middle Persian –I admit my Middle Persian is rusty these days. Gotta brush up. But through a history of transformations, Ahriman ends up being Beelzebub. No kidding.

But another reason Nietzsche may have chosen to rework Zoroaster as Zarathustra is because the real dude, 1500–1200 BCE, seems to have made up many of the ideas that now hold us back—such as God, heaven, hell, sin, angels, demons, and prophecy itself. He is immanent in the Big Three, Judaism, Christianity, and Islam. It seems that the influence of the Persian Empire at its height, filtered into the Hebrew religion. Cyrus the Great is referred to as "messiah" in the Book of Isaiah, the only person in Hebrew scripture to bear that title apart from David. The Persians liberated the Hebrews from exile in Babylon, sent them back to the Holy Land, and helped to finance the re-building of the Temple.

This wasn't from the goodness of their hearts. The Persians needed a reliable outpost in Canaan to keep the Egyptians in check, and there were those pesky Assyrians, who were probably done in by the Babylonians, but you never know. Better safe than sorry. World powers have a way of getting up off the mat before the ref counts to ten. So the Persians sent not only a powerful priest (Ezra), but also a pretty serious general (Nehemiah) to build not only a Temple, but a series of walls around their favorite city. In exchange, well, loyalty and a form of submission that didn't bother the Hebrews. In a hundred years or so, the Hebrews, with Persian military support, were able to subjugate the non-Hebrew peoples who had moved in at the invitation of the Assyrians that took the land of the ten lost tribes of Israel. The remnant of those tribes was legally absorbed into the tribe of Judah, and everyone in Israel was forced to keep the Law whether they were Jewish or not.

If this deal sounds a little bit like the current deal between Israel and the United States, well, welcome to Persia. My point is that there is this inheritance of Zoroastrianism that is all around you, all the time. Guess who knows this? Modern Zoroastrians. Guess who doesn't? Almost everyone else in the West, including most Muslims. Why am I telling *you* all this? Simple. Freddie knew it, and also knew the rest of us didn't get it. It's pretty interesting to be a practitioner of the oldest religion in the world, surrounded by people who know so little about their own religions that they do not know the debts, spiritually, philosophically, and in terms of practice, that derive from that much older religion. Now, to be clear, the version of Persian religion that descends from Zoroaster is *not* older than the Hebrew religion, but the Hebrew religion, as practiced in its first millennium, and has a lot of Egyptian influence, is very different from the Judaism that bears the influence of the Persian Empire. It has been a long bicycle ride.

Freddie's Dilemma

So, I want you to imagine: You live in a world where everybody has borrowed the most important truths and insights of your religion, and they claim these as their own. That is Freddie's situation. Even his best friends, who are not religious, don't know anything about this. But, like everybody else, if you depict struggles and conflicts and stories in images they can understand, they respond. To give only one example, the dualism of good and evil and its symbolization as darkness and light, works every time. Your friends love it when you tell them about *that*.

In particular, your religion, which you have been hearing about since before you could talk, has quite a cast of characters, and punishments for evil-doers. The always-creative writers for *The Onion* described some of the punishments and demons awaiting the 9/11 hijackers thus:

> Said Iblis, The Thrice-Damned . . . "Indeed, I don't know what they were expecting, but they certainly didn't seem prepared to be skewered from eye-socket to bunghole and then placed on a spit so that their flesh could be roasted by the searing gale of flautus which issues forth from the haunches of Asmoday."

And the *Onion* reporters add:

> exacerbating the terrorists' tortures, which include being hollowed out and used as prophylactics by thorn-cocked Gulbuth the Rampant, is the fact that they will be forced to endure such suffering in sight of the Paradise they were expecting. . . That can't be fun.

In fact, depictions of hell and punishment pervade the inheritors of Zoroastrianism. Freddie's flirtations with darkness are very mild compared to what your typical fundamentalist Christian believes he is enduring now, in hell, where he belongs, in their stupid view. It makes me very angry to contemplate it. You fundamentalists don't fool me, and you wouldn't like me when I am angry, so I am going to do my best to turn toward the light. It isn't easy in this moment. I want to send Gulbuth the Rampant to the nearest Southern Baptist Church for some new prophylactics. But Freddie wouldn't do that and he wouldn't like anyone else to do it either. I don't expect heaven exists, but if it does, Freddie is definitely there, as I will explain.

Creatures of the Dark

There were creatures of the dark before Zoroaster, of course, but in all those centuries, we never cultivated the demonic as a human type, let alone as a human aspiration, until Modern science made our souls problematic for us. This seems to be Goethe's point in *Faust*. The new learning meant that we had to rebuild the human soul, and that meant facing it, on its own terms, unsaved perhaps, not bound for heaven or even purgatory, but rather actually *choosing* the dark. Now that was part of Zoroaster's point, back in the day: we have to choose, and that imperative, that dilemma, would have been Freddie's experience all along. The rest of us run from the choice, but the Zoroastrians are taught to face it (alone). And these days, even they may have a hard time believing in the eventual triumph of good, and light.

Why were the Parsis in India? Persecuted by the Muslims in Persia. Why were the Bulsaras and other Parsis in Zanzibar? Persecuted in India. Why did the Bulsaras leave Zanzibar for England? Persecuted by the Muslims and other political factions that wanted power in the post-colonial era. Why did Freddie fall away from the practice of his religion? I think one could safely say "all the bullshit." But like any ex-Catholic, ex-Jew, ex-Baptist, ex-Muslim, there is a very *particular* God that *definitely does not exist*. It leaves what poet JP Jones calls "a God-sized hole." It is not a big step for lesser demons to share that hole, whether in turns or jointly. Freddie's behavior became erratic, self-destructive, detrimental to his friends and their music.

Demons? What Demons?

Let's begin with a description of these types of creatures, the ones so deeply at odds with the status of having been created, and who re-create themselves in darkness and defiance of the givenness of finitude. These are the very symbols of our finitude, these demons. More to the point: How, then, do we *make ourselves* immortal? Am I not Iblis the Thrice-damned? Asmoday and his flautus? Gulbuth the Rampant? Do we not fashion these demons from our own darkness?

We began with friendship. Creatures of the dark do not *have* friendships, but they do have 'society', in its broadest meaning. Their society mirrors that of mortal life in ways that ordinary creatures—of the light, of the dawn, or the dusk, or even the twilight—cannot see or quite fathom.

But just as we creatures of light and half-light have our scientists, we have our statesmen, our artists, and even our philosophers, so do the creatures of the dark. Their immortal vocations follow something of their mortal proclivities, talents, and interests. It is crucial to grasp that no one is *born* a creature of the dark. It is chosen. Just as Zoroaster says. There is a moment. We know it. It never 'happens' to a creature—it's an irrevocable step that we take knowingly. We bring the past along, but the past has no power in this new way of life. Fear has no power, it is simply gone. The future is no longer a form of time, but a playground of infinite desire, more of which shortly. We are super-sonic men, moving at the speed of light. Don't stop me. Never mind. You couldn't if you tried.

So, perhaps a creature of the dark still likes to draw or paint or write songs. Or experiment in medicine or physics. Perhaps it is Mengele or Sade, but the creature hardly lacks curiosity. We have seen these creatures, being curious. The issue of *genuine* creativity is far more difficult, but the demonic being aspires to be creative and will not tolerate the suggestion that it is not. That is why he has no friends, only producers, engineers, handlers, erotic lovers. The opportunity arising from choosing the dark allows for the development of beauty, knowledge, and power indefinitely. But real creativity? How can it go on? We have to discuss that. Why are Freddie's solo efforts so flat? I think you know.

But we are forgetful. Thomas Aquinas in the thirteenth century wrote the creatures of the dark out of existence in his greatest work, saying that immortal beings (presumably including those human souls who serve the light) could *not* possess carnal natures, and that among immortals, only pride and envy were within the purview of their "sinful" actions. You may consult this writing in English translation, *Summa Theologica*, Part I, Questions 63 and 64, the so-called "Treatise on Angels." He was struggling with St. Augustine's fourth-century doctrine of the bodies we possess in the "City of God." The Scriptures say these are "bodies of light" and in them there is no darkness. I wonder where an idea like that came from? Before becoming a Christian, Augustine had been a follower of Mani, who believed the universe was a struggle between the forces of light and those of darkness. Wonder where he got *that*?

Is This the World We Created?

Thus, creatures of the dark, although they had immigrated from the oldest regions of the world, were almost unknown to European mortals after Aquinas, and until the Modern science had stripped away the dogma. It was inevitable that Europe would have to struggle with the dark, as Egypt and Persia and India, and indeed China, had many centuries, even millennia before. The dark in the West took on a new configuration, including scientific knowledge as one of its many modalities. That would be Faust, or Mengele. This science is Romanticism, and in terms of the dark, it is this configuration, the technological will to power, that colors or even dominates the darkness in us even today. Our music must follow, but must remain on one side of the digital divide, Satan's realm, so no synthesizers. Just good old electromagnetism. It's like four alchemist magicians fighting against the information age. After all, life is real.

The creature of the dark suffers these days from an excessive refinement of taste. We need an analogy. What if we *drank* a creature of the dark? American creatures of the dark are like a heavy red blend, based on a Zinfindel, but by all means, add some Cabernet and Barbera, complex mixtures, some almost accidentally nice, others very difficult to endure. Dark Italians are like pure varietals. Sagrantino, sangiovese, the like. Dark Spaniards are Temperanillo, but leaning toward bull's blood. Dark Germans are like the finest Bavarian Weissbier (so deceptive, seems almost like light, no? Don't have a second.). Russians are akin to their own Imperial Stout, but used to chase an almost undrinkable vodka, to kill the taste. Dark Mexicans must be eaten as a mole, they are too thick to drink. What a mixture! It's practically chocolate. But it is gritty and they don't even notice. Perhaps you're beginning to understand. What about the refinements allowed by the dark? They are many, but somehow always the same. Don't drink too much, drink responsibly.

And what is it like to drink a Post-Zoroastrian Parsi Popinjay? Well, a lot of people got a taste. One would have to ask them, I suppose. And what of this deeper difficulty? What of an angel who plays the demon in order to be tasted by the whole world, if not literally, in the boudoir, then on stage, in our ears as audible candy, and in our hearts, darling? I don't know, but I am guessing he tasted like a Moët et Chandon, from a pretty cabinet.

How do we learn the dark creature? From those who dwell in the twilight, I think, so that will be none of our true friends. The creatures of the dark cannot know themselves, but they believe they have perfect self-knowledge, and it is useless to converse with them about what they are. But those who approach the choice of the dark, *without* so choosing, do know some things. I expect there are still some out there who knew Freddie's struggle with the darkness. And I want to say that in the end, he definitely did not choose the darkness, and that he was one of those creatures of the twilight. I think he did learn to know himself, and that when he returned from the edge, he was transformed.

Into the Light

Nietzsche is still waiting for his readers, I think. A book for everybody and nobody. But oddly, I think he is getting some help from an unexpected prophet named Farrokh Bulsara, who drew our attention to the struggle of light and darkness in his songs, and then, well, sort of died from and for *our* collective sin, namely homophobia. We feared, we punished, we hated, we killed with our refusal to care. Let them die, the religious hypocrites cried. With his sacrifice, Freddie moved our civilization forward, into the light. This is an important point, so I am going to say it again in slightly different words.

Let me ask, plainly: Why did Freddie Mercury, naming himself for the messenger of the gods, by the way, struggle with his own sexuality? Because he had been taught it was dark, by his Parsi culture and by our whole Western culture. He was taught that *love* was dark, was disorder, was chaos, and that Beelzebub had a devil put aside for him. He was led to believe, falsely, that the love he felt was condemnable lust, unless it was approved by his society. It was no easy time. I insist, insist, that he knew this: his dying of complications from AIDS would change *us* for the better. But even at the end, it was still a struggle to come out into the light with his truth.

Yet, he did enough, and it *did* change us. Because of him, so many people were finally able to say "screw it, I love him and everything he did, and I don't care whether he went to bed with men or women, or anyone he wanted." When his career began, *that* had to be a dark secret, even to himself. Of course his friends, his *true* friends, his band, and his true lovers, *knew*. They watched the struggle. Front row seats. The Musketeers and Constance. They had compassion and quite a bit of patience, and it wasn't just about his usefulness or pleasurable presence. They loved him. It shows.

They were simply more enlightened than most people who *followed* their music, and would come along later. They knew that *too*. It was quite a story.

III

A Night at the Concert

6
Be Free with Your Tempo

Douglas Rasmussen

Half a minute longer than "Bohemian Rhapsody," and with nearly as many distinct tonal shifts, Queen's "Innuendo" is just as grand and operatic a vision as its better known counterpart. Released on the album of the same name, it would be the last Queen record featuring Freddie Mercury before his death in 1991 from complications relating to his AIDS diagnosis. *Innuendo*, the fourteenth studio album produced by Queen, was released in February 1991, shortly before Freddie's unfortunate death that November.

Mercury worked through his declining health and put everything he could into the album, knowing it would be his last. The title track is Freddie at his most introspective, contemplative, and artistic. Gone is the rock'n'roll excess of his youth that marked a lot of his earlier work (like the party anthem "Don't Stop Me Now"). "Innuendo" approaches similar themes from Freddie's earlier works—such as nonconformity and individuality—but in a more mature and complex philosophical context.

We can look at "Innuendo" (with its themes of freedom and individuality in the face of a repressive society) through the philosophical lens of the American philosopher and essayist Ralph Waldo Emerson (1803–1882). Emerson was a nineteenth-century philosopher, and at one time an ordained minister. He wasn't exactly known for rocking out in a harlequin spandex outfit, but he *was* known for his unconventional views; in particular, his belief in nonconformity in the face of societal expectations.

Emerson advocated for individuality to the point where, despite (arguably) being a Christian himself, he often spoke out against religious orthodoxy (and organized religion generally) as a detriment to the spiritual nature of our character. The essay "Self-Reliance" provides an interesting synthesis of these views.

A Crazy Little Thing Called Self-Reliance

Written in 1841, "Self-Reliance" places an emphasis on the individual in opposition to societal expectations. Here Emerson advocates for nonconformity to an extraordinary degree: history, tradition, and institutions are cast as obsolete anchors keeping humanity rooted in one place and time. Emerson didn't believe in being chained to previous notions in regards to morality or ethics; especially as they were often mandated by small-minded government bureaucrats or preachers reciting from a prescribed text (and offering no wisdom or insight into God from their own conceptions).

The central philosophy of the essay is encapsulated by the very poetic, almost musically lyrical sentence, "Trust thyself, every heart vibrates to that iron string" (p. 19). The only path to happiness and true greatness in an individual is to have the strength of character to follow your own path and not concede to the institutional structures that weigh a person down. For Emerson it's the personal responsibility of the individual to live up to their own unique potential and not act like "invalids in a protected corner, cowards fleeing before a revolution" (p. 19). Hyperbolic language aside, this striving for nonconformity against the pressures of society is an important philosophical message shared by both Emerson and Queen.

For Emerson a person's path is clear: "Whoso would be a man, must also be a nonconformist" (p. 22). In order to achieve any sort of greatness, moral goodness, or even just happiness, an individual must actively strive against the confines of a repressive society. Emerson equates this nonconformity with a moral imperative, arguing that the sacredness of traditions don't matter if a person lives wholly within themselves (p. 22).

Emerson is critical of sectarian worshippers who only follow a prescribed tradition handed down to them by preachers reciting from a text—rather than following their own unique path to God. The path to God is contained within the self. Nothing is sacred to Emerson except the "integrity of your own mind" (p. 22). The so-called sacred, then, is merely a set of rules and regulations established by the church; it's only in the free expression of the individual that one can attain spiritual independence. For Emerson, only a nonconformist can get closer to God.

The consequence of this spiritual independence and nonconformity is that the "world whips you with its displeasure" (p. 27). Society has a social order to it that places restrictive demands on people, sowing the seeds of hate and division. Emerson provides a rallying cry—to confront the mediocrity of the times and the propensity towards squalid contentment that comes from following customs, trade, and office (p. 30). It's this intellectual stagnation that most of society falls prey to, contributing to the social ills of civilization. Only those brave enough to endure this constant opposition—by society, by governments, by religious orthodoxy, and by all manner of societal and moral institutions, imposed upon them at all times—will forge a distinctly new path towards greatness. Or at least a path towards contentment and happiness.

Emerson is quite clear in his condemnation of the social and moral institutions that govern society and the conduct of humanity. In his estimation they're obstructions to the innate goodness of an individual. Society never advances on its own, and the collective nature of society discourages the creative and unique individual with banal social customs and edicts passed down by the conspirators of history: "Do that which is assigned to you, and you cannot hope too much or dare too much" (p. 60). A person unwilling to risk everything to oppose societal conventions can't hope to achieve much in life (or affect positive social change in any meaningful way). Society isn't inherently moral or good in Emerson's view: therefore you can't be good or moral merely by conforming to its moral precepts and the established order of things.

Essentially, "Self-Reliance" is the nineteenth-century equivalent of rock'n'roll rebellion. Emerson's plea for individuality and nonconformity against the stifling hordes of society is an idea familiar to many artists. Indeed, many writers and poets (Emily Dickinson and Henry James, to name only two examples) were inspired by Emerson. Just as many artists are likely inspired by the eccentricity and innovation of Queen. It's an intuitive leap from Emerson's notion of an independent selfhood to rock music, and the creative expression of individuality in artists like Freddie Mercury.

Rock'n'Roll and the Independent Spirit

Rock'n'roll is premised on the idea that the social and moral authority of your parent's generation can't be relied upon or trusted as a valuable source of ethics. Invariably, the social mores of the previous generation tend to be rooted in obsolete notions and ethical principles applicable, more or less, to the previous generation only. The norms and traditions put in place by our parent's generation (and the generations that preceded them) often can't be trusted as an ethical framework to guide our actions. As Emerson points out, nothing can truly be gained from following the values and social customs embedded into society by the conspirators of history.

The appeal of rock'n'roll is in its rebellious spirit, and it's this aspect that resonates in the philosophy of Emerson. He declares that he's going to "speak the rude truth in all ways" (p. 22). Speaking the "rude truth" sounds quintessentially rock'n'roll! He goes further, stating that moral goodness "must have some edge to it,—else it is none" (p. 22). Rock'n'roll certainly embodies that "edge" that Emerson writes of—disrupting social norms with raunchiness, breaking social taboos of sexuality, identity, and race.

Queen are certainly speakers of the rude truth. Freddie Mercury uses rock'n'roll as a platform to express a desire for social order where freedom of expression—in his particular case that of sexual expression, but the principles can be applied to any field of expression—brings about positive social change in society. For someone to speak (or sing) the rude truth poses a risk; but what other kind can be of true value to the progression of society? This has certainly been the province of rock'n'roll and its innovative practitioners: disrupting the social order.

Rock'n'roll acts as a catharsis against familial constraints and rigid hierarchies. It makes accessible to a younger listener the vital function of self-reliance through its ethos of rebellion and nonconformity. Rock'n'roll in its best form brings an awareness to the idea that each generation inherits a world that's largely screwed up by the previous generation. A lot of the social norms imposed upon us by those in power (whether that's in our personal lives or on a political level), is formed by a corrupt and venal power base. This power base can emanate from the indoctrination encountered at school by narrow-minded educators, the domineering and controlling nature of families, racial and political oppression, or the demands placed upon the individual by society.

The systems of power and our social and moral institutions, as Emerson has observed, almost never have our best interests at heart. This is discovered empirically in youth, before many young (and not so young!) individuals are reading philosophers like Emerson. Instead, they rely on bands like Queen for help in shaping their world view. Popular music like rock'n'roll and rap perform a vital function in introducing sociological and philosophical concerns about these corruptive systems of power in an accessible format. Think of Queen as your introduction to Emerson!

This aspect of rock'n'roll resonates both in the popular music of individualistic artists expressing nonconformity in their music and in the listener whose ideas might be informed by their popular music tastes. It's quite a radical notion to disregard history as a major sociological force (as Emerson does) and see it as an anchor rooting someone in obsolete ideals. But it's a necessary removal from the conspirators of history that propels humanity's forward momentum. Rock'n'roll at its best is anti-establishment—inviting the listener to abandon the moral authority of school teachers, preachers, parents, and others. And to protest the divisiveness generated by these authority figures.

Freddie Mercury, the Artistic Spirit, and a New Society

Both Emerson and rock'n'roll share an important creative purpose: to actively disregard the forces of history—the social and moral values enforced by your parents, by school teachers, and the dogmas of society—for a new progressive vision of positive social change. Emerson advocates for freedom and individuality in a way that would be echoed by a number of rock'n'roll musicians, most notably: Queen. The song "Innuendo" is a prime example of the themes and ideas contained in Emerson's "Self-Reliance."

The second verse describes a world that would be familiar to Emerson: torn apart by sectarian divisions, racism, and strife. The verse begins with an ominous and heavy sound to accentuate the dark tone of the second verse. The horrible state of affairs that humanity finds itself in is dismal and oppressive. Freddie laments how as a society "we rule by blind madness / And pure greed." Emerson describes a similarly oppressive view, proclaiming that "Society never advances. It recedes as fast on one side as it gains on the other" (p. 61). There is a cyclical nature of violence and hatred that seems to afflict society. There is an inevitability to humanity's constant in-fighting.

Despite this bleak state of things, Mercury's chorus offers an optimistic hope that "we'll keep on trying / tread that fine line." Freddie was well-known for breaking barriers and defying social norms, echoing Emerson's plea for individuals to "affront and reprimand the smooth mediocrity" of the times (p. 30). Freddie and Emerson are inviting us not to listen to the conspirators of history—they're only motivated by selfish agendas and are stuck in their own dogmas, contributing to the perpetual struggle in which humanity always seems to find itself.

Much like Emerson, Queen is expressing discontentment with the corrosive nature of what Emerson refers to as 'dead institutions'. As Freddie sings in "Innuendo": "Our lives dictated by tradition / Superstition, false religion." Queen is dismissing the idea of traditions and religious orthodoxy. These are the source of societal divisions and a maintenance of the status quo, which seems to be violence and hatred. The discipline enforced on youth that rock'n'roll often rebels against is complicit in the coercive structures that are responsible for so much of our social ills. The past and its adherence to traditions and dogmas is an anchor weighing humanity down, negatively impacting our ability to progress socially and culturally. And, as Emerson and Queen have both observed, this appears to be the prevailing attitude in society. It's much more difficult to forge your own path in the world than to comply with authority (even when that compliance reinforces violence, hatred, and bigotry).

According to Queen, the answer to this problem is to encourage their listeners to be "anything you think that you could ever be" and follow their own path, their own inner voice. Autonomy can only come from within; only by refusing to adhere to society's imposed structures can humanity alleviate our misery and suffering. This is also one of the most difficult processes to undergo, for as Emerson notes, "The virtue most in request is conformity. Self-reliance is its aversion" (p. 19). On the whole, society seems overly concerned with maintaining the status quo, even if that status quo is harmful and destructive to the creative potential of a person. Often youth are indoctrinated by parents, school teachers, religious figures, and other assorted authority figures to follow in the same damaging path as they have followed from generations previous to them. It takes a brave individual to fight against that current.

When Freddie sings "Be free with your tempo," it's a philosophical mantra about freedom and individuality—and an invitation for listeners to express themselves in their own unique and creative way, without having to follow the norms and conventions of a repressive and hateful society. In this way "Innuendo" aligns fairly closely with Emerson's philosophy. They both advocate for a path to moral goodness that's not found in these imposed social structures. This makes "Innuendo" a more complex and mature take on their earlier music that promoted nonconformity. "Innuendo" calls for an active engagement with the world on the listener's own terms, for the purpose of the betterment of humanity. This brings the song more in line with the philosophy of Emerson by addressing the big metaphysical and political questions about the state of society and what form of justice exists: whether it's God or some other type of moral, ethical, or spiritual framework.

Freddie sings to the listener: "Show yourself, destroy our fears / release your mask." He's inviting listeners to shred their artificial constructions of identity—imposed upon them by familial or political structures—for an autonomy based on honesty and open communication. Only in this unconstrained sense of self can humanity ever hope to progress beyond the sad state of affairs it always seems to find itself in. The sentiment of nonconformity in "Innuendo" represents both a reflection on the political and sociological strife that occurs in humanity's interactions with itself, while also using this principle of nonconformity as a possible solution for ridding the world of its violence and divisions.

Legacy

A final point of comparison I'd like to make between Emerson's "Self-Reliance" and Queen's "Innuendo" concerns the biographical circumstances surrounding both works. In the year prior to the publication of "Self-Reliance," Emerson's son had died from Scarlet Fever, leaving him and his second wife Lidian inconsolable (Emerson's first wife Ellen died from consumption in 1820). The loss of his loved ones proved devastating to Emerson, and to his faith in God. At the time of writing

"Innuendo," Freddie was suffering from AIDS. He knew that he didn't have much time left. As a result, he spent as much time as he could, given his frail condition, to record the most music possible—to leave a legacy.

Both Emerson and Freddie were celebrated artists in their own right. Artists who expressed their despair through art, whether that was the poetic philosophy of Emerson or the rock music of Queen. The trauma of these events, however, imprinted on the artists a sense of importance in using their respective arts to convey a message: of freedom, individuality, and a person's true place in the world.

I think Emerson said it best when he wrote the immortal words that could easily have come from Queen themselves: "Insist on yourself; never imitate" (p. 58).

7
Performance as a Tour de Force

JULIE KUHLKEN

When Freddie Mercury bounded onto the stage at Wembley Stadium in 1985, he was clearly there to perform—musically, of course, but also in many other ways. That strong voice control and command of the keyboard are his musical performances.

The pacing tiger energy of his strides across the stage show that he is performing his role as the frontman of the band, letting the other members focus on their respective musical performances. His seamless pirouette from belting out "We Will Rock You" at the front of the stage to crooning "We Are the Champions" at the keyboard evidences the virtuosity of his performance, and the command he has over it.

He also "performs" his audience, clapping and fist pumping like one of the crowd, in order to mold a stadium of concert-goers into a co-ordinated squad with him just one of their number (a performance all the more amazing given that this was Live Aid, not a Queen concert where all of the attendees would likely have been fans).

All these aspects of performance distinguish the band's excellence on the stage, but what truly sets him (and Queen as a whole) apart, is that *Queen performs*

Queen. Queen both is and is not Killer Queen—more on this later.

In their infamous parties—most notably the one held in 1978 at the New Orleans Fairmont where strippers, drag queens, and dwarves supposedly dumbfounded four hundred guests—Queen performed itself as a rock band. The Mister Fahrenheit excessiveness of self-performance is what Queen grasps more clearly than many of their peers, who may have embraced the sex, drugs and rock'n'roll ethos, but did not necessarily also perform it.

By performing itself Queen undertakes a transgressive act against the culture industry of which it is an inescapable part. To perform one's self is to mimic the culture industry with a wink and a nod.

Instead of denying self-contradictions and ambiguities, Queen's self-performance underscores them: Brian, the Imperial College educated astrophysicist whose guitar solo could set Wayne and Garth headbanging; the shy, cat-loving Freddie who could command the rapt attention of a worldwide audience of two billion viewers.

The ability to suspend oneself between one's contradictions, the ability to be truly *mercurial*, allows Queen to give what the German philosopher Theodor Adorno dubs a promise of happiness.

Dynamite with a Laser Beam

The *promise* of happiness is the antidote to the *illusion* of happiness offered us by the culture industry. Freddie Mercury, in particular, would seem to embody the illusory kind. He is the boy with the ugly teeth and awkward, shy smile that grows up to be a rockstar: an apologist for a system that lets a few bask in glittered glory as a distraction from the daily grind demanded of everyone else.

Queen thematizes this illusory happiness in "In Only Seven Days," the "freedom" of the employee who is paid to not work for one week in order to ensure that he does the other fifty-one. Such a ruse goes back to the "bread and circuses" of the Roman era, when entertainments were organized to quell dissent against the elites' corrupt and violent rule. What is so insidious in the contemporary era is that the administration of these "circuses" is so total that it not only distracts individuals from dissent: it incorporates dissent.

Rock'n'Roll music is one long protest against authority—one long, mocking rendition of "God Save the Queen"—nevertheless, its administration is a marvel of tying the interests of bands to the economic interests of the record labels that make them famous (a situation that Queen repeatedly rebelled against, to their own expense).

The rock industry makes non-conformism a marketable brand, and hence quite conformist. Moreover, it is not just the rock stars themselves that come to identify with the power that controls them—it is the fans as well, whose likes and dislikes are further strings on the puppet musician's arm, moving him to tweak his musical output at their behest, belying his claim to originality.

This threat is serious, because the promise of happiness is a defiant claim to originality—the fat-bottomed girls of musical creativity, if you will. At the same time, trying to create something new is naive: like a child sitting at a piano searching out a never before heard chord, as Adorno describes it.

Only by retaining childlike wonder will one persist in the exercise, but just the same, this wonder is airy fairy—the land where "bees have lost their stings"—if not combined with hard-nosed consciousness that the "fairy circle ring" has indeed been broken. Musical originality ironically requires naive cynicism, a longing for the new (dubious of its fulfillment), an openness to the promise of happiness rather than a hard demand that it be presently manufactured.

Rather than manufacture, therefore, Queen performs. In a world where "nothing really matters," your acts are less important than the fact that you act. To put it differently, if (as Adorno famously says) the "wrong life cannot be lived rightly," we cannot truly believe that a rock song is going to change the world. But we can still believe that by performing it we maintain hope that such change is possible.

If, for Adorno, Hamlet's exclamation that "the play's the thing" exemplifies the essentiality of performance for the modern individual, for Queen, it's "Killer Queen" that does the same. The song perfectly encapsulates Queen's self-performance. At one level, it describes a high-class prostitute, just as Freddie says it does. But at another level, that is entirely disingenuous—especially for a band whose first two albums are eponymous and sing that they are coming to sell you their body (in "Let Me Entertain You").

In other words, Queen *is and is not* Killer Queen. Moreover, in the persona of Killer Queen coalesces the fundamental thematic dialogue of the Queen *oeuvre*: a back and forth between the entreating voice to Mother Mercury (of one who has fallen from grace) and the forceful shout at the moment of his master-stroke resurgence.

This musical conversation establishes itself early with the one-two punch of "My Fairy Queen" followed by "Liar" on *Queen*. This is followed by "Ogre Battle" and "The Fairy Feller's Master-Stroke" on *Queen II*. And the dialogue is quintessentially distilled into the six minutes of "Bohemian Rhapsody."

Both "playful as a pussy cat" and out to get you, Killer Queen is both disarmingly vulnerable and alarmingly vicious, and as the song refrains, you never know in a given minute whether you are going to encounter the gelatine or the dynamite. The self-performances of Killer Queen (as well as the band who plays it) are always viscerally direct and guaranteed to blow your mind.

Let Me Cruella DeVille You

Though as just noted, Queen's early work contains all the seeds of their mature lyrics and sound, it is the sociological situation of Queen that forges it into a band uniquely wedded to performance.

Their legal wrangle with Trident in 1974 (to extricate themselves from their label deal with the studio) left them both desperately bankrupt and angrily disillusioned with the rock industry. This disillusion detonates in the first track of *A Night at the Opera*, "Death on Two Legs"—followed in characteristically Queen fashion by the saccharine romp of "Lazing on a Sunday Afternoon."

It is revealing to compare the lyrics and tone of Queen's hateful dedication to their former manager, Norman Sheffield, with the cynical tear down of record companies by Pink Floyd in "Have a Cigar." Pink Floyd's record managers are patronizing, deceitful and greedy, but openly so, as is underscored by the tongue in cheek question, "Which one's Pink?" By contrast, Queen decries a blood-sucking betrayal of trust by their former manager, who is described as heartless, juvenile, and sleazy. The song echoes with the fury of a loss of innocence that thrusts the band precariously into the glaring light of the reality of the rock industry.

From this album on, Queen's self-consciousness of the particular limitations and opportunities of the rock genre become paramount, and they diverge from the pretensions that plague some other progressive rock bands.

They quit pursuing the rock masterpieces to which the earlier "Seven Seas of Rhye" would appear to aspire—though arguably and ironically "Bohemian Rhapsody" is one—and thereby start deviating from popular music in the traditional sense. From its beginnings in the medieval troubadours, popular music has fundamentally wanted to woo an audience (quite literally, in the historic case).

Don't get me wrong: Queen wants to be popular. But not by wooing its audience. Rather, by *unbridling* it. As many commentators on Queen have noted, their performance is uniquely generous to their audiences (and to each other). For them, music is a gift, a promise of happiness.

Queen's innovation is easier to understand if we challenge the commonplace notion that some music is serious, and some is mere entertainment. Classical music, patriotic marches (thanks, Plato) and religious hymns are usually lumped into the serious category, and popular music populates most of the latter. What if this distinction is bollocks?

According to Adorno—it is. Because in his view, all music (regardless of genre) needs to be both serious and lighthearted. Everything from Beethoven's "Ode to Joy" to "Bohemian Rhapsody" needs to mock its seriousness even as it takes itself seriously. (As an aside, this arguably explains the pretensions that plague some progressive rock; they fail to mock themselves).

That does not mean that one lumps all cultural production into one heap. In fact, quite the contrary, since the assimilation of all culture is precisely the aim of the cultural industry—something for everyone, so none can escape. Rather, artists must recognize whether their work is produced autonomously (guided by its own internal logic and rules) or heteronomously (characterized by an interweaving of internal and external influences and constraints). Rock music is inherently heteronomous.

Of course there are the internal influences from previous styles, songs, and musicians. But in addition, there is the relation to a fan base: the need to promote songs, that songs be popular enough to make the charts (which means in many cases that they be singable or danceable), and the reality that they must be performed in venues that range wildly from a football stadium to a bedroom radio.

Queen is kingly in its command of this nexus of apparently contradictory demands—deftly interweaving promotional opportunities into album titles and lyrics, and performance into composition.

Performance as a Tour de Force (Of Course)

In a bit, I want to look at the album *Jazz*, which is exemplary of Queen's innovation in handling the heteronomous threads just mentioned. Before I do, however, I want to enumerate various aspects of Queen's unique brand of performance. That will give us a better perspective from which to evaluate *Jazz* in all its glory.

The *first* important aspect of Queen's "performativity" is the persistent self-mockery. This takes a variety of forms. There is musical self-mockery in the eclectic grab-bag of genres and styles that the band works in, often in stark juxtaposition. The collision of Gilbert and Sullivan style operetta with hard rock in "Bohemian Rhapsody" is a classical example; it has the rare effect of making you marvel and laugh at the same time.

The lyrics themselves abound in self-jabs, such as the "poor boy" who needs no sympathy, the road to fame that was "no pleasure cruise," or Mister Fahrenheit himself who passes by like Lady Godiva. Also, and as we have mentioned, there is the exaggerated way in which the band's public persona typified the rock image, especially in its jarring contrast to their actual personalities.

The *second* key characteristic of Queen's brand of performance, as we have also touched on, is the constant dialogue. This occurs between the lyrics of their songs: such as the references to bicycle races and the refrain of "Fat Bottomed Girls" within John Deacon's song "More of that Jazz" on the same album.

There is also the thematic conversation between being alternatively down and out and then on top of the world, which the back-to-back play of Brian May's "We Will Rock You" and Freddie Mercury's "We Are the Champions" on *News of the World* perfectly captures—so much so that they are usually played together, despite being distinct songs by different songwriters.

Both of these cases also illustrate the degree to which there is tight musical conversation occurring between the band members as they compose their albums. And then lastly there is the spontaneous exchange with their audiences and fans during performances—which Freddie perfectly encapsulated with his signature, "Ay-Oh" call and repeat. Queen is playing with dialogue on a multitude of levels.

A *third* important characteristic is Queen's integration of performance (both in terms of promotional opportunities and stage conditions), into their compositions. The use of the Marx Brother's title for *A Night at the Opera* was not just in keeping with the spirit of the album—it also provided them a perfect name for their worldwide tour to promote it.

Similarly, the following album *A Day at the Races* was conveniently promoted by a literal day at the races. Queen seems to keep the conditions of performance before a live audience at the forefront of their imagination from the first conception of a song. The best example of this (even if apocryphal), is Brian May's line in the movie *Bohemian Rhapsody* about how amazing it would be to have a whole stadium of fans stomping and clapping to the beat of "We Will Rock You."

A *fourth* characteristic of Queen's performance is Freddie Mercury himself, and his transformation of the lead singer roll into a self-conscious performance of fronting a band. The Wembley concert provides an almost touching illustration, when he pauses his strut around the stage and listens to Brian May's guitar solo during "Hammer to Fall," guiding the audience's attention even as he moves it away from himself.

Finally, and *fifth*, there is Queen's innovative use of media technology, which allowed them to maximize what they could do both in the studio and in performance. Having maximized musical technology in the recording of "Bohemian Rhapsody" to such an extent that they created a song that could never be performed the way it sounds on the album, they turned around and created what was, in effect, the first modern music video to promote it. The music video was a new sort of technological performance in the rock industry, and Queen was at the forefront.

All five of these characteristics—self-mockery, dialogue, integration of performance and composition, Freddie Mercury's larger than life self-performance, and the innovative use of media technology—are all in play on the album *Jazz*.

(No) More of That Jazz

Of Queen's albums, *Jazz* is arguably one of their most self-reflexive. Four of the songs—"Fat-Bottomed Girls," "If You Can't Beat Them," "Let Me Entertain You," and "More of that Jazz"—are explicitly about rock music and performance. And a fifth celebrates the associated "go go go" lifestyle—"Don't Stop Me Now."

Queen was at the pinnacle of their popularity and had at their fingertips all the levers of the rock industry to pull in terms of promotions, parties, touring, and climbing the charts. And they delivered a *tour de force* (of course) to their fans. The thematic backbone of the album is the irreverent duo of "Fat-Bottomed Girls" and "Bicycle Race," where they "let it all hang out."

Given their importance to the album's coherence, one might have expected one of them to occupy track one, but no, self-mockery (number *one* above) is the name of the game. Queen launches the album with "Mustapha," a call to prayer style piece, only to pull the (prayer) rug out from under it, by following it with the *paean* to naughty nannies, "Fat-Bottomed Girls." The self-mockery extends to the composition, when the driving chorus of "Bicycle Race" disintegrates into a tinkle of bike bells.

In terms of musical dialogue (*two*), "Fat Bottomed Girls" ends with the call to "get on your bike and ride," whose response comes two songs later as "Bicycle Race." In addition, and as already noted, the dialogue extends to the very end of the album in "No More Jazz." So, what is this dialogue about? The culture industry, of course.

For Queen, the culture industry delivers Jaws and "blue-eyed floozies," but if this is not your scene, they implore you to make your own. The scene they stage is the absurd image—both wet dream fantastical and cynically real—of scantily clad women on bikes making the rock world go round.

It is pièce de résistance of the integration of performance into composition (*three*) in that this "bicycle race" mockery of the "rat race" pedals in the flesh onto the stage of Madison Square Garden on November 17th 1978, only weeks after their Mister Fahrenheit party at the Fairmont in New Orleans.

In both cases, Queen blurs the boundaries between the cynical employment of sex for commercial advantage and the truly edgy. The ambiguity is key. It turns on the recurring Queen dialectic theme of the fall from grace and the resurgent return—between the bad boy who "knew no good from wrong" and doing "all I want to do." As we said earlier about self-performance, it is about mimicking with a wink and nod.

Queen can't beat the culture industry, but when they "join 'em" they can make it look tepid in the lures that it uses to keep the audiences returning. They remind their fans that what the culture industry offers is the *illusion* of happiness, and that instead they should keep their eye on the prize, the *promise* of happiness.

The "promise of happiness" involves, as we have said, the refusal to resolve contradictions in favor of compromise. On *Jazz*, Freddie Mercury offers his anthem for that way of life. In "Don't Stop Me Now," he returns to the persona (*four*) that first appears as "Killer Queen," and lights a supersonic rocket under it.

Killer Queen does not apologize for her way of life: but under her viciousness lurks a vulnerability that her airs are meant to veil. Mister Fahrenheit, by contrast, has left such frailties behind in favor of the speed of light. He simply asks that everyone step aside while he soars to Mars. Even though he is by self-admission "out of control," he is not pleading for help; quite the contrary, he is inviting us to join him. To leave the regularity of the nine-to-five lifestyle for something out of this world. The auto-biographical nature of the song is not in dispute.

Freddie's two-hundred-degree lifestyle and sexuality are being performed for all to see (by a man who in his day-to-day existence was private, even shy). When Freddie performs Freddie, contradictions are embraced and celebrated in an empowering way. And when you sing along, as a great rock hit always invites you to do, you feel like a champion too.

Though the recording technology (*five*) of Jazz does not stand out, especially relative to albums such as *A Night at the Opera*, the use of media was at peak performance. Queen was at the *avant-garde* of using free coverage through media as part of their promotions.

To get such coverage they needed to be "newsworthy," which in practice meant "scandal-worthy." With *Jazz*, they promoted in two notable ways: First, they built the bicycle race of "fat bottomed girls" into the album that became an event that could be staged to outrageous effect.

Second, they chose to throw the most extravagant rock party of all time in order to launch the album. The initial budget of £200,000 is eye-watering enough, but is far surpassed in terms of the legend it created. It is difficult to decide which accounts of the party are credible; however, this is largely irrelevant given the media waves that the party generated.

The picture that Queen released from the party, showing Freddie Mercury signing his autograph onto the backside of a barely clothed (but carefully positioned) young woman was a perfect piece of "evidence" to support even the most outlandish accounts of the party (and yet be publishable at the same time).

Rock music is inherently heteronomous in terms of its artistic creation: but rather than try to cover this up, Queen celebrated it. They performed being a rock band in every dimension possible.

The performance at Wembley in 1985 has been cited by many as the quintessence of Queen. And it is: both in its exceptional and quotidian character. It is exceptional because, in that star-packed context, Queen stood out for its performance and professionalism. It is mundane, because such a focus on performance is what made Queen who it was wherever and whenever it performed. They would sing to you in Japanese and deliver rock *a la carte* day in and day out. And as Freddie says in his send-off at Wembley: they loved you for the chance to entertain, to create the new of that moment.

8
The Quintessence of Queen

RANDALL E. AUXIER

How can just four people make all that music? The question is often asked when people hear Queen. Of course, the band over-dubbed in the studio, as almost all bands do. But their ability to produce a live sound that was so full, even when Freddie was only singing and not also playing, has puzzled many people.

The answer is a little bit complicated, a bit like a car engine. Your car needs fuel, for sure, but that fuel is carbon-based, itself very chemically complex and highly refined. And you mix that with air, and additives (you want high performance, right?). So it's a mix, and the right balance is what makes the engine perform. It's like that with your body, too. Yes, fuel, energy, very complex. But there is more—air, sunlight for vitamin D, you know the list. Then there are additives, such as . . . music.

But as with engine additives, not all music is created equal, and, you do generally get what you pay for. The Queen sound only has four ingredients, but each ingredient is, shall we say, chemically complex. No one denies the chemistry itself. There is an emulsion of sound, and even if you take the parts separately, and think about them completely, you still don't get how it happens. It's an organic compound, carbon-based, and we know how complex carbon atoms can get. It's more than physics, although the physics has to be there.

Alchemy, Magic, Astrology

Music is alchemy. You scoff, but remember Kekulé's dream of the benzene ring. That was one pretty useful ouroboros. The movement from alchemy to modern chemistry is an incomplete story, and it deserves a little attention. Magic is the precursor of technology, the manipulation of energies by technique (whether in gesture or conjure or spoken command). You do all three when you send an e-mail. Astrology is a power of reading cosmic forces and their influences on us, and if you 'believe' in gravity, for instance that spacetime is curved by gravity in some proportion to mass, and that you are no exception to these 'forces', you believe in astrology. And if you believe that the whole of any compound can do things that the parts cannot do, you believe in alchemy. The truth is we don't know *why* any of this stuff happens, we only know *how*, and even that is incomplete.

There are a few insights from the ancient and medieval sciences that persist today. We still don't really know what 'energy' is. Aristotle invented the word by taking the word for 'function' (ergon) and setting it into movement, en-ergon. To this day we define it in physics as the capacity to do work, which means we now have to define 'work', and we point to change, and then we have to define 'change', and so we say 'difference over time', which means we have to define 'difference' and 'time', and good fucking luck with that. You'll bite your own tail, like that benzene snake, before you're done. I'll bet you an original, pristine Queen vinyl.

Those ancients wouldn't accept a pat answer. They wanted, in alchemy, the 'quintessence'. You've heard the word, but do you know it comes from alchemy? The ancients thought there were four elements, earth, air, fire, and water, and that chemistry was a matter of mixing them in just the right proportions, using their 'virtues' to create all the mixtures (compounds) we see. This isn't that far from what we do at the oil refinery, so you can get both your gasoline and your additives, which is the stuff that, well, it explodes in your engine and pushes that car you love from one place to the next. Alchemy. One compound dissolves releasing a force which "does work"—energy. The ancients knew this, but, like us, they didn't know why.

The idea of the quintessence was that there must be some "fifth" element that mediated among the four familiar elements. The alchemists thought this was the "base" and a full command of it would enable us to transform anything into anything else. Eventually we've gotten so good at transforming "this into that" that we stopped looking for the "why" of it, in the grand sense, and got busy selling our powers to make this into that, which turned out to be pretty lucrative. Better living through chemistry, sort of. We still believe there must be some universal principle or law that governs all the transformations, but the search for that is largely given over to the astrophysicists, but also the astrochemists.

Yes, there is such a thing as an astrochemist, I have seen one with my own eyes. There aren't many. It's hard to perform chemical experiments on elements you can't get in situations you can't create here on Earth. Yes, they are alchemists. There aren't too many of them. Most are, in fact, philosophers (including the one I have actually seen). They reason about the quintessence, even if they don't say so in those words. And what they use is a cosmic solvent, called 'reason' to help them break the compounds into elements so as to understand how they can and cannot be combined and re-combined. It turns out to be a frustratingly asymmetrical collection of nonlinear processes. Just because you can break down a compound doesn't mean you can re-create it by reversing what you did.

The Whole and the Parts

I don't believe that the four elements of Queen account for the music. Anywhere the whole is more complex than the sum of its parts, we are obliged to think as alchemists to understand it, and even then, our understanding is incomplete. You think this is just an analogy to what I said above, but it isn't. Trying to understand any good music involves alchemical reasoning. Good music critics do it well, from Hanslick to Klosterman.

Bad critics just treat the whole as the sum of the parts. Queen was subjected to much too much of the latter—narrow, linear thinkers who believe they understand how this music is created when they really don't even grasp how their digestion created what they leave in the toilet (requiring a good bit of nonlinear chemistry). They should probably study what they make of their lasagna and leave music criticism to people who know how to *make* lasagna, and who have other nonlinear abilities. I can see that Queen will not be fully understood by introducing a solvent, but I am going to do it anyway, and try not to assume that I could ever recreate the compound from the way it breaks down. For any solvent we introduce, there could be many more that would lead us to different assessments of the parts.

The Solvent

Let's take it apart, but we have to have a "principle" of division, some way to break down this complex, a solvent that leads us to the catalyst, the reaction we are seeking. I have an idea about that catalyst, and why it makes Queen such a super-sonic solution. But that's the end of this chapter. For now, the solvent. It's about the left hand, particularly Freddie's left hand, but let us think leftward more generally. One might begin with the right, but somehow it is intuitively clear that it is not as closely related to the base of the music, which is in the bass of the music.

When we get the super-sonic solution, all the parts are already complementing each other, but what are they like, as a whole? And then, how can we divide without completely dissolving? We need something we can build on. Since those left hands are pretty much indivisible from the bodies that wield them, I feel that we can find our way back to the whole using this solvent. That would not be true if I divided the melodies from the chord structures from the rhythms. If you do that, you won't ever find your way back to the whole. So, the solvent is the left hands, and not all left hands are the same. They are quite complex in their own right, and different.

A Human Body—Sound and Time

Let's begin with the compound. The sound. Complementarity—the creative overlapping of types and frequencies of waves—in musical sound follows non-linear patterns that the body feels *as a whole*, and *that's* the tricky part. What does it mean to *feel* something "as a whole"?

First of all, remember that your body, too, is one living organism, not a bunch of little parts cobbled together. The "parts" aren't even really "parts" until you abstract them and pretend they can be divided from the whole. Yes, you could cut off your ear, like Vincent Van Gogh, but then it's not really *your* ear anymore. Not a "part" of *you*. It is just *an* "ear." (I assume he could still hear afterwards. Kirk Douglas could, in any case.) So, all that is yours is *you*, one big sloppy experiencing blob hurtling *through* time and *with* time. You are a sticky, gooey part of the flux. Musical sound hits *that* blob, the *whole* blob (including the impurities), and *nothing but* the blob. (Actually, the sound hits everything, but I wanted to say that because it is clever, so I did.) Granted, some of us are blobbier than others. Fat bottomed ones, for example. But they make the world go 'round, so no body shaming here.

The encounter of the sound and the blob create an "energy" that I'll talk about in a different chapter. The point here is that your body gets energy from the sound, fuel of a sort, and like the fuel, the sound is refined: this sound is organized *musically*. It isn't noise, it carries structure, patterns, and even beyond the part we take in as fuel, those structures and patterns and forms enliven your body in a way that noise does not. Your body literally steals a little "order" from the musical organization of the sound, and uses it to intensify various aspects of your experience.

So, we come to 'parts'. One 'part' of you is your consciousness, one of your more rarified bits. We know it's part of you, but we don't know exactly how or why. It's a kind of magic, almost, but it's also astrology and alchemy, in the ways I have explained. Consciousness seems like a quintessence, a force, an energy, and almost a "why" rather than a "how." I am convinced it is a nonlinear process, and I am also quite sure that it takes in other non-linear processes such as music, language, and lasagna, without losing all of the structure that makes them hang together. If we knew how consciousness does this (and we do not), we might be closer to the quintessence –some philosophers have impatiently pronounced consciousness to be the quintessence, but they need to be more patient. We don't know, but I will say this: consciousness can transform lead into gold, as *ideas* at least. Even if you can't trade that for diamonds, you can trade it for the idea of diamonds. In fact, you just *did*.

I feel pretty powerful. Don't think of a pink elephant.

Music is like that. You can change the music by changing the sound, but it's a holistic process, and very delicate, almost infinitely delicate. Introduce even a small change in the *sound*, say, a sixty-cycle hum, and you might lose the *music* altogether. To alter the music radically, for better and for worse, requires only a tiny alteration of the sound. And so much of that delicate alteration is done with the left hand that it seems almost like consciousness itself in its power to bind or dissolve the music. So let's consider the left hands.

Roger's Left Hand

Starting at the bottom, for most drummers, including Roger Taylor, the left hand usually beats two and four, while the right hand decorates every beat and between the beats. The accents on two and four orient both the band and the listeners to the groove. The right foot drives, but the left hand responds, with a snare sound that cuts through everything else. You feel the kick drum, but you both feel and *hear* the snare.

The power of the snare sacrifices all fineness and nuance in rock music—it is not so in jazz. This communicates the main energy of the sound. This role is usually taken up and reinforced in the rhythm guitar, but with Queen, Brian and Roger have to be careful not to lose energy when Brian takes off on a solo, since they usually don't have a rhythm guitar—with notable exceptions like "Crazy Little Thing Called Love" where the rhythm guitar part is so important that Freddie has to play it. In bluegrass bands, the mandolin takes this job of the snare drum, reinforced by the guitar sometimes, answering the string bass.

The left hand punctuates and articulates the tempo, the groove, the feel and it is more part of the *sound* than of the *music*.

John's Left Hand

Things get a little more complicated now because the bass player does not always carry the bass line. That can be done on keyboards and with Queen it often is. Sometimes John's the one playing a keyboard, as in "You're My Best Friend," which has both piano and organ pound the left hand, meanwhile the bass guitar is just decorating the piece with ascending runs and counter-melodies. In this case, somebody's left hand is still the solvent, but it is super-saturated and pulsing on beats one and three, while the snare drum doesn't need any help with two and four (and rarely gets any in Queen's music, although there are a lot of hands helping on "We Will Rock You").

The bass player's left hand controls the *length* of the notes as well as which notes are played. If the feel is good, alternating in pleasing ways between staccato, short notes and legato, connected long notes, it almost doesn't matter which notes are played. For example, when the bass comes in on The Beatles' "The Long and Winding Road," John Lennon actually played the wrong notes on bass—an out-of-tune Db instead of a D, which is what Paul McCartney was playing on piano, but the timing is right, two double punches, and they left the wrong note in. It's interesting sounding, actually, although when the same punch comes back later in the song, John played a D. This, by the way, is the weirdest bass line in rock history in my opinion, and John was no bass player, so that may be the reason, but in some weird ass way it *works*. That's because the feel is right, and no one could explain why, not fully.

Well, John Deacon's bass lines are perfect. It's a little worrisome—many critics who don't know shit, including how they make their own, have said 'too perfect'. These bass lines are so perfect, meaning both the left-hand choices for length and connection, and the notes chosen, and the decorations and lack thereof, that it feels almost mechanical. What do you do with a bass player who never gets in the way, never trips, never over-plays, never under-plays? Well, you *keep* such a bass player.

It's said that George Harrison kept arguing with Paul McCartney over the bass line in "Something (in the Way She Moves)," which is a song about the Quintessence if ever there was one. George said Paul was "too busy." In retrospect, it is one of the greatest bass lines in the history of pop music. And if you listen to John Deacon's bass line on "You're My Best Friend," you may hear that he went to school on Paul McCartney, and maybe even that very song "Something." I wonder if John argued with himself for being too busy on his own song. Nah.

If you watch videos of John Deacon playing bass, he is so gentle and economical in his movements that it almost looks as if he isn't playing at all. He has a less-is-more left hand, and a composer's ear to match. More about this when we reach Freddie, but by way of anticipation, I have to say that John is the one who knew it was over when Freddie died—he finished the album because Freddie wanted that, played the last concert, and that was *it*. And John wasn't kidding. No Brett Favre or Tom Brady act here. He respected the integrity of the Whole too much to distort it with future efforts that would not have the alchemy.

Brian's Left Hand

And now our material becomes almost too complex to resolve into parts. Brian's left hand on the guitar is almost beyond comparing to any other guitarist, rock, jazz, classical, anywhere. The fingers are long and delicate and they fly over a fretboard too fast for the eye to track. There aren't five people in the history of rock in his league, and among those who might compare, none of them has the voice, the songwriting/composing, the producing/engineering, and the versatility that Brian May brings to the table. In short, there is no guitarist who can do all the things he does at the same level. His left hand on the guitar is beyond analyzing. I won't even try.

But for my purposes, I don't have to, because it turns out Brian May is human after all. On piano. And that is what leads us toward our goal. Brian was a fine but ordinary pianist. That is to say, his piano is technically excellent, but it doesn't shine like his guitar does. I could give any number of examples but I will settle for one that you can verify for yourself: <www.youtube.com/watch?v=yWULxtWCShk>. This is Queen's performance of "Save Me" at Hammersmith, December 26th, 1979. The song was written by Brian (on piano, obviously—his part sounds like a high school piano teacher's recital piece, some lost bit of Beethoven, frankly), and it was new at this time. The piece starts out with Freddie singing and Brian on piano, and I want you to listen to Brian's left hand. His piano teacher would be proud of the balance and precision, the way each finger separates and blends with the others, quite a nice recital.

But then, as the song progresses and builds, the time approaches for Brian to play a screaming guitar solo, and to maintain the energy (remember that idea?), Freddie has to take over on piano. The transition itself is stunning. Where did that guitar come from? And it attacks with such ferocity that you might not notice how very different the piano is now that Freddie is playing it. But listen—especially to his left hand. It is doing a lot more than blending and balancing.

Freddie's Left Hand

Now that we have noticed Freddie's left hand, let's isolate it. Here is Brian May on Freddie's *right* hand: Freddie "had a wonderful touch on the piano. He could play what came from inside him like nobody else—incredible rhythm, incredible passion and feeling" (Ian Inglis, p. 51).

There's no question that Brian is right. He's a first-rate music critic among other things, and he probably also knows how the body makes what it leaves in the toilet to boot. What a great touch with the right hand (on the piano I mean), superb, extra-ordinary, and perhaps Freddie is among the top ten rock pianists ever, as good or better than Elton John and Leon Russell, if not quite Billy Joel or Rick Wakeman. But there it is, the right hand, tinkling, decorating, accenting, occasionally punctuating, but not *pulsing*. That's his left hand.

A contributor to *Quora Digest*, Matt Rimmer, gave this analysis of Freddie Mercury's piano playing:

> **Freddie playing was predominantly percussive.** Every note was intended and had a specific place in time. He didn't seem to allow his fingers to just wander over familiar patterns. In an interview Brian noted how low Freddie kept his wrists and that there was **a lot of power being applied**. Freddie was a rock piano player (like Jim Steinman but with an in-tune piano and a heap less reverb). **Very precise.** Loads of cool little piano riffs that were every bit as much fun to play as Brian's guitar riffs. Somehow Freddie managed to have his own sound on an instrument which has one setting (it's just a piano after all).

Getting an ordinary piano to sound like nobody else's piano is no simple task, but Freddie did it. I like to imagine that Beethoven himself must have played with such passion—oh, to have a recording of *that*. But we don't really know. We know that people loved it and critics hated it. Beethoven was a rocker I'll bet. Anyway, it does remind us how great is Queen's debt to classical music, but I think that is mainly Brian's influence. Freddie found and played weird, weird chords, things not in the Western scales, normally—that education in

India wasn't lost, nor the youth in Zanzibar. Freddie's compositions are out of the cannon, but they come from the canon of his left hand. His left hand is to Queen's music what artillery is to an infantry—send this up and into their bodies first, and you can capture the whole audience: they surrender. Call up some Queen videos and start watching the left hand. Then you will *see* what you have been *feeling*.

The Blob You Are

So this brings us back to the physico-chemico-temporal compound that is you. You and your total feel of the *sound*. A lot of the 'blending' work that creates a 'total feel' is done by the way rock musicians—on all the instruments—use their left hands, especially those who play keyboard instruments (which includes three members of Queen). I want you to think and arrange your actions with *your* left hand, because the principles apply to more than just music. This works even if you are left-handed, indeed, *especially* if you are. You already do this kind of blending, but you might not have thought about it. It might help you keep yourself alive.

You don't do your blending step by step; it isn't one moment after another, rather, the total feel of anything you do, from giving a speech to cleaning the toilet, is created whole and *then* becomes moments. So, you are right-handed, say, and some critic has left your toilet soiled with he knows not what. You shall clean the toilet. There the task is, whole. Now, find the brush and the Comet. You will be working that brush with your right hand, and with the left? Yes, that's right, dump the Comet, and now wait, brush-brush-brush, and left-hand forward, flush it. Go on. It's a bit like playing the piano. Now repeat (this was a bad, bad critic who didn't like Queen).

It would be pretty silly to set the brush down just to flush right-handed, unless you have only one hand and one arm. I notice that often (it used to be always) they put the handle on the left. What's up with that? Butt, even if you only use your left hand to balance yourself, there it is, blending the moments of brushing into one process, and now that critic's mess is gone and you can forget about it.

Making music is analogous. The creation of the sound is one bodily action of both blending and articulating, and then they come into physical sound as moments. These musical structures and patterns intensify your *rarified bits*, including the parts of you that are really just waves, like your brainwaves, which we can see, sort of, with some technological magic. They look quite different when you listen to music, and even depending on what kind of music you're experiencing. The music organizes your body in sympathy with its own dominant patterns. The pulse is the most dominant among the patterns, and that is Freddie's left hand, in the case of Queen. Or at least, I think that is a solvent that does the least damage to the super-sonic solution.

This Is Your Brain on Queen

Consciousness is surely related to brain waves, but it is so rarified and delicate, we can't quite find it among the other physical things that exist, although I think most sensible people agree it must be physical in some sense. Whatever it is, you can bet your fat bottom it is altered by musical patterns. You are "conscious" of only a tiny portion of what your body encounters, the sound as a whole. Only a ripple of all that sound survives after our blobbie bodies filter and baffle. But the part of the music that makes it through to your consciousness and organizes the patterns is the most refined part of the music. The rest is exhaust.

So these big, heavy sound waves assault your time-blob of a body, and they are then separated into the different senses you separate out in your consciousness, sound, sight, smell, touch, taste. But the truth is that you really can touch and see and smell and taste the music, just not as well as you can hear it. The waves affect your whole time-blob. When musicians know this, as Queen always did, they are able to refine the energies for your whole body. Small adjustments make a big difference. They can create musical experiences that move in and through us *as* nonlinear wholes. A song is a temporal event that happens to your body and changes it, over the course of, say four to seven and a half minutes.

Yet, sensation, and its five major modalities, (seeing, hearing, smelling, etc.) is only a small part of "feeling." *Feeling* is far more complex and subtler than *sensing*. We only "hear" the music *after* we have *already* rocked to the feel of Freddie's left hand. Most musicians don't think about this so much as master it by practice and intuition. But there are exceptions.

Guess which musicians understand this best? Yes, I think you know. And yes, it's just my opinion, but it is a reasoned opinion. You should agree. Don't be a critic.

9
Vulgar Romanticism and Prog Rock

JAN OLOF BENGTSSON

"How Prog Were Queen?" asks Dave Everley in the title of a recent piece in *Prog* magazine. This is the important question. While his answer is exaggerated ("very prog"), the article adequately accounts for some of what, to a limited extent, makes early Queen so-called progressive rock.

Needless to say, rock isn't always philosophical. But what's important to understand is that even when it's not, its non-philosophicalness is the expression of a particular view of life and the world. This view, common to all or most rock, was described and analyzed by Robert Pattison in *The Triumph of Vulgarity: Rock Music in the Mirror of Romanticism*.

At least a philosophical discussion *about* rock is always possible, and in particular against the background of the defining characteristics of the imaginative universe and general sensibility of rock.

In a way that might at first appear somewhat provocative, Pattison applies some traditional aesthetic and other criteria in order to lay bare the profile of this worldview, which may otherwise be hard to discern in a society that is itself deeply shaped by it.

Following Irving Babbitt and his classical humanist (indeed *classicist*) criticism of romanticism, Pattison explains that rock is a *vulgarized expression of romantic pantheism*, including its political manifestation, *democracy*: "Rock is the quintessence of vulgarity. It's crude, loud, and tasteless. Rock is vulgarity militant, and modern vulgarity is one incarnation of Romantic pantheism." And "American democracy provides an ideal setting for the growth of romantic pantheism"; "Rock begins in America, and its roots are deep in the same soil that gives birth to the great experiment of vulgar democracy"; "Believing in Whitman, the democrat should also glory in the Ramones" (*Triumph of Vulgarity*, pp. xi–xii, 4, 9).

"I Want It All," Queen sang a few years after the publication of Pattison's book. "I want it all, and I want it now." Although this song was typical of their music since the mid-1970s, whose crudeness, loudness, and tastelessness had become more pronounced, it was an expression of the same naked ego psychology and self-affirmation, often nihilistic and shaped by the modern cultural dynamic of romantic pantheism in its vulgarized form, to which they had given more complex expression in their early work. Actually, I *am* it all. You, society, better accept it. Now.

The Lure of the Daemonic

Throughout their early albums, Queen's lyrics are far more ambiguous and obscure, but they too express the defining moral ambivalence and undiscerning expressionism of romanticism and pantheism, as more or less opposed to the traditional, transcendent and dualistic morality of the classical and Christian traditions.

Pantheism is a different kind of religion than theism, and both in rationalism and, especially, in romanticism, it was reduced to a purely immanentist, worldly affirmation with no basis for the moral order, and in which that order was consequently often negated or reversed. The religious nature of pantheism was lost in a closed, this-worldly monism and moral relativism.

In rock, or at least rock'n'roll, romantic pantheism is normally trivialized and, as Pattison stresses, reduced to what he calls Chuck Berry's "doctrine of fun"—even when raised by Bob Dylan to "the highest level of rock art" (p. 198). But not in the distinct new developments of the second half of the 1960s. Not just in progressive rock, but in the hard rock that emerged at the same time, romantic pantheism is expressed in a different modality.

In early Queen is found, for instance, a recurring, chilling theme of potential (or more or less actualized) evil—of a strange state of gracelessness in a religious sense, of God-forsakenness, of having to rely only on oneself in an empty, meaningless, and cruel world whose nature is that of a merciless fight.

There's also the lure of the daemonic, perhaps even an element of the cursed glamor of the fallen angel. Whatever inspired the songs, and whatever else they may be about (and this is often hard to determine), this theme is identifiable, although it's unclear to what extent it can be said to amount to a proper artistic idea.

Freddie Mercury, whose shyness off-stage was attested by many, flamboyantly impersonated this bleak existential state, with a distinctive air of cruelty and criminality—although it was quite as often Brian May who wrote the songs. "Keep Yourself Alive," the first song on the first album, was intended by May as a critical depiction of a character displaying some of these traits, but, according to himself, it assumed a different meaning when Mercury sang it. This makes for a fundamental ambiguity. Is it about a "death on two legs," or the predicament of the romantic hero himself, having turned cynical naturalist in his disillusion?

The meaning is clearly nihilist. No striving, no trying to get better makes any difference. Regardless of how many rivers are crossed and miles are ridden, "I'd still be where I started, same as when I started." Only a basic, primitive, egotistic or even philosophically egoistic keeping alive matters. Only "time and money" is needed to stay alive and "satisfied." There's nothing more to life. "Great King Rat," on the same album, seems explicitly to gauge the depths and attractions of evil, whomever it may be about. "Where will I be tomorrow?" It doesn't matter. "Will I beg or will I borrow?" Nothing matters, in fact. So wouldn't I like to see, wouldn't I like to know the evil of the "dirty old man"? The "Liar," also on the first album, seems to be stuck with a criminal character.

At their best, Queen conveyed this sensibility with a degree of cold, alluring sublimity. "Bohemian Rhapsody" epitomizes the theme, on a less hard rock and therefore higher artistic level. Life has already been thrown away, the disillusioned romantic hero has killed a man (Queen are, as they declare in the title of a live album, *Killers*). Nothing really matters, the wind blows any way—but you can't "stone me and spit in my eye," "love me and leave me to die." The fight, although meaningless, somehow still goes on. Must go on. It's even that now, *anyone can see* that nothing really matters. Yes, we had seen that, from the beginning.

"In the Lap of the Gods" presents the more modest romantic hero, a misunderstood "beautiful soul" who at least accepts the gods, although they are plural gods and perhaps of an uncertain nature. They might be on his side in his fight for authentic selfhood against the deaths on two legs that only want to talk about his money, or conventional society and what it wants him to be.

"We Are the Champions" is said to be a gay anthem, but is there anything in the lyrics to support that except the abstract emptiness that needs such an interpretation to give the championship any meaning at all? Some see Queen's theatricality and operaticality as effeminate, not least in comparison with the simple hard rock of the 1970s.

But despite the band's name and what at a late stage became known about the distinctly non-effeminate Mercury and what therefore many critics nowadays say, I can't remember any explicitly and unambiguously gay themes. Moreover, there's nothing in the gay interpretation of "We Are the Champions" that contradicts the romantic theme.

Maybe it's just that I'm not familiar with the codes. But it seems to me it could just as well be simply a crude, singalong, ballgame version of the self-glorification of the authentic but unfairly misunderstood Rousseauian heroes, reduced to a banal—vulgar—winner-loser paradigm. "They"—conventional society—"say we're all fools," as they sing in "Teo Torriatte (Let Us Cling Together)."

Even in "The Show Must Go On," from 1991, there's perhaps a faint trace of the theme, at a time when the daemonic power had long been waning. When the artistic refinement and the daemonic spell falter, Queen certainly become vulgar. But early Queen could be real evil, as it were: serious darkness, not the clownish evil and darkness of Black Sabbath.

A Triumph of Vulgarity

Now, describing rock as signifying, as such, a triumph of vulgarity looks like a condescending, elitist view from a scholar of literature. But that's not Pattison's view:

> Vulgarity finds itself condemned on all sides by enemies as disparate as President Reagan's Secretary of Education, who wants to restore the legacy of cultural refinement, and the Marxist critic Theodor Adorno, who looks to socialism to purge the world of its capitalist crudities. But vulgarity by its nature is impervious to condemnation. The point is not to condemn it, which has been done without success, but to describe it, which has yet to be undertaken. Since we live in

> a vulgar world, and since the world seems likely to become more not less vulgar, the time has come not only to say what vulgarity is but to enumerate its benefits alongside its sins. (Triumph of Vulgarity, pp. 3–4)

Contrary to Babbitt, we find in Pattison's book an *affirmation* of vulgarity as a manifestation of romantic pantheism. Yet that too is problematic. An adequate critical perspective is needed, and not just because much of the vulgarity he defines (as manifested in rock and as exploited, ever since Elvis, by the music industry), is in some ways one of the many expressions of bourgeois decadence—one of the consequences of capitalism in decay. Properly understood and creatively renewed, the criteria and distinctions provided by the traditional perspectives are still necessary in order to understand these things at all.

According to some critics, including Greg Kot in the *Encyclopedia Britannica*, rock as such is not, strictly, rock'n'roll, but a specific new development during the 1960s, whose distinctness was fully apparent towards the end of the decade. It's indeed a more philosophical genre.

Some of it was what is called hard or heavy rock, which was also clearly vulgar in a way that could not quite be accommodated by postmodernism (that other product of romantic pantheism), no matter how hard it tried to extend its relativistic tolerance or see it as studied provocations: witness the names of the bands, the albums, the songs. But at the same time, there evolved progressive rock, defined by its ambition to progress beyond the genre-specific confines of contemporary rock as a whole.

Disciplining the Guitar

Queen are far too influenced by hard rock and far too dominated by what I think is its most important defining feature—the cold and loud electric guitar. As Roger Scruton says: "If a machine could sing, it would sound like an electric guitar" (*An Intelligent Person's Guide to Modern Culture*, p. 91). Queen's inordinate guitar solos, insufficiently integrated into the compositional wholes of the songs, are atypical of progressive rock.

But on the early albums, there are at least clear streaks of progressive rock, or prog. From the beginning, there were some overlaps between hard rock—and soon metal, heavy metal—and prog. We find it in some songs of Led Zeppelin and Deep Purple. This is the category in which early Queen belong. But although they aren't prog proper, what's *important* about them is prog: the easily recognizable elements of prog both in the music and the lyrics.

At least at its best, prog is characterized by a rigorous disciplining of the electric guitar, which is uncompromisingly subordinated within the integral sound picture of the respective bands and songs, and not allowed to destroy their other elements by formless, wild, and too long solos or too heavy riffs. The subdued guitars are sometimes even made to sound almost like some other instrument.

Brian May occasionally achieves this, although far too seldom: much more commonly, he destroys songs with his solos. A good example is "Brighton Rock," an intelligent, original, and melodically strong hard rock song in their defining, cold and evil style. It has only just begun when it's interrupted by May's unbearable, primitive, metallic cacophony. This turns out to be its main part, and it continues until its end.

Still, the extent to which their first four albums are prog makes Queen one of the instances that show why Pattison's general analysis needs to be modified and supplemented. Prog is something different than the rock he writes about. "The title was the most prosaic thing" about *Queen II*, Everley writes; the music "was as fevered and baroque as rock gets, informed equally by Zeppelin, Yes and crazed Victorian artist Richard Dadd, whose 1864 painting The Fairy Feller's Master-Stroke inspired one of the album's most prog-leaning tracks. It may have been rooted in the heavy rock of the times, but its cavalier approach and sheer sense of scale pegged Queen as a defiantly progressive proposition" ("How Prog Were Queen?"). This second album, *Queen II*, is full of the typical fantasy themes of prog.

Higher and Lower Romanticism

While clearly related to the bourgeois decadence of the Sixties counterculture and of some New Left ideology, prog at its best transcends it. In order to understand this, I suggest the needed revision of Pattison be made along the following lines.

First of all, the concepts of romanticism and pantheism need to be dichotomized. There is the distinction between religious or truly spiritual pantheism and wholly secularized pantheism. And, as suggested by so-called personal idealism as well as Claes G. Ryn's synthesizing of Babbitt's humanism and Benedetto Croce's Hegelianism, there's also a distinction between a "higher" and a "lower" romanticism. The former rises towards moral objectivism, dualism, and transcendence, while at the same time affirming modern personal autonomy; the latter descends to the manifold and equally modern phenomena that are the ultimately nihilistic products of impersonal pantheism in its romantic form.

Second, and as already suggested, all rock is not vulgar in Pattison's sense. Prog, with its distinctive innovative, experimental, rock-transcending aspirations, including its willingness to reconnect with "classical" music (to use the silly, common term), is at least not vulgar in the same sense as most rock. Although it shares the general romantic pantheist outlook, it explores the themes of lower romanticism on a higher aesthetic level. Genesis and Pink Floyd are both good examples of this, although in radically different modalities.

The artistic expression of higher romanticism is always more difficult. In prog, only Yes, in what Bill Martin calls their "main sequence" of albums in the 1970s, (*Music of Yes*, p. xxv) were consistently successful in this, and it's not least for this reason that they're the greatest in the genre. In general, the seduction of the lower is stronger for listeners and readers than the pull of the higher—as paradigmatically seen in the preference through the ages for Dante's pre-romantic *Inferno* rather than his pre-romantic *Paradiso*.

Much great and most modern art, including prog, is exploration of partial, imperfect, lower points of view, including the distinctly modern, romantic inferno; exploration which is "valid" as representing significant human existential experience. Early Queen are perhaps, at their best, complex enough to have at least a little bit of this in common with the greatest prog groups.

Pattison's characterizations of rock simply fail to do justice to prog. And it's striking that even Roger Scruton, a great philosopher of music, only found examples that confirm Pattison's account, on the few occasions when he made an attempt to say something positive about the rock of which he was a sharp critic. He never even discovered prog.

Third, contrary to Pattison's *assessment* of the triumph of vulgarity, the concepts and categories of his *analysis* are still relevant for rock criticism, not just for cultural history. The aesthetic expressions of vulgarized romantic pantheism shouldn't be undiscerningly accepted.

The Destiny of Modernity (and Rock Criticism)

The same Babbittian criteria themselves allow for a more positive assessment of some rock, given the reality of a higher romanticism. Pattison's analysis is influenced by Babbitt's highly critical *Rousseau and Romanticism* (1919). But another of Babbitt's books was *Democracy and Leadership* (1924), where he also explored aspects of higher romanticism.

He argued that modernity, shaped by romanticism in its shifting reciprocal interrelationship with rationalism, should be affirmed. But it must be affirmed as able to retain, adapt, and creatively renew (in its changed historical circumstances) the traditional criteria of the classical and Christian worldview. By means of them, modernity can overcome the excesses of both romanticism and rationalism.

For Babbitt, vulgarized romantic pantheism was, after all, not the ultimate destiny of modernity. It could be handled, managed, reduced, even overcome by proper moral and cultural leadership. Democracy had a higher potential. Babbitt saw the limitations of conventional society, and rejected the narrowly decorum-based pseudo-classicism that, through its fusion with an equally narrow, utilitarian rationalism, had come to dominate the society and the literature that Rousseau revolted against.

The true traditional criteria, further elaborated as those of higher romanticism by means of distinct conceptual developments in aesthetics such as that of the "moral imagination," are in fact eminently suited precisely for rock criticism, and, indeed on Pattison's own showing, more needed there than perhaps anywhere else.

I suggest they be reasserted against the influence of romantic pantheist postmodernism and its rejection of the very conditions of possibility of such criticism. A vantage point is again made available, from which well-founded judgment also on the dominant, contemporary artistic explorations of lower romanticism in rock becomes possible. Some of Queen's evil can actually be *moralized* about in a meaningful way.

The Neo-Liberal Fall of Prog

Prog and prog criticism is where this becomes the most significant and important. But here, we have to face the historical fact that in the strange mass psychosis, fueled by neo-liberalism, that was the 1980s, the great potential of prog was temporarily lost. Indeed, the decay started already in the second half of the 1970s. Queen were, needless to say, not the only victims.

Not a single promising development of Seventies rock—not just in prog, but also in the broader genre of art rock, and even in much ordinary rock—survived the onset of the Eighties. These musicians all deteriorated at the same time. Why? Tony Banks of Genesis was once asked why they didn't continue to make the kind of music they had made in the early Seventies: His answer: "It wouldn't be allowed," or something to that effect.

Roger Taylor had contributed one ordinary, vulgar rock song to each of Queen's early albums, but now Mercury, May, and John Deacon too started to write such stuff: hard, heavy rock, but also with much regression to ordinary rock and pop-rock. To the genre diversity of their vaudevillian and music-hall moments was added a kind of funk and disco. Both the music and the lyrics lost their complexity.

The shift to a new level of "crude, loud and tasteless" vulgarity, indeed "vulgarity militant," becomes offensively clear already in the brutal opening hard-rocker "Tie Your Mother Down" on *A Day at the Races*, from 1976. It goes quite as far in its base immediacy as "Get Down, Make Love" on the following album (*News of the World*), and, in fact, much further than "I Want It All" ten years later.

It's "all right" that the hero gets his way not just by tying mother down and locking father out of doors, but by taking little brother "swimmin' with a brick." Killers indeed. "Don't stop me now": nothing must stop the romantic hero, he and his desires are right and just, since in reality he's naturally good and the conventional family in which daughter is held captive is evil, and can't understand he's just a "peace-lovin' guy." This is the romantic theme on its crudest level.

The line about little brother is from the guitarist who was later invited to play "God Save the Queen" on the roof of Buckingham Palace at the queen's golden jubilee, and would soon become a university chancellor.

It should, I suggest (in the way that postmodernists dismiss as wholly vain), compel us to ask serious questions about the state of our vulgar democracy.

Things like this were forced by contemporary mass culture upon teenage ears. It was all a wild and degraded siren's song, the seduction of a Dionysian orgy.

Quite obviously, there were deliberate, calculated attempts to do away with the criteria of high culture and to break down moral restrictions, for the sake of cynical commercial exploitation of the forces already long let loose in the cultural dynamic of a lower romanticism powered by the fruits of rationalism in the form of technology. And for the related sake of a general cultural and ideological dumbing-down. One was under attack.

A pop-cultural rape of youth was going on, and there were no adults in the room—for instance, no qualified rock critics with adequate standards.

Most hard rock was part of this attack. Queen's early hard rock songs had been comparatively sophisticated and complex; they too evinced a degree of musical and compositional intelligence. But this was only because there was always material of a different kind in them, which made the metallic heaviness more tolerable.

This was the prog element in early Queen: it consisted not least in the admixture of unusually long, highly original, and varied soft, vocal- and acoustic guitar-dominated sections in the hard rock songs themselves, which mitigated their electric-guitar-dominated rawness.

And interspersed with such songs were short ones that, in their signature coldness, were quiet and gentle in their entirety, and remarkably beautiful: "The Night Comes Down," "Nevermore," "Lily of the Valley"—early songs that weren't somewhat overstated banality like "Love of My Life" and "You Take My Breath Away."

Everley thinks the album *A Night at the Opera*, where "Love of My Life" is found, is "Queen's grand artistic statement and their most unashamedly prog album." But the multiplicity of genres makes it less consistently prog than *Queen II*. And I mean, "I'm in Love with My Car"? But of course, along with "Bohemian Rhapsody," it contains the peak prog "The Prophet's Song," another eerie expression of the recurring theme's moral ambivalence, in which their most distinctive contribution to prog, the mock-operatic, layered vocals, is quite as fully developed.

Love is the answer, but what is depicted is the evil and darkness warned against, and the vision fades, a voice says "Listen to the Madman," and "still I fear and still I dare not" laugh at him. Here too, we are very far from a full, redeeming vision; the song is about the lure and danger of the evil lower, and the higher is barely aspired to.

Queen: Capital "P" Prog?

But in the genre, this music was something new and different, inspired by the neoterism of the second half of the Sixties. Prog had begun, and by the time of *A Night at the Opera*, its so-called first wave was already approaching its end. While still stuck with many of the conventions shared with rock in general, and more specifically with hard rock, early Queen were part of it. "While Queen weren't a capital 'P' prog band," Everley notes, "they were infused with the spirit of the movement, combining its forward-looking values with its absolute disregard for the existing rules" ("How Prog Were Queen?").

The reason why they remained behind the greatest prog bands, which had already progressed beyond all ordinary rock and hard rock, was not that their prog elements were less prog, but that there were so many other elements. Early Queen were an exceptional, sophisticated hard rock band with a prog potential that was only imperfectly realized. A real prog band never really rocks: as soon as it starts to rock, it becomes non-progressive. To rock is vulgar. But in the context of vulgar rock, Queen were clearly exceptional.

All of that exceptionality was lost in the general collapse that started already in the second half of the Seventies. First, rock purism was relaunched in the wave of punk, which, in hindsight, can be seen to have been to some extent a corporate reassertion of, if not faux-working-class, at least very deliberately sought out and reconstructed rock roots. And they were reasserted precisely against the truly radical—not least because partly traditional—avant-garde of prog. Queen adapted by simplifying everything.

Their best streamlined power ballads from the early part of this era of decline had a certain pompous, anthemic grandiosity ("Spread Your Wings," "Save Me"), there was some lingering, elegant, lightweight sophistication in the versatile plurality of genres ("My Melancholy Blues"), and some compositionally disciplined hard rock ("It's Late").

But the songs had lost all the distinctive prog qualities. Camp exaggeration now lacked any connection with worthwhile substance. Attempts at chart rock and pop—and lots of "fun" ("Let Me Entertain You")—began to take over, and it was all increasingly unlistenable.

"Fat Bottomed Girls" was perhaps studied vulgarity, but if so, the studiedness didn't make it any better; like "Tie Your Mother Down" and "Get Down, Make Love," it was simply repellent.

Vulgar Rock Stars or Repressed Prog Royalty?

Contrary to prog musicians, Queen had always been "rock stars," with rock stars' tour lifestyle of provocatively offensive vulgar debauchery. But by now, everything was crude, loud, and/or otherwise tasteless. The incipient artistry was gone. Mercury's stage performance, including his manner of dress and his rock choreography, began to resemble those of an athlete rather than a singer. He wore gym vests, with white trousers with red stripes and Adidas shoes. Or he appeared in a royal robe with ermine fur and a crown (I don't remember and cannot mobilize enough interest to find out which lyrics this was supposed to illustrate, if any).

This was undiluted vulgarity through and through, in an age when MTV helped further reveal whole new dimensions of rock musicians' vulgarity, or the vulgarity now mandated by the industry (the musicians themselves clearly weren't always responsible for the music videos). Compare Queen's Eighties stadium shows with the London Hammersmith Odeon version of "White Queen (As It Began)" in 1975, where Mercury's flamboyance is restrained, disciplined, integrated into a consistent performative whole—as he appears, in Zandra Rhodes's white satin outfit, as the winged messenger whose name he took. *That* was prog.

The only redeeming moment in their subsequent career is the remarkable and surprising "Innuendo," the title track from the 1991 album. Despite its hard rock moments, it so clearly reconnects with the early period that it becomes almost incomprehensible how they could have done what they had done since the second half of the 1970s.

It even features a flamenco guitar solo by Yes's Steve Howe. Had Queen, like all others, merely been forced to suppress their prog potential all those years? If they could suddenly manifest again such relative sophistication at that late stage, it seemed it must somewhere have been there all along, almost intact.

But this only underscores the tragedy of the Eighties, the depressing truth about what happened to our democracy. Under neoconservatism, the vulgarity of bourgeois decadence in fact continued apace, in new forms, on the road to the imperialist woke freakshow of today. But "Innuendo" confirmed at least some early Seventies intuitions of what Queen could have become, intuitions which had not just long been doubted, but definitively disbelieved.

IV

The Show Must Go On

10
Is Adam Lambert a Killer of Queen or Somebody to Love?

MEGAN VOLPERT

Freddie Mercury is a minor deity who exited his earthly form in 1991, leaving behind a rock'n'roll band in need of a glorious front man. From 2004 to 2009, there was Queen + Paul Rogers. From 2014 to present (as of this writing), there is Queen + Adam Lambert.

So, to what extent is the band still the band if the lead singer is swapped out?

The Ship of Theseus

Heroic founder of the city of Athens and mythical son of the sea god Poseidon, Theseus was a badass with a boat. Most of his awesome battles, such as slaying the half-man and half-bull Minotaur, occurred as part of a quest on land. But when he returned to Athens at the end of defeating six Underworld enemies and dozens of minor bandits, he arrived on a ship.

In commemoration of his incredible deeds, Athenians kept the boat afloat in the harbor for several centuries. As anyone with a boat can tell you, boats are a money pit. Boats always need so many repairs that you may as well just drop your load of silver drachmas right into the sea itself.

Yet the Athenians were determined to use this boat once a year to go to the island of Delos and properly offer some big-time worship to Apollo in order to celebrate the achievements of Theseus—so the ship's rotten bits had to be constantly replaced to keep it in good enough shape for its annual voyage.

After very many parts of it were replaced, this naturally led local thinkers to ponder whether it could be said to be the same boat at all, since it had changed a lot over time. Philosophers now refer to this scenario about the soul of a patched-up thing as the ship of Theseus, and it's a puzzle that clearly can be brought to bear on the replacement of Queen's front man.

How many parts of a band can you replace and still feel like it's the same band? Many philosophers have attempted to answer this question in detail, and we shall reflect on each of their insights in turn.

Old School

One very ancient Greek, Heraclitus, argues for a surprisingly modern answer to this question. He says the question stacks the deck because it presumes that Queen was always Queen as long as Freddie was at the mic. Heraclitus was the guy who said that nobody can step in a river the same way twice.

The band is like the river: and thus Queen has never been the same Queen twice, even if all the original members are present. The Queen you saw at the iconic Madison Square Garden show in '77 is not the same band as the Queen you saw at Rock in Rio in '85, which is not the same band as the Queen you saw at Live Aid at Wembley a few months later in '85, and so on. The identity of the band may not have a fixed position over any length of time, as their mojo rushes like a river.

Beyond the obvious changes to each band member like aging and additional life experience, is it reasonable to compare Queen to an ever-changing river? Yes, because of the nature of rock star performances. Freddie often talked about the audience being the most important component of the band's work.

They only ever wanted to play stadium shows and no fans ever expressed a desire to see Queen in a more intimate venue. The more people you pack into the show, the more of an ocean of energy it creates for the band to feed upon. Or as a Zen Buddhist would say, the only Freddie you get at Queen's stadium shows is the Freddie you bring in there.

Defining the fandom as an essential part of the band really makes a lot of sense. To keep using the river metaphor of Heraclitus: what makes a river? It takes a lot of drops of water, but also a path carved out of the earth by rocks and trees or whatever else. Queen is comprised of the band members of course, but also their musical instruments, their roadies and techies, the stadiums, and the fans.

Contemporary science backs up the metaphysical prospect of Heraclitus through our newfound understanding of wormholes and the fourth dimension. A band exists not only in space, but also in time. The identity of Queen in the Seventies is just as real and true as the identity of Queen today. Queen is a band that occupies many slices of time. Perhaps the older time slices are worth more to you personally.

The reason you'd pay extremely expensive ticket prices to inhabit the space of a front row seat is the same reason you'd pay ridiculously high prices for a bootleg of a show, whether you attended that show or not—to indulge in the rare privilege of inhabiting a long-ago time slice.

Yet we would not say that replacing Roger Taylor's drum sticks makes Queen a totally different band. Nor even if we replaced his entire drum kit. Perhaps even if we replaced Roger himself. Of Queen's four original members, his personal fanbase is perhaps the smallest. Drummers never get the respect they deserve.

Maybe we should even wonder whether Queen would still be Queen if we replaced Brian May. If Brian got a new guitar, it's doubtful anyone would conclude Queen is no longer the same band. But what about a new guitarist?

Consider the case of Van Halen and tally up the number of fist fights between the devotees of David Lee Roth versus those of Sammy Hagar. Some might say there are two entirely different Van Halen bands. But others would disagree. When Roth returned after Hagar's tenure, was the resulting band the original Van Halen or was it a third iteration?

In some ways the point is moot, because the position and contribution of a guitarist within any given band doesn't feel quite the same as that of a lead singer. After all, Eddie Van Halen was there continuously through all iterations of the band. So, let's turn our attention to whatever special sauce the front man is bringing.

Consider that Blood, Sweat and Tears had eight original members and none of them are a part of the band presently touring as Blood, Sweat and Tears. The same goes for Ratt, Thin Lizzy, and The Flying Burrito Brothers. But perhaps the total fandoms for all four of those bands doesn't approach even half of the fandom of Queen, so we want to consider that the replacement of Freddie Mercury somehow represents a special case.

Perhaps the closest parallel, because the new iteration of the band seems to be a lasting one, would be the replacement of Steve Perry with Filipino YouTube sensation Arnel Pineda as the frontman for Journey.

He's been going strong at the mic since 2007, with ticket sales continuing to hold steady over the years. It is commonly known among Journey fans that although Pineda looks nothing like Perry whatsoever, he has a relatively exact match for Perry's vocals.

How much of an exact vocal match would it need to be to convince Journey's fans that they don't have to stop believing and can remain faithfully? Perry is more than a voice—he's got moves, he's got fancy outfits, he's got a certain kind of presence on the stage. So, what bit of Freddie Mercury is the essential component that made Queen?

New School

With apologies to Heraclitus and Bruce Springsteen, contemporary philosophers thought the river was a dumb metaphor for these types of questions. Noam Chomsky would argue that there is no reason a band's identity must be psychically continuous in the first place.

In other words, there are as many versions of Queen as there are people who perceive the band because the way Queen is in our minds doesn't necessarily have any connection to the way Queen exists outside of our minds.

Queen, as a band and as an awesome stadium concert experience, has no innate characteristics like guitars or costumes or musicians that make it Queen. Queen may only have what Chomksy called "qualia," elements that answer the question 'What is Queen like?' for each of our own individual mental states.

And so, what you interpret to be the essential ingredient of Queen may have nothing to do with what I interpret to be the band's essential ingredient. This is also why two people who attend the same concert may have wildly differing experiences and subsequent judgments of the show's quality.

Your nosebleed seats can't convey half the power of the band that my VIP backstage passes can. And I might be too drunk on living my best fandom lifestyle, or you might have gone to wait in line for the restroom during my favorite moment of the concert. Therefore, we cannot apprehend anything close to the band's reality anyway.

Yet this attacks our common sense in a way that doesn't feel so good. No matter our individual differences of perception, we all bought a ticket and took the ride in some transcendent few moments of concert-going togetherness.

When you look out over the ocean of arms waving in that stadium, all their voices lifted to sing along with Adam Lambert, there's a genuinely familiar sense of somewhat spiritual oneness that feels in contradiction with the old school notion of infinitely different river flows.

English political philosopher Thomas Hobbes would say that Queen ultimately becomes a new band, and the latest version of it featuring Adam Lambert would be unrecognizable to Freddie Mercury except for the memory of his own iteration of the band evoked by the newest iteration.

In this way, Hobbes uses common sense to bridge the gap between Heraclitus and Chomsky, because Queen today can be understood in the context of your personal experience with the Queen of yesterday—even if it is simultaneously true that no two slices of Queen are ever identical.

This is also why nobody would ever dare to say that Queen + Adam Lambert is better than the previous Queen with Freddie Mercury. Most of us would agree that it's disrespectful to say the newest version is the best version, in part thanks to the fact that there is no Adam Lambert without Freddie Mercury as a precursor.

It's absurd to think that Adam's band could exist without Freddie's band having come before it. Adam Lambert cannot be a copy of nothing. He admits that Freddie Mercury has been the most fundamental musical influence on his own work since he was very young, when he first watched *Wayne's World* and encountered that awesome scene in the car featuring the full version of "Bohemian Rhapsody."

During interviews, Adam has consistently spoken of Freddie in the most reverent tones, saying he felt a kinship with Freddie's fearless showmanship from an early age, that he considers himself a vessel for homage to Freddie and that the gig has helped to secure a lengthy legacy for the legendary original singer.

Hobbes and Chomsky compel us to ask: to what extent is Adam Lambert 'like' Freddie Mercury? What qualities does he possess that enable him to adequately step into those iconic black and white Adidas samba sneakers, to channel our memories of earlier iterations of Queen?

Future School

To answer this, we now turn to Jean Baudrillard, the French cultural theorist who pioneered media concepts like "simulation" and "hyperreality" that are now common ideas to most of us, thanks to movies like *The Matrix*.

Baudrillard agreed with Chomsky that we have no access to genuine reality outside any perception of our own minds, and extended this idea by defining four stages of symbolism through which we construct our reality. Everyone's perception of Adam Lambert will fall into one of these four stages.

The first stage is when people believe Adam is trying to be an exact copy of Freddie. While it's true that Adam is now growing a beard and doing his eye make-up in a way that strongly resembles Freddie, he will never succeed in physically impersonating Freddie. And of course, their vocals are different in a thousand small ways that make it easy to tell the two voices apart.

Adam himself rejects this idea of creating a faithful copy of the original, as he has repeatedly said in interviews that he does not wish to be Freddie but only to do him justice. His own thoughts about his role are perhaps most like Baudrillard's *second stage*, wherein any copying of an original is necessarily inexact but still capable of hinting at the fact of Freddie's previous existence. His fellow band members tend to agree with this notion, citing Adam's concert presence as a focal point or channel for memories of Freddie.

But Brian May has emphasized that Adam's role goes beyond making any kind of copy of Freddie. This is a nod toward Baudrillard's *third stage* (involving a symbol still somewhat pretending to be a copy and thereby masking the fact that there is no original), and his *fourth stage* (involving a pure symbol that makes no pretense of having any relation to an original).

Confronting Baudrillard's territories of simulation helps us uncover what makes a cover band. Yeah, that's right, I'll say it: Queen is now a cover band of itself. That's *probably* a good thing—but it's at least an inevitable one, according to the logics of the hyperreal.

As Adam has now been fronting Queen for the better part of a decade, he is less and less tied to the details of Freddie's showmanship and even the trajectory of his legacy.

This is as Freddie himself would want it, as he appeared quite serious in televised interviews when he said that the group must always carry on and that if he left, they should just replace him.

When Freddie bit the dust, Brian May told the crowd gathered in homage at Wembley in 1992 that it was going to be the biggest sendoff in history. Indeed, the massive tribute show included David Bowie, Robert Plant, Def Leppard, Elton John, Axl Rose, Liza Minelli and very many more.

They needed twenty people to do what Freddie alone could do, because the range of the band's catalog is so incredibly diverse. Who knows what Freddie may have become if he'd lived to be older than forty-five.

He contained multitudes, and perhaps he might have become a lot more like Adam Lambert. The Paul Rogers version of Queen was not eclectic enough, falling mainly into a blues and soul area that was only a small part of what Freddie could do.

By contrast, Adam also seems to contain multitudes. Rogers's early impression of Adam's magnetism was that it made him a sort of campy Elvis that Freddie would appreciate. Surely the man who only announced his AIDS diagnosis to the world one day before he died from it would also appreciate how out of the closet Adam has always been as a gay man. What would it have meant for Freddie to officially come out in the Seventies?

An Effortless Affinity

Adam has said that he can feel Freddie's loneliness as a closeted gay genius rockstar and has learned from that: how to use that onstage and channel it into the music. Freddie's own limited campiness opened doors for Adam, and Adam believes Freddie would've gotten more open as the times have changed.

Brian has commented that he's happy for Adam to be pushing forward the conversation about prejudice against gay people. Adam even gave a brief speech about the Pulse nightclub shooting onstage at the Isle of Wight Festival with the band's full approval.

In the end then, we're not looking for the essential piece of Freddie that Adam possesses to make himself worthy of fronting Queen. Instead, we must simply reflect on the ways that Adam has evolved the band in keeping with the spirit of Freddie.

Brian has been emphatic that Freddie would hate for things to be reproduced exactly the way he did them, that Freddie would want the music to be open to interpretation and flexible and changing—like a river, I daresay. Freddie wouldn't want them to be a straightforward cover band but a new iteration in tribute to his original works.

Perhaps the most we can say is that Adam has consistently demonstrated an effortless affinity with

Freddie, a kind of two-way flow of influence with a powerfully present ghost. Brian has likened Adam to a blood transfusion and Adam has said his relationship to Queen is symbiotic.

These biological metaphors make clear that although Freddie Mercury may be dead, Queen is still very much alive.

11
Is Red Special a Member of Queen?

STEVEN GIMBEL

What's the relationship between player and instrument? Are instruments mere tools used by musicians? Is the instrument a part of the musician, an extension of their body? Can an instrument itself be part of a group?

On the one hand, Roger Taylor's floor toms through the years have changed, but these are standardized and mass-produced items. There is nothing particularly unique or important about them except that they happen to be played by the drummer of Queen. If someone swapped out his floor tom for that of the opening act's drummer, there would be no difference.

On the other hand, Freddie Mercury's instrument was his voice. That clearly is unique to him as a person, as a performer, and an essential element of the band as an entity. With the loss of that voice, Queen itself changed. Notice how the band is billed as "Queen with Adam Lambert." Lambert's voice is *with* Queen in a way that Mercury's voice *was* Queen.

But what of Brian May's guitar, Red Special? Handmade by May and his father, it has a number of unique features no other guitar has. It is a part of what created the "Queen sound" on so many of their most memorable songs. Without that specific instrument, Queen would sound different. Red Special is more than a floor tom, but it raises the question of whether an external, constructed object can rise to the metaphysical level of Freddie Mercury's voice? Brian May is a member of Queen. That much is uncontroversial. But is Red Special, independent of Brian May, itself also a member of Queen?

Realism versus Instrumentalism

Metaphysics is the philosophical field that examines what's real. It considers questions of existence and the properties of those real things. Metaphysicians, for example, consider whether God exists, whether the mind is something different from the brain, and whether humans have free will.

But there are more seemingly mundane metaphysical questions that deal with things we can see and hear. Consider, for example, whether groups are things independent of the individuals that make them up. If, for example, we want to say that corporations have moral responsibilities, then those corporations have to have an existence that does not depend solely on the membership. In considering this sort of metaphysical question, we need to try to understand the nature of different sorts of things, as well as which of their properties are essential—that is, the qualities that something has to have to be included in that category of real things.

"Realism" is the view that something is real. That is, that we ought to assert it as an actual, independent existence. Consider Harvard University. A realist about universities would assert that it is itself a thing. In the list of all entities that make up the world, the furniture of the universe, Harvard University is one of those things.

"Instrumentalism" is the metaphysical view that some "thing" is a mere tool, a useful fiction that we can use to speak shorthand about other things that are real, but that "it" itself is not real. If someone were an instrumentalist about universities, then that person would say that Harvard University does not exist. That does not mean it is imaginary like, say, Hogwarts. Students go to Harvard. Professors profess at Harvard. Researchers research at Harvard. But, for the instrumentalist, it is only the people and the buildings that are the real things. "Harvard" is just a shorthand way of referring to that collection of those real things, but not itself a new thing apart from them.

In our case, we're asking metaphysical questions about bands. For the sake of argument, let's be realists about them. We will say that Queen exists. Queen, as a thing unto itself, is real. It is the sort of thing that has parts—that is, there are independently existing things that when brought together form the new real thing, Queen. But what is included in it? What makes something (including someone) a part of Queen?

Let's start simple. There are humans that are part of Queen. Which humans? Clearly the musicians considered to be members of the band must be parts of Queen. Why? Because the music could not have been made, and made as it was made, without them. Their doing what they do individually as existing entities, when brought together, allows Queen to do what it does.

Of course, that does not mean that everyone whose actions contributed to the music is a part of the band. Roadies, for example, work hard and without them the band could not play as they do. The roadies may be part of the organization, but they are not part of the band.

Similarly, David Bowie sang with Queen on "Under Pressure." He contributed musically. But we want to say that he performed *with* Queen, not *as a part of* Queen because his was a passing contribution.

But there are trickier cases. Consider David Richards, Queen's producer. His contribution has been sustained and creative, not merely technical. He helped shape the sound, create the music as it is. Like George Martin with the Beatles or Alan Parsons with Pink Floyd, the contribution was artistic and formative. The music would not be what the music is without his continuing aesthetic labor. So, did Richards help Queen make its music or was he a member of Queen making their music? There is a debate to be had—and engaging in that sort of debate is what philosophers do.

We will leave this tantalizing question open because it helps to show that there are engaging philosophical questions that require more than simple intuitions: where there is intellectual work that needs to be done, and for which easy answers are a waste of time for these interesting, intricate questions.

We can view certain individual humans—Freddie Mercury and Brian May, for example—realistically. That is, they are really part of Queen. We can view other humans—the roadies, for example—instrumentally. That is, they are tools of the band Queen: people they use to help them create their music, but they are not real members of the band. And then there are the gray cases, cases where we have to think hard about whether someone's work is realist or instrumentalist. Is it work done *by* Queen (since they are a part of the band), or is their work *for* Queen (since they are outside of the band helping)?

It seems as if we can have this same sort of conversation concerning musical instruments. There are some instruments that have to be understood realistically: that is, as real parts of the band itself. Consider Freddie Mercury's instrument, his voice. That voice made Queen's music what it is. It would not be what it is without it.

This example may seem odd because, in this case, the instrument is literally a result of a material part of the performer. But the voice is an instrument. It produces sound according to the talent and artistry of the performer, just as any other instrument. But wouldn't we then say that it is the singer and not the voice that is the part of the band?

Suppose we could separate them. Say it became possible to run the microphone through a box the way guitarists can and the result would be that whoever sang would have an electronically altered voice that would be indistinguishable from Freddie Mercury's. Sure, the timing would be different; the inflection would be different; the attitude and presence would be different. No one else, after all, will ever be Freddie. But the voice would be the same. In this hypothetical case, it would seem like a part of the band had returned (even if we would have to say that Queen had a new singer). So, for Freddie's voice, we have a case of instrumental realism.

There are also easy cases of what we can call, "instrumental instrumentalism." Instrumental instrumentalism are those cases in which we privilege the player as the sole member of the group (and not the instrument played). Consider one drum of Roger Taylor's kit, say, his floor tom. He has played a number of different drum sets through the years. While he has come to play more upscale kits over the years, the drums are of the same sort as those generally available. One could be substituted for another and the resulting playing would be the same. In such cases, we can assert instrumental instrumentalism, that is, these instruments are mere tools played *by* the band and are not themselves part of the band.

Previously we found that there were easy cases for people (who clearly would be in the band or not in the band) and hard cases that we would need to think about—such as the case of producer David Richards. Similarly, we have a hard case for the question of instrumental instrumentalism: Red Special. The floor tom is just a thing, indeed, it is a mass produced thing. There are others that sound just like it. It has no sentimental value because it was simply purchased. There is nothing unique about it. Freddie Mercury's voice was unique. It was a part of him. For those reasons, we think of it realistically, that is, as part of Queen. And then there is Red Special.

The Birth of a Guitar

Picture Brian May on stage. We see the hair. We see the wild, yet stylish, outfits. But what we never fail to see is that guitar in his hands: Red Special. And special it is.

When he was young, May fell in love with the sounds he heard on the radio: American blues, rock, pop, and the sounds of the early British rockers and skiffle bands. He wanted in, got himself an Egmond acoustic, and learned to play. He found some mates and they started to perform. The acoustic just wouldn't do. He needed an electric guitar, but couldn't afford one. He may not have had the cash, but he had two things almost no one else had—a father who was an electrical engineer and the brain of Brian May.

> We made my Red Special, my Dad and I, in my Dad's workshop—converted from the spare bedroom in our small suburban house in Feltham, Middlesex—in about two years of spare moments, and it was all done with hand tools—planes, chisels, and saws, and a lot of sandpaper, fashioning the thing out of bits and pieces. For the neck, we used part of an old fireplace that at the time was 100 years old; it was just kicking around the workshop. If you look really closely, you can still see the wormholes that I filled up with matchsticks. My Dad and I had all kinds of stuff that he'd made, things like test instruments for radios and TVs, and he had the tools as well. He had lots of stock he thought might be useful one day and if we wanted something for the guitar, we could normally find it in the workshop. (Brian May's Red Special, p. 19)

The entire guitar—the body, the bridge, the frets, the scratchplate, the electronics—they made it all. It took trial and error, a lot of creativity, and extreme amounts of ingenuity to figure out how to create the parts from the scraps they had.

> The materials that went into the Red Special were, in so many cases, just made from part of one of those things that happened to be lying around in my Dad's workshop—little pieces of steel, brass and aluminum, washers, nuts and bolts and screws, and occasionally less common objects. The tremolo arm was made from a part of one of those things that support your saddlebag up on a push-bike. The tip of the arm was made from part of one of my Mum's larger knitting needles, filed down using . . . my improvised lathe—a hand drill held in a vice. (p. 60)

With no experience making instruments and no model on which to base their work, they had to figure out from scratch things that professional instrument makers knew. When making the fretboard, for example, where exactly do you put the frets? May measured the placement on his Egmond, but did not just want to duplicate it. Electric guitars standardly have twenty-two frets. The idea of stopping there, just two short of two full octaves, bothered him. He wanted twenty-four. So, he needed to figure out *where* the frets go. And because he's Brian May, he also needed to figure out *why* the frets go where they go.

> I was fascinated by the idea of why frets were set at particular distances: why did they get narrower towards the body? I figured out what happens is reproducible. If you want to convert the string length that produces a certain note to the length that makes a note a semitone higher, there must be some factor (less than 1) that would multiply the string length by, to get the semitone. So, if you call that proportional factor 'x', you multiply the total string length by 'x' and you get the

> distance from the bridge to the fret that makes the next semitone up!
>
> Now the trick is . . . you multiply that length by the same factor x, again, and you get the fret distance for another semitone up, and so on. Do it again and again with the same proportion and you get all the fret positions. But what is that factor? Well, it's defined by the fact that if you perform the operation 12 times, you get the octave, which must be half of the length of the whole string. So multiplying anything by 'x' gives you a half. This is a simple equation to be solved which, in words, looks like this: x raised to the 12th power equals a half. Solution: x is the 12th root of a half.
>
> A simple equation with a simple solution, but to actually find out what the 12th root of a half actually is? Not so easy. Initially, I worked it out with a slide rule, and made a table of results so I'd get them exactly right.
>
> Strangely enough, when I was working at EMI Weapons Department (!) during my school holidays, I had access to one of the first computers in the world. It was the size of a small factory, but of course had much less computing power than your average smartphone of today. I wrote an iterative programme to determine the 12th root of a half, to 100 decimal places. So, if anyone wants accurate fret positions to 100 decimal places, I have them! (p. 36)

Yes, May and his father had to reinvent the wheel; but along the way, they also gave it a hubcap, making advances that commercial guitar makers would copy or later discover.

> Actually, there are quite a few innovations on the guitar. The roller bridge was, I think, unique in those days and everybody was saying I should have patented it, but patents are a pain in the neck, and why not share everything with the world? A fingerboard with 24 frets was unusual, so I introduced an extension of the marker dots to save me from getting lost. Instead of two dots at the 12th fret I put three—so the twos could go elsewhere. The truss

> rod was anchored on a massive bolt which also fastens the neck on to the body . . . so tightening it up really held the neck rigid. The tremolo uses compression springs (borrowed from a British Norton Motorbike—they're valve springs) rather than springs in tension like most units. And, unusually for the time, it sat completely in equilibrium in the centre position, so I could rock the pitch smoothly either way. Also, I devised my own system for switching between combinations of three pickups, so, for the first time, I think, all the combinations of three pickups, in and out of phase, could be used in performance. There are a few other things, like the acoustic pocket in the body . . . It also has a slightly shorter scale length (effective string length) than most commercial guitars, making the fingering a little easier, and the tone a little brighter. (pp. 35–36)

There are a lot of guitars in the world, but there is only one Red Special. May's guitar tech, Brian "Jobby" Zellis put it this way: "It's not like a Stradivarius where you can just go and buy another one: it's the Red Special, there isn't anything else like it."

It is not only the guitar May plays: it is a part of his life story. It was a labor of love that kept him connected to his family. It has a unique sound, part of what gives Queen the Queen sound. It is not a mere object. As May himself wrote, "I think everybody in Queen saw my Red Special as part of the family; it was very much a part of our daily lives" (p. 89). Part of the family—that is usually something we only say about people. Of course, being a member of a band is also something we only say about people . . . .

A Member of Queen?

So, we have two questions: 1. should guitars in general be thought of as instrumental or realist? 2. Is the case of Red Special different? (not the case that the guitar gets carried in, but the example . . . you know what I mean.)

I am a musically talentless philosopher, so to help me answer these questions, I consulted a friend and colleague, Jocelyn, who is a professional pianist and professor of music. The fun part is that we disagree. She will tell you that one thing you learn as a pianist is that pianos are too big to carry, and as a result when you go someplace to perform, you will be using their piano. One might think that pianos are all the same, but this is absolutely not true. Each piano has its own personality, quirks, and distinctive elements. This is true even if they are made by the same manufacturer.

If, for example, you were to go to the Steinway factory in Queens, New York (which she has) and played several pianos of the same age, built in the same way, using the same materials, with all the same technical attributes (which she also has), one could still tell the difference between them. They will have different feels, different sounds, different properties—they play differently.

When "Jobby" Zellis tried to distinguish Red Special from other instruments by saying "It's not like a Stradivarius where you can just go and buy another one," he was wrong. Even among the limited number of surviving violins made by the legendary Antonio Stradivari, there are important differences from instrument to instrument.

In philosophy, the distinction is made between "types" and "tokens." A type is a category, a set of objects of the same kind, and a token is an individual member of that set. When we speak of instruments, we cannot speak merely of types. Rather, we must speak in terms of tokens.

When a musician plays, the music is the result of a relationship that must be formed between the musician and the particular instrument: the token of the type of instrument the musician plays. The relationship one will have with one instrument will be different from the relationship with another, even of the same type. Some pianos will make certain sorts of playing come alive in ways that might not be true on others.

This is even more true in a case like Brian May and Red Special. The guitar is not only a guitar. It's a reminder of family relations. It's a connection to his past. It's specifically designed for certain ways of playing and certain effects May wants. It's a special relationship, a unique relationship because of his history with the instrument.

It is not the only relationship May has as a member of Queen, of course. He also has relationships with his guitar techs, with the roadies, with his manager and accountant, and with his bandmates. These are all very different sorts of relationships.

Some are artistic relationships. Because Queen is an artistic entity, it is the artistic relationships (and the artistic relationships alone) that are the essential elements needed to make something a member of the artistic entity that is Queen. What makes a relationship artistic?

A relationship between two entities is artistic if the particulars of the individuals involved in the relationship are a part of the cause of the art that results. Brian May may therefore have very close relationships with his accountant and with the roadies, but that relationship in no way influences the artistry of the music he makes. It may be necessary for the music to occur, but it does not in any way influence the form or content of the music.

This can also be seen to be the case with the floor tom. This is an instrument, but unlike Stradivarius violins and pianos, they are mass produced in such a way that they can be switched one for another with no (or at least: minimal) artistic effect. Therefore, the relation is with the type and not the token. Hence, we now understand why we want to say that Freddie Mercury had a different relationship with his voice and Brian May has a different relationship with Red Special than Roger Taylor to his floor tom.

But the most important artistic relationship, of course, is between band members. The relationships among bandmates are every bit as artistic as the relationships between individual members and their instruments. But—Jocelyn wants to stress—only relationships among musicians are reciprocal artistic relationships (in other words: the relationship to the instrument is not reciprocal). Musicians play their instruments, but they play *off* of each other. The instrument is unique. The instrument has qualities that artistically inspire. But the instrument is played by the player to make art. The player has a relationship with the instrument, but the instrument does *not* have a relationship with the player. The players do not play each other, but rather play *with* each other. The musicians relate and interact with both instruments and other musicians to create the art, but the instruments do not relate back. They do not play together, they are played.

To be a member of a band is to have person-to-person artistic interactions; those, Jocelyn contends, are the only possible relationships (within the confines of artistic creation in the band) that confer membership. As such, Jocelyn is an instrumental instrumentalist. Instruments, even those as special as Red Special, are in the end just instruments, not members of the band—because they are incapable of the proper sort of artistic relationship.

I agree . . . in the usual case. But unusual cases like Freddie Mercury's voice and Red Special are different. In these cases, the instruments are sufficiently unique (and the relationships inspirational enough) that they may inspire artistic creation that otherwise could not have occurred. Put any other guitar in Brian May's hand and you don't get the Queen sound—which would have changed how he thought to compose. The ancient

Greeks called the goddesses of inspiration the Muses. In the rare case of an instrument like Red Special, it can serve as a muse, as a compositional/artistic partner without which the art would have been different. The guitar may not have ideas, but because the relationship with it is unlike the relationship with any other instrument, it may give rise to ideas as if it came from the instrument—because the musician would not have had them otherwise. As a result, I am, in this unusual case, an instrumental realist.

This leaves you with a question. Who do you agree with, the musician or the philosopher? Is Red Special a special instrument played *by* a member of Queen, or is it itself *a member* of Queen?[1]

---

[1] Special thanks to my friend and colleague Professor Jocelyn Swigger for her invaluable help concerning the content and structure of the arguments, and insight into both music and the lived experience of musicians. This chapter could not have been written without her gracious and generous input.

V

Made in the Heavens

12
Hot Spacetime

KRISTINA ŠEKRST

You knew you wanted to be an astronaut since you were five years old. Your biggest historical role model, who obviously wanted it all, was Brian May, both a rock star and a scientist with a PhD in astrophysics. After years of education and training, you accept an offer to go on a one-year mission in search of a new planet. You return after a year only to realize that everybody you knew has grown old and died. In order to figure out what has happened, we must first visit the two most fundamental concepts of them all: time and space.

Time Waits for Nobody

Newton's mechanics was essentially unchallenged until the twentieth century, both from the physical and philosophical standpoints. At that time, what we today know as science was actually called *natural philosophy*: the philosophical study of nature and the universe around us. So, Isaac Newton wasn't a physicist back then, he was a natural philosopher.

In his *Principia*, Newton stated that time, space, and motion exist both as absolute and relative phenomena. Being *absolute* meant that there was nothing external to the space-time-motion complex. If space is absolute, that means that there exists a reality *independent* of bodies inside it, like a container. It's there even if you empty it. The same goes for time, it exists *independently* of any observers. The fact that 'time waits for nobody', in Mercury's words, would be an accurate description of absolute time: we as observers aren't important, it has its own reality and its own pace.

For Newton, therefore, space was something distinct from objects inside it: there is space and there are bodies. Philosopher and polymath Gottfried Leibniz was one of the first to argue that space only makes sense if we take the relative location of bodies into account. The main criticism was often directed toward our inability to conceive absolute space as something completely independent of anything else. If you turn right in empty absolute space, that's *right* relative to what exactly?

Eventually, Ernst Mach, physicist and philosopher, proposed the so-called "Mach's principle." Imagine this: you're standing in a field, looking at the night sky. Maybe expecting a shooting star. You see the stars above you're not moving, and you've been waiting for this meteor shower for quite a while. You're standing still, eagerly, with your arms resting at your side. "Okay, I'll create my own shooting stars!" you say, and start spinning. The stars seem to be whirling around you and your arms are pulled from your body (and we won't stop you now!). But why would this happen? Why aren't your arms being pulled away from your body when you're not spinning?

Mach states that we can only talk about rotation in terms of things that are *in* the universe. If everything was spinning, we wouldn't call your spinning "spinning," since that would be normal. So, Mach's idea was that everything in physics and philosophy is based on *relative* motion, space and time. This paved the way to modern relativistic theories. Until Einstein, concepts of time and space were treated as distinct and separate realities. It was the advent of special relativity theory that merged the two into a single notion of *spacetime*. However, first there was light.

At the Speed of Light

Einstein's special theory of relativity is a theory regarding the relationship between space and time, the same question that has been bugging philosophers for decades. He proposed that the laws of physics should obey *the principle of relativity*: the laws of physics must be the same for all of the observers. It doesn't matter whether I'm spinning in a star field, riding a train, or sleeping in my bed, the laws of physics are identical or *invariant*.

The second big postulate of the special theory of relativity is that the speed of light in a vacuum is also the same for all observers. Light will travel at the same speed in a vacuum, no matter what I'm doing now. The speed of light in a vacuum is defined as approximately three hundred thousand kilometers per second, and what Einstein has proposed is that this is the upper limit at which *anything* can travel through space. So, when Mr. Fahrenheit is 'travelling at the speed of light' in *Don't Stop Me Now*, he's actually at his maximum. In order to stop him, we would have to be faster since we don't want to use violence. And that's impossible. But we might join him if we can travel at the speed of light as well.

For centuries, philosophers have theorized that the light was moving in a certain medium. If sound travels in air, if waves travel through the water, then the light must travel through *something,* so let's call it *aether*. After decades of arguments and discussion about qualities of such a medium, its properties became practically magical. It had to be a certain type of a fluid in order to fill space, but it also had to be stronger than steel to support the physics and high frequencies of light waves.

And this monstrous thing was nowhere to be found. Do you see anything like that around? No, but what's interesting is that all the philosophers and natural scientists were taking the existence of aether for granted. It just had to be there. There was even a decades-long experiment that tried to find it, and it was first performed by physicists Albert Michelson and Edward Morley. They didn't find any magical substance, and the only logical answer was to repeat the experiment since they had obviously done something wrong. 'There's no aether' simply wasn't a valid statement.

The experiment continued for decades, and it has been called the most famous failed experiment in history. In 1905, Einstein noticed the lack of evidence for the existence of aether and thought: hey, maybe it just isn't there. But in order to fully develop his theory, time and space had to merge into another inconceivable monster called *spacetime*.

"'39"

Back in the nineteenth century, there was space and there was time. And there it was, the twentieth century stating: no, they're actually the same thing. Einstein saw them as two different sides of the same coin. Mathematically, it's the same if you travel at a certain velocity as if you're rotating in a four-dimensional spacetime. Space has four dimensions now: up/down, left/right, forward/backward and one time dimension. In a Newtonian universe, if all the things disappeared from the universe, time and space would still remain. In Einstein's spacetime, they would disappear as well without any matter inside.

Imagine you want to join our old friend Mr. Fahrenheit. You power up your spaceship and want to disturb him a bit, maybe using a laser to satisfy your inner child. If you were traveling at a constant speed of say, half the speed of light, you wouldn't even be able to tell you were moving, the same way it might seem the other trains are moving when your train starts to exit the station. If you had a mirror on top of your ceiling and a detector on the floor, you might test that laser and shoot a beam up, which would come back down and be detected. The beam wouldn't miss the detector just because your ship is moving at half of light speed

But behold, Mr. Fahrenheit was way smarter, and he called Dr. May, who was practicing guitar back on Earth, to help and observe whether there are any villains in spaceships around. May would see your laser light travel upward diagonally, strike the mirror, and travel downward, diagonally again. Dr. May isn't slow or drunk, it's just physics. Not only that the light paths of your laser light were different, according to our spacetime equivalent, but because that means the time passed must be different as well, in the spacetime frames of Dr. May and Mr. Farenheit. Such a phenomenon is called *time dilation*. If a ship is moving very quickly, traveling close to the speed of light, time passes slower than on Earth.

In "Dead on Time," written by May, a person can "leave on time," but "never can tell." The fact that you left at a certain time might not mean anything since there's nothing like absolute time. It might go slower or faster for you, depending on your velocity. Maybe the guy in the song has a ticket for a spaceship, in that case you really cannot tell how and, more importantly, *when* you'll end up.

In a 1983 interview for BBC Radio One, May has stated that the song "'39" is a science-fiction story about a person who goes away to visit a new planet, but then time gets in the way. The time dilation effect makes the traveler age a year, and his loved ones back on his home planet age more than 100 years. In "'39," we find out that a group of volunteers used interstellar travel to find a new world, perhaps in 2139, or maybe May was optimistic and thought of 2039. A hundred years later, in another "'39," they return home with the good news of finding a habitable planet. He looks at his daughter, presumably an old lady now, seeing her mother's eyes in her eyes. Even though "many years have gone," the narrator finds himself just "older but a year."

Many Years Away

Well, if there was one thing that philosophers thought was the same for everyone, that was time. It had been inconceivable even for an ordinary layman to think that there was some funny business here. Why don't race car drivers age slower than couch potatoes like most of us? They're going faster all the time, right!

Actually, they do. But the effect is so negligible since they barely even move compared to the speed of light. Astronauts who spend a great deal of time in space age more slowly, but it's barely measurable. After six months on the International Space Station, an astronaut would have aged about 0.005 seconds less than her family on Earth. A Nascar driver is going to experience a third of a nanosecond less time than its audience. Don't stock up on fast cars in order to get younger, such an effect becomes important only when you're approaching the speed of light.

May also wrote another song, "Long Away," haunted by the same feelings of loss and nostalgia as "'39." Both time and space are of the essence here: "who know when now, who know where." These are two sides of the same coin. If you pack your suitcase and leave this place, you might end up as a 'new child'. I see this song as a kind of twin to "'39," talking about a long way behind the people who embarked on a sad sacrificial journey. The same can be said for "All Dead, All Dead": if the "'39" narrator's wife is long dead, he's really "old but still a child."

As with *Interstellar* (Christopher Nolan, 2008), "'39" tells a story about an astronaut leaving everything behind, and coming back still young, while everybody else has grown old. Communication was probably impossible because of weak signals, which meant that everything they could have sent would just end up as "letters in the sand."

For everything mentioned to work, science needs to treat space and time as a single phenomenon or entity: spacetime. The narrator in "'39" is aware of that, telling his loved one she's *many years away*. This might be taken both literally, since light years are measures of astronomical *distances*, or as the other side of the coin, being aware that time passes differently for her and for his daughter.

Keep Yourself Alive

What if the astronauts were away for what the people on Earth would perceive as thousands of years? In your lifetime, you don't have proper time to visit the far side of the Milky Way, and go back to report it to your children, since it would take you over one hundred thousand years for such a trip. But who would be right? Did it take you one hundred thousand years or just a couple of months?

It seems that there's no correct answer. However, there's one important question here: can we talk about people in such a situation existing at the same time at all? In philosophical *presentism*, it is thought that neither the future nor the past exists. All that exists, all that's physically real is the *present*, a system of events simultaneous to each other. However, even if you were to know everything there is, according to the special theory of relativity, you wouldn't be able to know *what* that system is. Freddie and Brian might see events A, B, and C unfolding in different orders, and no one is right here.

On the other side of the ring, there's *eternalism*, which seems to better fit the findings in physics. Such a philosophical approach takes the view that all of existence in time is equally real. There's nothing like an *objective* flow of time. Many philosophers have argued that the special theory of relativity implies eternalism. But the advent of relativity wasn't the first thing to trigger such a philosophical concept.

For example, in some philosophical doctrines of *fatalism*, every statement about the future exists, and it's either true or false. In the words of *Who Wants to Live Forever*, it's all "decided for us." In special relativity, different observers experience the so-called *relativity of simultaneity*. Dr. May spying on us is going to see a different trajectory of a light beam than we would in our spaceship, but neither one of us is in a privileged position.

Even though eternalism is often embraced by physicists, there's something counterintuitive here. You would feel weird stating that Socrates exists right now. One of the standard answers to this problem is to state that 'exists' means existing in a general sense, without assuming some temporal location.

There's also one philosophical alternative, which seems to be more aligned with our general common sense. The *growing block view* states that the past and present both exist, while the future does not (yet). Imagine you had a huge spotlight, and you would gradually increase its range and shine over more and more objects. More and more spacetime would come into being. After all, light is the evidence that the block grows.

If you believe in presentism, you'd probably embrace the concept of *endurantism*: if an object persists through time, it needs to exist completely at different times. But if you support eternalism, then if a thing exists in time, it has to exist in another continuous reality. In a doctrine called *perdurantism*, an object is an aggregation of all your temporal parts: all of your past, present and future selves.

This might seem like a difficult concept, but it's rather intuitive: I consider my past self myself as well, and my identity now is an aggregation of all my previous experiences. Rarely would we consider ourselves being just what we are at the moment, but let's leave some hope for turning over a new leaf.

There are some interpretations stating that "'39" is about time travel, which doesn't seem to be the case, but we might see it that way. We're all familiar with time travel stories, but philosophy was also intrigued whether it's logically possible. If you could go back in time, you would be able to kill your grandfather before your mother was conceived, and that would lead to a famous paradox. Do note, if presentism is true, then neither past nor future objects really exist, so there's no time travel.

One other common argument is the concept of backward causation where an effect precedes its cause in time: your usage of a certain time-travel machine would make you pop out of nowhere somewhere in the past or the future! However, it seems that many physicists and philosophers believe that what we know about the laws of physics is actually *compatible* with time travel.

Another World

May's astrophysical and musical duality does not end with Queen. In his "Another World," there's a main motif of parallel universes, "across time and space," while the single named "New Horizons" was inspired by the eponymous space mission and the human indomitable spirit eager to explore the universe around us. May has famously stated that music is about our internal lives and being able to touch each other, while astronomy is the opposite: instead of looking inwards, we're looking at things beyond our grasp. Our goal is that, after reading this book, you have a strong feeling that philosophy does the same, and notice May's wondrous ability to illustrate the strangest concepts of modern philosophy of science with ease.

Current philosophical theories of time and space need to take physical findings into account. But vice versa should be valid as well. Even though you're just a bunch of elementary particles interacting, we can talk about a *human being* since we perceive an organism made of atoms different from the atoms external to it, such as the air around you or the ground you're standing on. Human intuition, perception and experience are also a part of philosophy, no matter what the underlying physical mother theory seems to be.

If one day neuroscience shows with complete accuracy that the human mind is a combination of neurons and that's it, you'd still feel as if you're something other than *just* that. The same goes for fundamental concepts of time and space in physics and philosophy, two disciplines strangely connected, in this case, with music.

13
The Mystic Art of Music

RANDALL E. AUXIER

We have to talk about three things. We need to talk about the physical nature of sound. Then we have to talk about how music is made from sound. We also need to talk about how sound is experienced. Is this science? In a way, yes, but there is more to Mr. Fahrenheit than you think. That may sound a bit off topic, but it won't be, because we'll be talking about Queen the whole way, and especially how they made sound into music, and what it did to you.

Since Queen did it better than anyone, and since they had a physicist on guitar, it's fair to assume that they understood this science stuff better than most bands. John was an electrical engineer, and it is not as if anything I will say here would be news to him. Further, Roger was trained as a dentist and thus had a science background in general. We assume that physics wouldn't be new to him either. Freddie? Freddie was smart. Yes, yes, art school, I know. No physics there. Probably not much. But c'mon, that dude was music *itself*, so I'm not going to worry about it. He'll show up at the appointed moment.

Good Company

Before we get to sound, let's get a few things straight about the band, and part of what makes Queen better than other bands. I am not saying that they are to everyone's taste. When I say they are "better," I mean that they occupy a certain extreme, at the highest possibilities of a certain kind of music. Their music is both pop and rock; it is highly melodic, and so has a certain relationship to folk music, in that sense. And it is complex, combining tropes of classical music, prog-rock, and occasionally jazz.

Then there is the weird stuff. There might be a few other bands that share most of these characteristics. For example, take away the classical and touch of jazz, and REO Speedwagon is a comparator. Take away the pop and Yes is a comparator—I mean the real Yes, not what became of them in the 1980s, in which case you could add pop back in. Styx has almost all of the same elements. So did Kansas. In short, this *sort* of band *existed*. But Queen had the weird stuff. The others really didn't.

Yet, I want to say that Queen was quite a bit more flexible and wide-ranging in what they *could* do, and what they *did* do. I would also give Queen the slight edge on every single instrument.

- Brian May is, in my judgment, better than even the best of the guitarists in these bands, in style being most similar to Gary Richrath of REO, but better.
- Was John Deacon seriously better than Chris Squire? Maybe not, but Deacon's range of styles was wider. Squire only did Squire. And Deacon didn't give much away on the virtuosity either. He is, in my judgment, at least a close second.
- Comparing drummers is not easy, but for fullness, groove, power, tastefulness, and musical reach, Roger

Taylor has to be near the top; when you add in the vocals and songwriting, he comes out MVD (Most Valuable Drummer).

- Then there's Freddie. No one has ever been quite like him, although Elton John will come to mind for some people. I think Freddie definitely learned some things from Elton, and as a front man, from Bowie and Jagger. But unlike Bowie, who pretends to be a star man but was really a jazz sax player, Freddie really was from another planet, called Zanzibar, a Zoroastrian from Zanzibar. Sounds made up. But no, he was with us for a short time, but now he's gone back where he came from.

We have a cast of characters here who're in a position to know some things most people, let alone most bands, don't know.

Some Facts about the Universe

There probably was a guy named Pythagoras. We don't know for sure, so this isn't one of the facts of the universe. Some people say he's only a legend, not a historical man, but it doesn't matter. If he didn't exist, he sure left a lot of traces as if he had. You learned a famous theorem, that was either his or someone else's. This guy, or someone like him, is sort of the daddy of a number of discoveries about order in and of the universe. And here is the important part: his discoveries don't come from *how we* experience the universe, but seem to be *part of* the universe, itself, even if *we* never existed. Hard to say for certain, but it sure looks like it.

The objectivity of musical order is one of these discoveries. Pythagoras noticed that musical sound is complex. But now just focusing on musical sound, which is sound rarified and refined into music, there is no such thing as just a pure tone consisting of just one wave vibrating at one frequency. Actually we *can* make such a sound digitally, and it's most unpleasant. Thankfully, it doesn't exist in nature without our 'help'. It's like a laser beam. By itself, light doesn't arrange itself that way. Neither does sound. So there is a difference between what *we* can do with sound and light and what they do by themselves.

Does the universe make music without us? My answer is yes, but I get challenged on this by very smart people, so you may want to take a different view. Here's the rub: it depends on what you mean by 'music'. The philosopher Charles Hartshorne (1897–2000) wrote a book called *Born to Sing* arguing that birds sing because they enjoy it (not just to attract mates or stake out territory). He says *that* makes it "music." Lots of people think that what makes art different from non-art is that art isn't practical—we do it because we like it. I buy this. So, birds make music, and therefore music exists in nature without help from humans. You can decide for yourself.

A Kind of Magic

When it comes to sound, it arranges itself in surprising ways. There are waves within waves, crisscrossing all over the place so that what we call a "tone" is an average of these vibrations. A tone can, by a kind of magic, become a note. The dominant tone, that is, a note, when we surround it with other such tones before and after, carries a whole series of overtones, and the more of these we combine, the richer the sound. The richer the tone, the more order it may impart to our bodies.

For most of our history we just fiddled about looking for and refining material objects that make tones we can use as notes. Drums probably came first, but it's impossible to know. Somebody may have picked up a conch shell or a dead sheep's horn and let loose. The point is that we made instruments from stuff that would make musical sounds. This took on a new meaning when somebody got the idea of stretching a string across some kind of hollow box and plucking it. It was a revolution in our level of control over tones, especially in combining them. I guess you see where this is going. But cool your jets. We will get there.

Princes of the Universe

Now, the Pythagoreans, our princes of the universe, came along some time after the stretching of the strings, but still way back, and they noticed some things about these odd boxes. If you place your finger exactly halfway between one end of the string and the other (when it is stretched tight), you get a tone that is just like the tone of the whole string, but higher in pitch. These guys said, hmm. Then they placed a finger a third of the way down the string and got a different but complementary tone. And you could get that same tone from either end of the string a third of the way down. They said, hmmm. One to two, and also one to three, are cool ratios. We'll call this "harmony" when tones like each other this much. Except they said it in Greek, like this: Ἁρμονία—, and it was so lovely they said "she's a goddess, daughter of Ares and Aphrodite!—war and beauty—you don't want to meet their other daughter, Eris. For the Romans these were the daughters of Mars and Venus, Concordia and Discordia.

The Pythagoreans were intrigued. They tried the same thing one fourth of the way down and up the string and got a different tone, and lawdy be, it was the same tone as the half-way tone only still higher, and they said, hmmmm. Then they started placing fingers everywhere fingers would go and started hearing all sorts of relationships, but some were stronger than others. When they stopped fingering everything, they had counted eight 'steps' between the lower and higher tone that were the same, and they said, hmmmmmmmm. And when they listened very closely, they could hear that these tones were complex, including a whole mix of tones, but making one dominant effect.

Breakthrough

The 1/2, the 1/3, the 1/4, the 1/5, and the 1/8 were sort of special, more powerful and assertive than the other spots on the string, and so, being mathematically inclined, they started looking around for other things in the world that favored these ratios. And they started finding all kinds of stuff. If you want to try this for yourself, you can pick up any guitar and make these "harmonics," just like Pythagoras may have done. If you don't have a guitar, you can use a bugle—it plays the same ratios. Play taps or reveille. Those are the same tones, and they show up as complementaries on every instrument, not just stringed.

A good drummer, such as Roger Taylor, will tune his drums in these ratios. A rock drummer will probably tune his bass drum and snare drum to the tone we call 'E' or perhaps 'A' for a concert. It's too much trouble to retune the drums between songs, so the drummer goes for the average key the concert will use. But in the studio he will retune his drums to the key of the song, or in a harmonic relation to that key. I'll bet you didn't know that. It makes a difference.

You don't get a choice about the physical structure of music. It is what it is, and it does to your body what it does. Resistance is futile. You want to be assimilated. We have become so accustomed to music these days (it is everywhere), that we tend to forget that it was once a fairly rare thing to hear music, and when some was being created, people came out of their holes and shacks to hear it. They wanted some of that order in their bodies. The omnipresence of music in a technological age has led us to take it for granted. That is a pity.

Teo Torriatte

During the "no synthesizers" era of Queen, they were studying their Pythagorean ratios. You think I'm making this up, but I am not. You are dealing with some very scientific composers here. In particular we have an engineer (Deacon) and a physicist (May) screwing around with sound. You know about Brian's guitar and John's special amplifier, I hope. But maybe you want more proof that these guys are Pythagoreans. I suggest you look at Brian's composition at the end of "Teo Torriatte." It's an instrumental which uses "Shepard tones." What's that, you say? Well, they were newly discovered when *A Day at the Races* was recorded. It is "a sound consisting of a superposition of sine waves separated by octaves [that is our 1/8 and our 1/2, and our 1/4)]. When played with the bass pitch of the tone moving upward or downward, it is referred to as the *Shepard Scale*. This creates the auditory illusion of a tone that seems to continually ascend or descend in pitch, yet which ultimately gets no higher or lower." Thank you, Wikipedia. Read the whole article yourself, it's really interesting.

My point is that when you are hanging with Queen, you are hanging with dudes who actually think about and study the effects of sound on 'a human body' (Roger's biological education?). Allowing that Freddie was a pure musician in the sense of 'artist-not-scientist', you still don't want to underestimate what his friends would do with his sonic ideas, which were decidedly outside the Western canon sometimes. Yes, he played Persian scales and other bends and quivers that did not abide with those clean Pythagorean ratios. But his friends were pulling his creations back into the ratios we Westerners all love.

One interesting example is "Teo Torriatte," where the verses are decidedly modal, before a Western symphony kicks in at the chorus. Yet, even in the first verse John is dancing around melodiously on the bass mid-neck using a Western major scale. These guys know what they are doing, relative to the physics and acoustics of music, and they know way more than you do, and they are doing all this for your aesthetic gratification. And they know how and why you like it. People thought they were cocky, but the truth is they were just unusually smart, as well as good, and they knew it.

Pythagoras in Persia?

Let's go a little deeper into this, well, let's call it back chat. Way back when music was really special (before it became cheap and spotified), people marveled at the kind of *order* they experienced when they were in its presence. It was 'found order', not entirely made by us. It was natural for them to attach religious significance to it. Here was something the gods had prepared for our edification, no? And so there was no real debate that the order in music was something divine. It was. And so Pythagoras and his bunch were regarded as a religious order, for a good while. The 'alternate history' folks, who don't let the truth get in the way of a good story, say what if Pythagoras made it to Persia (which some people claim, but then they claim anything they want when it comes to Pythagoras):

> Imagine the consequences: much of the abstraction of the early Ionian philosophy, together with the mathematical obsessions of Pythagoras, fused with the almost-monotheistic and dualist Zoroastrians. Both groups are highly spiritual, and the result could have all the cosmological and ethical trappings of Zoroastrianism, the war against evil, light and darkness, fire as a supreme element, the demiurge etc., to-

> gether with philosophical reasoning and a belief in the underlying reality of mathematics. (Faeelin 2004)

Does this sound like any rock group you know of? If so, I want you to ride the wild wind with me the rest of the way to the lap of the gods.

Blending and Memory

So we have passed through what sound is, and how it becomes music, we need a bit more on how Queen does the deed. We have seen that they know their physics and acoustics and how to blend and bend ratios. But the blending and bending is where the weird stuff happens with this band.

The blending is what makes the articulated sound intelligible to the ear—not as the sound hits the body, but as the body sorts out the sound as an experience of music. The blending makes a whole sound, deliverable in a flash, but the body separates the noise from the music in that sound, and it takes a little time. You might think of it as the difference between listening and really hearing. But you don't really hear the sound, you feel it. You hear the music *in* the sound. The musicians create the blend, quite on purpose, and if it's Queen, with technical and even scientific precision. It is pre-fitted to your range of experience.

I asked Luke Dick, a prominent producer, songwriter, and recording engineer about how Queen does this. He said:

> I think there is something to the way people experience popular music that contributes to this 'sound.' "Another One Bites the Dust," for example, has a lot of simple but original studio tricks that are so awesome they couldn't be duplicated live. The reverse piano swell for one. The weird echoes before the outro, and so on. Because the songs are

> blasted out on radio and become hits before they're played live, the fans have an experience with these very awesome songs, so there's anticipation. That anticipation helps fill in gaps, as well. Add that to the utter volume of a live show, and that helps create the effect of blending a live arrangement with a studio arrangement.

So your listening now uses what you heard before to add to the order of the whole experience. You are making the sound using your memory and even your body. Many musicians know you will do this. I once played in a three-piece band and we wanted to do Beach Boys songs for frat parties, and with only three singers you can't cover all the harmonies. When the harmonies started, we would leave out the main melody, knowing that the audience would fill in that part with their memories (not to mention that's what they were often singing along). Queen had the same challenge. Really only three singers (extremely good ones of course) and all those thick harmonies to reproduce live. But Pythagoras helps—the overtones are *there*. John could add a bit when needed, but no fucking way are they doing Bohemian Rhapsody with what they had—yet, your anticipation makes it work. Luke continued:

> Once people just hear the bass line [of "Another One Bites the Dust"], they're excited at the vibe. That excitement can help ice over discrepancies in recordings. Add the volume and the fact that the main feel is there, plus the visual element of THE ACTUAL BAND IN REAL LIFE, and it's actually almost always better to fans than the recording itself. "They're even better live," they say. Of course, if you just played back the live recording and A/B'd with the studio recording, there's no way fans would say that. But the combination of all these things adds up to being an even more exciting experience to fans. BUT, that excitement wouldn't happen if the studio recording of 'Bohemian Rhapsody' didn't happen FIRST.

Feeling the Bends

So that's the blending, what about the bending? Those Pythagoreans had two sides, a scientific and mathematical side, and a mystical and religious side. In fact, eventually these two aspects of the Pythagorean community led to a split between the "mathematikoi" and the "akousmatikoi." These are two different kinds of order, one spiritual and dogmatic, the other scientific and progressive. The teachings of the akousmatikoi are quite similar to those of Zoroaster, which has led some people to speculate that Pythagoras did go to Persia. In any case, Freddie can easily belong to the same bunch, so long as they don't have a problem with his mysticism—and they didn't.

And so it is with Queen. No, the three scientists were not religious, although they weren't anti-religious either. But Freddie was raised in a strict religious household, and that religion was weird and old. I talked about it in a different chapter, but now I want to add something I didn't say there. Just as with "Teo Torriatte," there is an Eastern twist in this music, and I credit it to Freddie. I give as one of a thousand examples, the Persian-sounding religious chant at the end of "Another One Bites the Dust." Freddie's strange vibrato is a Middle Eastern trademark. It took some getting used to, for good English lads, I expect. It bends the scales.

Freddie always knew how to find his way back into the comfortable scales the Westerners liked, but he never ceased his chanting. It's everywhere in this music. Call it the bends. In a way, this is the element that distinguishes and spiritualizes all this sound. You feel it long before you hear it, and you remember it long after you hear it.

VI

Supersonic Men

14
He Will Rock You

MICHAEL F. PATTON

Is this the real life? Is this just fantasy? Caught in a landslide, no escape from reality.

This is quite an interesting Berkeleyan idyll to show up in a pop song, wouldn't you say? These lyrics raise questions that deal with the very nature of his perceived reality. In another song, the same lyricist discusses a man who has, as the song goes, played in the street and generally been a big disgrace—all the while waving his banner and kicking his can all over the place. And the guitarist who complemented those lyrics with his screaming guitar tones was one of the few that the late, great, Frank Zappa said he admired and considered a peer.

Of course, I'm talking about Freddie Mercury and Brian May—two of the iconic members of the legendary band Queen.

Not everyone knows that Freddie Mercury has a D.Phil. in Metaphysics. Oh, wait—no, he doesn't. That's why so many people don't know it. But he does have an MA in Applied Ethics. Oops! That's false too. At least Brian May really does have a PhD in Astrophysics from Imperial College London and was awarded the CBE. Really. Look it up.

Perhaps these facts can help explain some of the ways in which the music of Queen continues to engage and fascinate us. Besides singing along in the car with Garth and Wayne, maybe there's more to think about in these songs . . . and maybe their content is a bit more philosophical than it seems to be on initial listening.

Let's look at three timeless Queen songs, "We Will Rock You," "We Are the Champions," and "Don't Stop Me Now." By considering these songs and the actions of Socrates in the *Apology*, we'll attempt to gain some philosophical insight from them or, failing that, *cram* some philosophical insight into them. No matter how it turns out, let's set off to our day at the races.

We Will Rock You

I think the attitude of the anthemic "We Will Rock You" is more than just unfocused teenage (and later) rebellion and the desire to stir things up. I believe that "rocking" someone in the sense of this song is meant to be a more subversive and philosophical act.

Queen's front man and songwriter Freddie Mercury certainly wanted to push social barriers and sexual mores to extremes—and did so by exploring themes in the music he and his band mates made very widely known. Queen have sold over 300 million albums (and still counting) and some of its members have been made MBEs (Most Excellent Order of the British Empire). Their music has been immortalized in film, and several of their songs are instantly recognizable to members of several generations, my own included—many of whom have never so much as bought a single produced by the band (or downloaded an MP3, or whatever you do these days).

I'm pretty tech-savvy for a sixty-year-old, and frankly it's getting hard to keep up well enough not to sound geriatric to my students. I made it from eight-tracks to cassettes to LPs to CDs to MP3s and now I'm exhausted. I'm just happy I can still work the Spotify. Anyway, I think Queen's music does have philosophical content and jumping off points for more philosophical discussion and reflection. More specifically, I think the attitudes involved in a set of late 1970s Queen songs place us in the vicinity of one of the most important episodes of Western Philosophy: the life, death, and legacy of Socrates.

The songs all deal with alienation from society and the desire to change the *status quo*. The short form rock'n'roll song may not allow for as much complexity and thoroughness as the philosophical monograph. After all, you need to keep the song to about three minutes and change if you're going to get any airplay—outside of those snooty FM stations whose DJs think their tastes are sooooo much more refined than mine . . . but I digress.

Anyway, back to the Queen songs. The story of the protagonist in "We Will Rock You" goes through three phases: first, a boyhood characterized by a dirty face and wandering all over the place, then, a middle period where he is shouting and waving his banner (now with a bloody face) and, finally, old age, where he is poor and still seeking peace. All the while, our hero is stirring things up and, it seems, upsetting the status quo.

Why else would the author of the song make the claim that he's a big disgrace and that there's a crying need to put him back into his place? In "We Are the Champions," the singer is vowing to go on until the end, whenever that may be—claiming victory against unnamed forces who, presumably, don't really perceive that there's much of a threat at all. After all, this is not the sort of song a group in power would write. People in firmly established positions of power tend to gravitate towards blustery national anthems and the sort. Think "La Marseillaise" (the French national anthem) or the "State Anthem of the Soviet Union"—those songs' lyrics are overconfident, to say the least. Seriously. Google them.

It's obvious that the protagonist of "We Will Rock You" is a philosopher. Like Diogenes, Socrates, Spinoza, Russell, and many others, he is unwelcome in his time and place. Nonetheless, our song's hero keeps pushing on—trying to change the world even though it's a dirty, dangerous job. I submit that this is one of the true functions of any philosopher: to be the gadfly Socrates claimed he was. Always challenging the accepted pieties and pushing for better understanding and action.

This is also a function that we contemporary philosophers have mostly abandoned. At least in terms of saying things that break through enough to disturb the people outside of our notoriously self-contained profession. Whether we philosophers no longer say very many things that are revolutionary at a societal scale—or whether we simply aren't getting enough airplay—it's very rare to see anyone other than another philosopher get upset by what philosophers have to say.

We Are the Champions

Perhaps a few like Peter Singer manage to upset some laypeople now and then, but that's the very rare exception. I mean, seriously, do you think Socrates would have stooped to writing an advice column for the *New York Times*? "The Ethicist" was in more appropriate hands when the novelist Chuck Klosterman wrote it than it is now with Kwame Anthony Appiah at the helm. Hey, I don't have a gripe with any PhD in philosophy who can make a living, but Dr. Appiah recently addressed the question "Our Colleague Had Covid. Should Our Supervisor Have Told Us?" (*New York Times*, November 16th 2021). While he was admittedly dealing with some serious issues of potentially life-and-death behavior in the workplace, dealing with employer-employee relations is hardly the same as grappling with the questions in, say, the *Apology*.

It's precisely in Socrates's performance in the *Apology* that we see a person like the hero of the Queen songs we're considering. In the dialogue, Socrates is laying out the case for co-authorship of both "We Are the Champions" and "Don't Stop Me Now."

After pointing out the confused nature of those who're sure they're right (when they're not), Socrates says he is wise because he knows that he does not know—he is aware of his own ignorance. This is the true nature of wisdom for Socrates, and his self-awareness allows him to be ever-questioning. To be a seeker of truth, rather than a dogmatic fool, set in his ways and resistant to change. Whether truth is ever reached—or whether it's an ideal approached but never attained, like an asymptote—is a question for further discussion. But Socrates emphatically rejects the self-satisfaction and stagnation of the alleged experts in favor of his own brand of motivational ignorance. And he really did go on fighting till the end.

Even while on trial for his life for constantly asking questions and embarrassing all the experts and corrupting the youth (what could be more rock'n'roll than *that*?), Socrates upholds his love of ignorance in the face of the death penalty (which he ultimately receives). He pointed out that no one knows what death holds: it could be like dreamless sleep, it could be something pleasant, or it could be something unpleasant. Since we don't (and can't) know, we shouldn't be afraid of death.

The real thing to fear, in Socrates's view, is being wrong. And Socrates wants to avoid every error—after all, you never can tell which belief will be one that gets you into trouble. Even if the only incorrect belief you have is that Pierre is the capital of North Dakota, that could turn out to be the question in Final Jeopardy (sue me, I'm a Jeopardy purist) when you're finally in a position to win it all. And that would really blow. So, Socrates will keep asking his questions—even when faced with death.

And boy, is Socrates not afraid of death! He taunts the jury (a group of Athenian senators), practically begging them to sentence him to death for asking questions. And they do it. Socrates explains that he will never stop questioning the received opinions, or even his own opinions. He knows he could beg and plead for his life and possibly be set free, but he considers this course of action beneath his dignity. It shows too much love of life, Socrates argues, to stop at nothing to hold on to one's life, while giving up one's most dearly-held principles.

In combat, a coward can always avoid death by running away from the battle. But that act of running would expose the character flaw of cowardice—so you should never risk being a bad or flawed person, even to save your life. Socrates holds fast to the belief that what matters most is your moral well-being, and how you ought to live to maintain it. He says he will never stop seeking the truth, whatever the consequences. To stop seeking his answers would be to risk settling for false answers to the most important questions in anyone's life.

Don't Stop Me Now

For his entire life, Socrates has, as the song goes, played in the street and generally been a big disgrace—all the while waving his banner and kicking his can all over the place. He certainly has mud/blood on his face, as he faces the jury to answer the charges of corrupting the youth and making up gods and so on. But though the jury expected to put him back into his place, Socrates stands undaunted.

He explains his action as having been commanded by the gods. Given the words of the Oracle at Delphi, that Socrates was "the wisest of men," Socrates claims that it would be folly for him to act otherwise—since he knows he is not wise, he must continue to ask allegedly wise people for enlightenment. It is only after repeated disappointment in the advice of "experts" that Socrates comes to believe that the only truly wise person is the person who knows his own ignorance. Once he knows this, he sets out to convince others of this one truth and to educate them as to their own unrecognized ignorance. This is not a way to win friends (though in the long run it *did* influence a whole bunch of people).

Socrates also taunts his accusers, declares his love for Athens, and basically dares them to execute him—suggesting that his penalty should be to be revered as a hero of the state and to be kept in luxury at the state's expense in perpetuity. Toward the end of the dialogue, the historical co-author of "Don't Stop Me Now" emerges—a person who will keep going on, no matter what. Almost reluctantly, it seems, the jury finds him guilty. When he is offered the chance to pay a fine to atone for his offenses, Socrates offers an insultingly small amount of cash. When offered the chance to be exiled, Socrates says that Athens is his home, and he will not choose to leave it.

Given the possibility of just agreeing to stop his questioning and live a quiet, normal life, Socrates rejects that proffer as well, citing the oracle's seeming charge to find someone wiser than himself. In the exchange, Socrates justifies and defends his behavior admirably, but the jury still condemns him. It certainly seems like they have dug their heels in, as if engaged in a playground fight. My reading of the whole affair is that they were left with no choice but to wield their ultimate power to try and save face. Basically, backed into a corner, the jury sentences him to death.

After the verdict is announced, Socrates rightly points out that all the jury is doing is saving a little bit of time—he is old and would have died soon in any event. He then urges the assembled senators to treat his sons the way they have treated him. He asks that the jury continue to take further revenge on him, scolding them if they think they have worth (if they do not) and for neglecting the most important thing—living the good life. If they do this, Socrates says he will have had real justice at their hands, both for himself and his sons. He will be the true champion of the whole encounter.

As Socrates goads the jury—even as he is about to be led to his prison cell to await his death by poison—he urges others to pick up where he is leaving off, and says he regrets none of his past actions. In doing so, he recalls the last lines of "Don't Stop Me Now"—"Yes, I'm havin' a good time. I don't want to stop at all."

And while he accepts his fate and is at peace with it, he expects (or at least hopes) that the fight will go on and on and on because, well, he *is* one of the champions. And in doing this, Socrates enjoins all of us to pick up the mantle of Philosophy and keep fighting—arguing and pushing for change as an extension of who we really are, or at least should strive to be. Surely we can keep the spirit of purposeful disputation alive, even while hoping that few of us have to drink the hemlock in the end.

After all, we all know how this whole life thing ends, at least in this world. After hearing Socrates's explanation of his actions (you *did* know "apology" doesn't always mean having to say you're sorry—it can mean "explanation" as well, right?) they chose to execute an old man—in his seventies, near death anyway—because they were tired of being shown up as ignorant by an old man who claims to have no knowledge.

Where does this leave us? Maybe we just have to keep fighting the good fight, as philosophically-minded people. The execution of philosophers merely because they are acting like philosophers is pretty rare these days. The usual penalty for overly philosophical behavior is some degree or other of social isolation. But hey, that's what philosophy conferences are there for—to give you the semblance of a normal life. Maybe we just have to hope that Freddie and Socrates are still rocking on with Wayne and Garth, defying authority and getting ever closer to that elusive goal: leading the Good Life. It might be a better fate than mindless conformity and the acceptance of the *status quo*. As Socrates's final words put it so eloquently:

> Now it is time that we were going, I to die and you to live; but which of us has the happier prospects is unknown to anyone but God.

15
My Uncle's Delicacy of Taste and Passion

CHRISTOPHER M. INNES

Uncles can be severe critics of a rock band's musical talent, and mine was the most severe of all. In 1975 we watched Queen perform at Hammersmith Odeon in London, on a live Christmas Eve BBC-2 television broadcast. I was on my family's yearly Christmas visit to see my cousins (Malcolm, Greg, and Michael) and their unyielding father. My trips to Bradford in the north of England were often laced with threads of unrestrained criticism.

The barrage of unflattering comments—aimed at Queen and their ability, or lack of it—was expressed in seemingly uncontrolled emotional outbursts. The main line of criticism was that Queen is "talentless." The focal point was Freddie on the piano, accompanying his singing of "Bohemian Rhapsody." The piano playing is hard and purposeful and gives the song a dramatic moment of expectation; by many accounts, a masterpiece. But to my uncle, Freddie can't play properly. He is talentless.

It was Malcolm's facial expression that tipped me off—my uncle was off on one of his tirades and he should give it a rest, at least for this evening. But the criticisms continued, setting me to wonder: was my uncle right? Were there good reasons behind the tirade? How could I know?

Talent Spotting Needs Talent

Of course, the first question should be: does my uncle have what it takes to criticize a rock group and conclude that they have no talent? Criticizing a rock band for not having talent is like any other type of artistic criticism: it involves an understanding of their art. Here, an understanding of music in general and understanding rock music in particular is needed to allow a true aesthetic appreciation of Queen. Like spotting a great painting or sculpture as a work of art, spotting a rock band's talent involves much of the same artistic critical skill.

Being an art critic is part of what it is to be a philosopher. We're expected to ask how music is to be appreciated. My uncle was quite capable of pointing out the best orchestral composers. This is easy because they've stood the test of time and been compared, judged, and appraised by experts—with the best examples provided for *him* to appreciate. The aesthetic appraisal has already been made.

Maybe *his* skills of appraisal lie in appreciating the best examples of singers in popular music of his era. This is the genre of crooning jazz and big band singers of the 1940s and 1950s, commonly known as American Standard repertoire (with such names as Frank Sinatra and Dean Martin). This music is also known as swing; it was new at the time, and being appreciated for the first time.

Is this where my uncle got his ability to criticize music and allow him to successfully critique a rock group as great as Queen? Is it an adequate basis for comparison? Brian May's use of guitar distortion in the opening number "Now I'm Here" is unfamiliar to my uncle—not part of his music appreciation, and out of my uncle's range.

Appreciating Queen's Talent

It's a well-known fact (at least in certain circles) that my uncle's emotions often get the better of him. He expresses his views with a passion that gives the impression to the family that he's personally affected by the object of his criticism. Yet, Queen is a rock band that doesn't make sense to him. Should he have been making such comments?

This is where David Hume (1711–1776) comes in handy. He wrote "Of the Delicacy of Taste and Passion" in 1742. He was a Scottish philosopher who, much like Freddie, thought that his art should be performed in a flamboyant way. Hume recognized that human emotion is at the heart of a person's evaluative response to art—the driving force. But he also made it clear that emotion should not be the final judge. There needs to be an objective criterion: where a person's sense of touch, taste, sight, smell, and hearing is mediated by reason. A superior beauty might not be recognized without a bit of time and use of reason for reflection.

It follows that my uncle's argument that Queen lacks musical talent shows he is placed in the middle of a social and artistic situation where there is no objective aesthetic guide for the appreciation of music. It is the *person* who gets the aesthetic impression stamped on his mind; being emotional is expected. We are emotional creatures, and such a disposition is what drives our sense of taste. Hume sees passion as a far better guide than the one provided to us by the likes of Socrates—who demanded that music be appreciated in a formal way, devoid of human emotion. Study form, rhythm, and lyrics, says Socrates, without the inclusion of human passion.

As my uncle looked at Queen to evaluate their talent, he needed two human characteristics: sensitivity (but not too sensitive), and self-control (to not let little blemishes in the art make him too upset). Being emotional creatures, we get a lot of enjoyment from the details and intricacies of music. The more temperamental, the more enjoyable the music, *if* controlled by reason.

Being too emotional will result in devastation or overexcitement. My uncle should relish his *passion* and cultivate his *delicacy* (delicate disposition). This is to say that his delicate disposition (once he develops it) should control his passion. But not too much!

This is where my uncle needs to look at Hume's five criteria for being a good arts critic: *delicacy*, *practice*, being able to make *comparisons*, having *no prejudice*, and having *good sense*. What Hume means is that the art critic should look at the art and notice all its details. The critic then needs to be practiced in the art of criticism, to be able to make comparisons, to avoid prejudice (and not be side-tracked by the artist's looks or character), and to have a good sense of taste, which requires knowing the art and what it stands for.

Being Delicate Has Its Limits

I get the impression that my uncle has a delicacy of taste and passion, allowing him to enjoy his perception of beauty, but is offended by any perceived mistreatment or offense. This is to say that he likes the crooners and their music, but finds Queen to be offensive. Brian May's guitar in "Guitar Solo," played halfway through the evening, is well played, but not to *my uncle's* taste. May's vast technical knowledge of eclectic guitar playing, even in 1975, is recognized as exceptional. Needless to say that his solo in "Bohemian Rhapsody" creates the desired crowd appreciation after Freddie's melody, and (most of all) his downward play on the treble scale on "Sons and Daughters" shows his applied skill. My uncle appreciated the crooners for their musical skill and showmanship, but experienced disgust while watching Queen. This certainly removed any joy he might have gained from such a work of great rock. Hume argues that the art critic should look at the art and notice all of its details. Sense of hearing and sight should be put to use, without getting too offended.

As Hume said "delicacy of taste is as much to be desired and cultivated as delicacy of passion is to be lamented, and to be remedied if possible." My uncle might not have been able to control his over-sensitive tastes—or his disposition to outbursts of negative criticism. We might not be used to something new or different, but a sound education, says Hume, will "make a tolerable critic in such performances" and "our judgment will be strengthened by this exercise." Hume makes it clear that passion is needed, but in a refined and controlled way. The emotions will be made softer and more tender, creating a tranquil disposition and making the person more sociable. Meaning, in my uncle's case, more open-minded to Queen's talent.

Enter the Liberal Arts

The five senses are seldom arranged in a perfect way to truly perceive the thing of beauty. It's the liberal arts—where the study of philosophy, humanities, and physical sciences are distinct from the study of professional subjects—that teach us to be considerate of other pieces of art. Unlike my uncle, my cousins had such an education, and appreciate music composition.

This is what allows "Ogre Battle"—with May's heavy accelerating and pulsating guitar riff and Roger Taylor's drum and cymbal accompaniment—to be noticed and appreciated. Taylor's percussion skill, shown in his drum solo in "Keep Yourself Alive" would also be appreciated by those with some knowledge of the genre. This is not to forget the perfect blending of the band members' vocal harmonies to create a mesmerizing medley of voices. Freddie's vocal range surpassed four octaves; he spoke in a baritone and sang in tenor (where he would go from F2 to an F6).

As a result of their education, my cousins were able to appreciate the delicate details of Queen's music and of Freddie's showmanship—entering the stage with his epic cat-like walk, and finishing off with a Christmas toast as he holds up a champagne glass and drinks to the audience.

There's Nothing Like Practicing and Comparing

My cousins had practice in appreciating this type of music—where my uncle had little. We all listened to BBC Radio One, which played the latest hits. At that time, Queen was broadly part of the glam or glitter rock genre. Songs like "Killer Queen" and "Seven Seas of Rhye" were on the charts that year, heard many times. My cousins' use of reason and good sense enabled them to create a fair comparison of one piece of music with another. My uncle may have heard the music in the background, but would not likely have paid attention to it. He would have been likely to simply relegate it all as "no talent" without ever giving it enough attention to understand it.

His music was the Rat Pack: crooners such as Dean Martin and Frank Sinatra.

On the surface his music might seem remote from Queen, but there are comparisons to be made that allow for appreciation. At the very least, Queen's showmanship shouldn't go unnoticed. The Rat Pack often paid homage to singers like Alice Cooper for their showmanship. Freddie's flamboyant gestures to the audience, his gestures of gratitude, and most of all his Dionysian ability to get the audience to participate was the envy of many other bands (including David Bowie). They all dressed flamboyantly, and Roger Taylor put glitter on his drums (creating a mist of sparkles) demonstrating their ability to put on a spectacle. The Rat Pack would be able to appreciate that talent.

I guess my uncle might not have tried enough to make a link that allowed some type of appreciation. In all fairness, rock music and the American Standard repertoire of the Rat Pack are essentially different. But there are some musical similarities. The crooners were known to break for drum solos, and there was a lot of bass. In fact, the big band jazz groups often performed instrumentals that were quite frenetic. And showmanship is, well, showmanship.

Maybe he should have referred to my cousins as the ultimate referees. They had the ability to make the comparisons and would be the better judges. As Hume said, "a true judge in the finer arts is rare" and we might say that a true judge in rock music is rarer. And I must say that Brian May's distortion in "Now I'm Here" on his guitar might not have a comparison. If Queen were incomparable, can I blame my uncle for finding no basis for comparing?

Being Opened Minded Is Nice

Well, here we get to the crux of my uncle's criticism of Queen—my uncle seemed to have unbridled prejudice. Hume says that this is something every music critic has, but it should be put aside (and steered clear of) when appreciating art. In the music world we are talking about being prejudiced about other genres of music because they are not familiar or they are too different. Queen's "Killer Queen" might be viewed with bias because it had that glam rock feel that Queen perfected—with May's lead guitar, Deacon's rhythmic bass tying the music together, and Taylor on drums giving a sense of movement and progression. Such bias is understandable, but it gets in the way of appreciating it as a good example of that type of music.

Allowing bias to flourish will create distortion in the apperception of Queen (and we want distortion to stay in Brian May's wailing guitar solos, where it belongs). This is to say that my uncle grew up with the crooners. A number like "Brighton Rock" comes across to the seasoned rock aficionado as having a great guitar sequence with May playing his throaty riffs. But to someone who is prejudiced, it comes across as a bit too hard to appreciate.

Having the Good Sense to Listen to Others

Years after the Hammersmith concert of 1975, Michael Jackson advised Queen to release John Deacon's disco creation, "Another One Bites the Dust," as a single. It was well-liked and made it to number two in the UK Charts. It was this kind of good sense to listen to others and appreciate Queen's high standing that my uncle lacked.

Good sense is shown when an art critic is reasonable, and tries heartily to develop an appreciation for a type of art that they are not yet familiar with. The rock music aficionado already appreciates rock music and, usually, has little trouble in listening to different types of rock. For a fan of crooning jazz and big band, such impartiality is not going to be so easy.

We're quite confident in saying that my uncle is being headstrong in his criticism of Queen's live performance. This is where good sense is needed to direct music appreciation and perfect his ability to develop taste.

We might have to say that the comparison of Queen with the Crooners might not be fair. For example, comparing pineapples with another type of fruit, especially if you have never tasted pineapple before, is not a fair or sensible comparison (and the culinary appreciation will be inaccurate).

This is where good sense directs us to get musical insight from others when our passion and delicacy of taste are not balanced. Like the person who has tasted pineapple for the first time, we might need to turn to a trustworthy source to receive guidance on what is good rock music. This is where the rock aficionados will become useful.

Up to the Christmas of 1975, Queen was gaining notoriety and fame with a number of top ten hits in the UK charts—"Bohemian Rhapsody" being at the UK number one spot at the time of the Hammersmith Odeon concert. Good sense would inform anybody that Queen was a formidable rock group. My cousins considered them a formidable group, and their expertise should have been trusted.

Time is also a formidable judge of a group's talent. Queen was initiated into the Rock'n'Roll Hall of Fame in 1996 because of their special contribution to rock music. This is an authoritative claim to having more than enough talent. The criteria for induction are based on the nominating committee's evaluating the rock group's talent (and its influence on rock'n'roll). The committee, consisting of rock'n'roll historians, decides who will be on the ballot. They then send the ballot to a thousand rock'n'roll experts. Those with the highest number of votes (and over fifty percent of the total vote) are inducted into the Rock'n'Roll Hall of Fame. No more than seven groups are inducted each year.

Taking for granted that these rock aficionados know what they're talking about, and that the Rock'n'Roll Hall of Fame is not blighted by lack of good sense, we can say that my uncle should (after years of reflection), have accepted Queen as a formidable rock group. Their accomplishment also includes being inducted to the Songwriters Hall of Fame in 2003. They were the first group to be inducted. If Queen doesn't rock my uncle, then good sense should guide him to at least accept that they are talented.

It's Nice to Be Appreciated

Being an art critic is a tragic occupation; my uncle's appreciation of Queen is no less tragic. You have to be sensitive to the nuances and fine points of art, while still being in control of your passion and prejudices. Rock music criticism is like any art form of art appreciation: it looks at the talent needed to create such an art. Queen has that talent. It's only through a lot of practice, through comparing Queen with other rock groups, by not being biased, and by using good reason that a critic is able to appreciate Queen's talent.

As Queen finished their set that Christmas Eve, Brian played a guitar solo of "God Save the Queen." As for Queen, they are certainly saved in the annals of rock history—as the best. Regardless of my uncle!

VII

Sheer Head Attack

16
Don't Lose Your Head

KEVIN TAYLOR

As a band, Queen was one of a kind. You might say, there can be only one.

But for fans of the decapitatingly delightful Connor MacLeod—of the clan MacLeod—in the 1986 fantasy franchise *Highlander*, there cannot be one without the other. The *Highlander* franchise launched a half-dozen movies, video games, animated series, and a television series (that saw Duncan pick up where cousin Connor left off).

And yet I think most fans would agree that *Highlander* would have been laid low if not for the sublime singing of Freddie Mercury, the bombastic bass of John Deacon, the dynamism of Roger Taylor's drumming, or the intergalactic guitar of Brian May. All of which is so quintessentially Queen.

Six songs. Queen contributed six songs to the *Highlander* soundtrack—and to this day no fan can hear "Princes of the Universe" without imaging a New York–born French-American (Christopher Lambert), portraying a Scotsman, wielding a Japanese sword fighting for survival against a bloodthirsty immortal (Clancy Brown) who just happens to also be the voice of Mr. Krabs on *SpongeBob SquarePants* (his IMDB list of villainous voiceovers and acting roles merits a moment of your time).

On its surface, the plot of *Highlander* is straightforward. The hero of the movie is a sulky Scotsman named Connor Macleod, and the villain is a murderous Russian called only the Kurgan. They are immortals—yes, they exist, and they live among us in secret. In explaining his immortality (to his friend and assistant Rachel) Connor tells her more than once: "It's a kind of magic."

They have a power known as "the quickening" which they take when one decapitates another in a duel to the death. But in the end, there can be only one. The immortals are drawn to one location in what is called "the gathering" when only a few immortals are left. The survivor will have the power to rule all mankind. In the end, Connor defeats the Kurgan and allows himself to love again.

The movie seems to want to have a samurai philosophy: the Japanese way of the warrior known as bushido. But on closer examination, warrior philosophy is surprisingly thin in this movie about warriors fighting to the death. Yes, *Highlander* is famous for its dragon-headed katana—which Connor received from his trainer and mentor Juan Sánchez-Villalobos Ramirez (played by Sean Connery, who is Scottish, but here plays an Egyptian born 2,500 years earlier under the name Tak-Ne).

Ramirez tells Connor that his one-of-a-kind sword was gifted to him by a blacksmith named Masamune (not *that* Masamune though, because this was way back in 593 B.C.!). The swordsmith gave Ramirez the sword upon his marriage to his daughter: a Japanese princess named Shakiko. This not only predates the historical Masamune, whose name graces every video game's most powerful sword (I'm looking at you, *Final Fantasy*). But it also predates bushido philosophy. Connor Macleod further romanticizes the concept of a ronin (or masterless samurai) as he travels around the world fighting evil immortals, righting wrongs, and helping the defenseless.

Even the climax of the movie echoes the famous battle between Miyamoto Musashi (Japan's greatest swordsman) with his antagonist Sasaki Kojiro. Kojiro is known for his oversized Japanese greatsword, a *nodachi*, whereas Connor's nemesis is a great sword–wielding Russian referred to as the Kurgan.

Connor's mentor Ramirez even lays out a fundamental code all immortals adhere to: immortals hide because people fear them, they must fight until only one remains, they are safe on holy ground, and when one immortal takes the head of another immortal, they gain their power in a storm of explosive energy (the aforementioned quickening).

All of this may sound like some kind of samurai showdown, but actual bushido philosophy is pretty hard to find in this movie. Except, that is, for the soundtrack.

Queen gave *Highlander* more than box office numbers; they helped articulate *Highlander*'s warrior philosophy. If you think a movie about immortals fighting each other to the death has a bushido philosophy, it's because the soundtrack provided by Freddie, Brian, John, and Roger was able to express the Buddhist and Confucian concepts found in samurai philosophy.

The music that accompanies Highlander is sensitive to samurai philosophy and virtues. "Princes of the Universe" may be the tell-tale celebratory anthem to fans of the movies and television show alike, but "Who Wants to Live Forever?" is the foil to that anthem—which laments the inherent impermanence of existence, watching loved ones die while remaining unchanged for hundreds or thousands of years. "Gimme the Prize" is a cautionary song of going to battle with a head full of hubris and hedonism.

Even though only six songs made their way into the movie, the 1986 album *A Kind of Magic* includes nine songs. "Hammer to Fall" actually originated two years before the album (or the movie), but was such a good fit that it made a brief appearance in the film—although it was not replicated on the 1986 album. All told, between the movie, the album, and the 1984 song, these help tell the story of fighting for survival against immortal head-hunters.

But each immortal has a unique perspective forged by hundreds of years of experience. So, why should we cheer for Connor Macleod? Here, I think, Queen tells us: it's because with Connor Macleod we see an end to a rage that burns a thousand years (with a protagonist who hears secret harmonies). It is, after all, a kind of magic when there can be only one.

Who Wants to Live Forever?

Brian May explained in an interview that the band Queen was not terribly interested in recording music for the movie *Highlander* at first; they had just finished a 1984 tour and were hesitant about taking on a new project. "We actually said no. Because we just didn't want to be . . . we wanted a rest, to be honest. And then we saw that twenty-minute cut of this *Highlander* film and thought 'Great, that's us'" (Queen Official, "Queen—A Kind of Magic Interviews," YouTube).

Though the project was probably not a huge shock for fans (who were familiar with Queen's 1980 soundtrack for *Flash Gordon*), the film would present the band with a different take on fantasy. Those twenty minutes gave the band a lot to work with and, of the three major songs that define Highlander, Brian May's contribution ("Who Wants to Live Forever?") was most influenced by what he saw as the tragic side of immortality:

"What actually moved me was the sort of subplot. The main plot is a kind of violent tale of immortals fighting each other to the death… There's a kind of subplot which is a tragic love story. It comes about because the hero cannot die but nevertheless, he falls in love with people who can die. So he falls in love with this girl in the highlands and she gradually grows old and dies in his arms. And he has to say goodbye to her and he has to go on. Strange kind of tragedy. And that really came across to me very strongly and I related it to my own life, as well as in everyone's life, I thought, you know, love always does come to an end at some time, so I had this song immediately in my head which is called 'Who Wants to Live Forever?'" ("Queen—A Kind of Magic" Interviews).

What Brian was quick to observe was actually a central Buddhist teaching that samurai philosophy was adopted (albeit for different reasons). In the end, everything goes away and our attachment to the things we love causes us to suffer at their loss. Samurai philosophy recognizes that warriors are ultimately expected to fight to the death.

They live with that possibility every day, and as such they must re-orient themselves to the world in such a way that they could die at any moment. Buddhist philosophy teaches that nothing is permanent: including the idea of a soul that may be reincarnated.

When Connor learns that he is immortal, Ramirez tells him to leave his love, Heather. Ramirez explains that he himself has had three wives and he had to watch them all die. "I would spare you that suffering" he tells Connor. Buddhism understands that attachment to impermanent things, especially a loved one, will result in suffering.

Connor may be happy with Heather, but she eventually dies of old age: and the result for Connor is suffering. In fact, like some Buddhist monks, Connor becomes a world renouncer. He cuts himself off from most of the people around him so that he doesn't get attached to mortals—so that he does not have to experience loss when they inevitably die.

This is a practice Connor breaks twice in the film: first in World War II when Connor saves a little girl from a Nazi soldier (this is Rachel), and second when Brenda gets too close and Connor risks telling her the truth of his immortality. Another song from the album that does not appear in the movie speaks directly to this dilemma.

"One Year of Love" speaks to Connor's predicament. Even though the immortal Highlander has removed himself as much as possible from interacting with mortal humans, he finds that he can't resist confiding in Rachel, admitting his secret, and opening himself up to physical and emotional love. All Connor can do is surrender to the moment.

But Connor is still suffering from the problem of attachment that Buddhism warns us about. Even though he has allowed himself a moment of love, rather than a lifetime alone, he is still distant. Rachel says as much when she tells Connor, "Most people are afraid to die. You're afraid to live."

But that's the point that Brian May zeroed in on: who wants to live forever when love must die? On the other hand: whereas the awareness of impermanence caused Connor to escape from the world, the Kurgan was instead driven mad by his desire to see it all end.

The Tragedy of the Kurgan

The antagonist in *Highlander* is a greatsword-wielding black knight who, in the modern period, looks more like a punk rock scene troublemaker. He originally seeks out Connor Macleod before Connor has learned of his immortal nature.

The Kurgan hires himself out as a mercenary for an opposing Scottish clan—but his price is that he alone must be allowed to kill Connor Macleod and take his head. In the chaos of battle, this fails. The Kurgan kills

Connor but fails to take his head, thus triggering Connor to be reborn as an immortal.

What follows in the movie is a villain who becomes increasingly unhinged as the Gathering draws to a climax. One of the characters even remarks that "The endless killing has driven him mad," which it very well may have. As the third act of the film draws to a close, it's evident that the Kurgan has lost it.

The screenwriter for *Highlander*, Gregory Widen, described in an interview how the Kurgan was different in his original screenplay:

> He was much more tortured. The Kurgan in Highlander as it is is pretty much like Freddy [Krueger]—he's just a cackling psychopath. I envisaged him as a guy who loses everything over time. The only thing he could hold onto, to give him a reason to get up in the morning, was to finish this thing—finish it with our guy [MacLeod]. It was more about that . . . it was just a reason to get up in the morning. Otherwise, what is the point? Everything is impermanent, everything is lost. That made him much more serious—in a weird way, a sympathetic bad guy. (Ed Power, "There Can Be Only One")

Despite the change in tone from screenplay to big screen, Queen was sensitive to the Kurgan's descent into insanity. Two songs play in the movie when the Kurgan is on screen: "Gimme the Prize" (also known as the Kurgan theme), and "Hammer to Fall" (which was recorded two years prior to the film).

Now, I can handwave "Hammer to Fall" as "this is a very literal song that heightens the tension when our villain is about to start some trouble" but "Gimme the Prize" delivers on the message that Greg Widen was getting at.

A central teaching of Buddhist philosophy, of which warrior philosophy has absorbed, is the impermanence of everything. Nothing lasts forever: but we often find ourselves acting as though some things are permanent. If only I could find true love, I would be happy.

But Connor had love with Heather in the Highlands of Scotland, and she eventually died of old age while he remained immortal. The result for Connor was pain and suffering. The woman he loved died, and his happiness died with her. As a result, he isolated himself from most of the rest of the world to avoid the pain that comes with impermanence.

But Buddhism teaches us that we must accept the fundamental truth that everything is impermanent; even immortals can lose their heads! The Buddhist answer to this problem is first to accept that impermanence leads to suffering, and then to change how we view reality so that we are not hurt when things go away.

Whereas Connor muddled stoically through life, keeping himself at arm's length from everyone, Greg Widen notes that the impermanence of everything causes the Kurgan to become unhinged. Just as Brian May was sensitive to the strange kind of tragedy of Connor Macleod, the band saw a similar tragedy in the Kurgan. It's a rare hard-rocking song from the band that lays out the Kurgan's single-minded pursuit: "Just gimme the prize," it says.

The Kurgan cares nothing for being a ruler of humanity; he wants the power to defeat his enemies so that he can become the God of kingdom-come . . . but really, he just wants to finish this thing. The problem of course is that, if the Kurgan won, it wouldn't be finished.

It would continue—his immortality would have forced him to find an outlet for his immortality. But after centuries of existence, the Kurgan was unable to find one thing to bring him satisfaction. As Buddhism teaches, the fundamental truth of reality is that all things are impermanent and satisfaction can't be had if you're looking for something lasting.

Princely Virtues Are Samurai Virtues

When Ramirez trains Connor in the ways of combating fellow immortals, he explains that in the end, there can be only one—and that one person will have all the powers of the quickening, making them rulers of mankind. Okay, yeah, it's pretty dramatic.

But Ramirez is concerned with who that last immortal will be: and with a psychopath like the Kurgan actively head-hunting his fellow immortals, he's right to worry. "Princes of the Universe" tells of immortals fighting for dominance as rulers of mortals; not a great message if you ask me.

We heard a similar argument in the Greek philosopher Plato's *The Republic*: when asked what justice was, one Athenian named Thrasymachus calls justice the advantage of the stronger, or rather: might makes right (*The Last Days of Socrates*, p. 589).

"Gimme the Prize" features in the film as the Kurgan's theme song, laying out the Kurgan's single-minded pursuit: "Just gimme the prize." The Kurgan cares nothing for being a ruler of humanity; he wants the power to defeat his enemies so that he can become the God of the kingdom yet to come.

But even if the Kurgan won, he would have been one unhappy tyrant. Should the Kurgan win the prize, his rule would be authoritarian and self-interested. The Greeks called such excessive self-confidence *hubris*, and stories often portray hubris to be a person's own downfall. As a contrast to Thrasymachus's might-makes-right approach (which threatens a Kurgan style authoritarianism), Connor just wants to be friends.

What little we know about Connor in the movie tells us that he does not want to fight. When a fellow immortal, Iman Fasil, attacks Connor in a parking garage, Connor tries to avoid the fight and make nice. We see during Connor's training with Ramirez a scene in which he had the option to end his friend's life and take his power—but Connor chooses to grasp his brother by the hand and rejoice.

Near the end of the film, Connor meets up with an old friend, the immortal Kastagir. Rather than cross swords, the two share a drink together and remember fond times. Friends will be friends right till the end.

Despite his emotional detachment, Connor is a nice guy, moral exemplar who would make Aristotle or Confucius proud. And if I had to pick an immortal ruler of all mankind, I'd definitely go with Connor before the Kurgan!

Confucian philosophy also features prominently in samurai thought. The word samurai comes from the verb "to serve," and a samurai serves their master. But here the masterless samurai, if Connor Macleod can be called such, seeks to serve humanity. And to serve harmoniously, like the ways suggested by Confucius.

Confucius wrote at length on being an ethical leader: and with good cause. Confucius taught during what is known as the Warring States period. Crazy rulers constantly waging war on one another is enough to cause anyone to reflect on what makes for a good ruler!

Confucius famously made the case for a ruler who can create harmony between humanity and heaven; a kind of natural, spontaneous, un-self-conscious harmony that once prevailed in the Golden Age (of the kind that came before Confucius, with the reign of the ancient sage-kings). Princes of the universe: one might be tempted to say.

Confucian philosophy teaches that a good ruler is kind to the people. To be a ruler is to be altruistic—that is, to think about others before oneself. Unlike the Kurgan, who would rule with force, a Confucian ruler is expected to bring about harmony through charismatic, non-coercive power.

Connor makes the case at the end of the movie that because he can hear the minds of everyone on Earth, he can help humans understand one another. Keeping his powers secret, Connor would be exerting his influence in such a way that world leaders would not know that they're being helped along. Confucius calls this effortless action.

It's not that you're not acting—but rather that you do something so perfectly that it looks like you didn't do anything at all. An athlete or a dancer makes it look easy. Such a Confucian ruler is said to be like the North Star. When you look up to the heavens and see the stars, they all seem to rotate around the north star.

If Connor can help people understand each other, then he would be like the North Star, guiding others on the right path while seeming to do nothing. And when it comes to Connor Macleod of the clan Macleod, even though he was born to be king—he doesn't seek the limelight.

With the power of the quickening, he hears secret harmonies in how he experiences the interconnectedness of all beings. A good Confucian ruler brings about secret harmony, and Connor sees the possibility to do this with one voice of love and trust.

If the movie *Highlander* wants to evoke samurai and their bushido philosophy, Queen's contribution to the *Highlander* soundtrack succeeds at drawing out the warrior philosophies of justice, compassion, friendship, and loyalty. The band's impact on the *Highlander* franchise is fundamentally intertwined. There is no *Highlander* without Queen. They may have their princes, but they'll have to bow to Queen.

The music video for "Princes of the Universe" featured the band on the set of the climax between Connor and the Kurgan. The band performs on a rooftop in front of a neon sign. Everyone other than Freddie wears trench coats identical to Connor Macleod's.

As Freddie sings his heart out, Connor Macleod makes his way to duel Freddie Mercury—Connor with his dragon-headed katana and Freddie with his mic stand.

Can there be only one?

17
Hammer to Fall in the Shadow of Death

ROBERT DEVALL

In the fall of 1990—while deeply immersed in playing 1st edition Dungeons and Dragons, and fresh off going to many weekends at our local Renaissance Faire—a fellow D&D player asked me to watch a movie with him. "You'll like it," I recall him saying, "It's about a bunch of immortals who use swords to try to cut each other's heads off."

The movie was *Highlander*, and it sounded right up my alley. In our D&D campaign I was playing a demon-slaying paladin of Tyr, flirting with demi-god status—and I too had a sword to deal out death.

Not only was the movie super cool, but it also had a soundtrack made up of exclusively Queen songs. I found this original and very novel (what I didn't know at the time was that Queen also did the song-track for a not-so-great-remake of Flash Gordon).

While watching the movie, I first got to hear Brian May's searing riff on "Hammer to Fall," thanks to a scene that depicts a paranoid Vietnam vet in his Pontiac Trans Am. While he cruises along looking for criminals to confront, he blares this on his car stereo. I thought this was the best song in the movie—so I was surprised to find out it's not even on the original song-track.

At the time I wasn't a huge Queen fan. My exposure to the band was limited to my first-time hearing of "Another One Bites the Dust" from my buddy's boombox, and what I heard on our local rock stations.

Regardless, I knew them as a good, solid rock band with a flair for the theatrical. Queen complimented my otherwise heavy rotation of heavy metal and prog rock.

"Hammer to Fall" is the fourth single from Queen's *The Works* album: a rocking antidote to their previous effort, *Hot Space*, that focused on enticing the dance-floor crowd. Apart from Freddie Mercury's "yeahs", "you knows" and howls, what first struck me as a simple jamming anthem of the likes of AC/DC or Kiss, turned out to be a surprise.

The lyrics propelled me into a rich landscape of deeper meaning concerning death that the song does a good job disguising. Its focus on death makes the song a very existential experience.

Existential Fall

I say existential because the lyrics to "Hammer to Fall" echo uncannily the work of a twentieth-century philosopher named Martin Heidegger. Heidegger died around the time of Queen's rise to prominence (as they filled a niche between the glam rock of David Bowie and the hard rock of Led Zeppelin).

Today, many find Heidegger to be a polarizing figure. Some see him as a pompous, bullshitting member of the Nazi party. Some see him as an original thinker whose work, *Being and Time*, transformed twentieth-century philosophy.

This latter camp smooths over his Nazi affiliations with such euphemistic phrases as "his commitment to National Socialism" (oh, do you mean his collusion in a system that systematically murdered ten million Jews, blacks, Catholics, disabled persons, and other "undesirables"?)

Despite these attitudes toward him, I argue that Heidegger had some interesting things to say about death and our relation to it. He would point to "Hammer to Fall" and say: "this is what I was trying to say about death!"

Due to his tendency to be wordy and sling bullshit, he lacked the ability to boil down to the essence of his philosophy—which "Hammer to Fall" inadvertently achieves in four and a half minutes.

Much like the movie that brought it to my attention, "Hammer to Fall" is clearly about death, an event we all must face some day. As Brian May (who wrote it) says, "The song is about life and death and being aware of death as a part of life."

Most of the time we're not consciously aware of our finitude. We subconsciously envision ourselves like the immortals in Highlander, going on for eternity. But like a swing from a sword, or the crush of a hammer, we face termination regardless of whether we are "rich or poor or famous."

Death is the great leveler, the ultimate equalizer with no regard for who we are or think we might be.

Heidegger was preoccupied with death. He would have listened to "Hammer to Fall" on infinite playback because it captures, I think, what his obscure style of writing put off communicating. The beginning verse establishes us in the world. "Here we stand" on planet Earth, not quite sure why we are here, we just happen to be.

Heidegger uses the term "thrownness" to describe our arbitrary arrival in the world, as if some god grabbed us from a bag like a worm and threw us maliciously into a pond to fend for ourselves.

In our more somber moments, we also know deep down that we will also die here, and in the grand scheme of things no one (except maybe a few close relatives and friends) will really give a shit that we ever existed.

To sum up, I think what Heidegger means is that we don't get a choice when and where we begin to exist in the world. We just do, and we must deal with it. How we deal with it depends on our relation to our own death, and the actions we take in this life.

Death in Life

As we all come to know, death is a big part of life—just look at the number of funeral homes and boneyards that exist. Think of how the death of Freddie Mercury affected fans and fellow band members alike (supposedly Freddie's death affected John Deacon so much that he refuses to play on stage anymore).

Think of how the death of a close relative affected you. Hearing about the death of someone makes us ponder our own mortality, and gives us a choice in how we respond.

Death is such a monumental event that many of us don't want to think of it. We tend to distract ourselves from such thoughts, and find comfort in the ordinary and everyday life. The thought of death gets pushed subconsciously into our mental closet. We find solace in the "Western Way" of life.

Meaning we focus on acquiring things, trying to be popular, and focusing on trivial gossip and cheap entertainment. We use the "anesthetic" of consumerism, drugs and alcohol to tranquilize us. When we run away from our true selves, we run into the comforting arms of what Heidegger calls the "they."

They Are Sayin'

What helps us along is the voice of the all-pervasive "they." "They" tell us to sculpt our bodies to meet the expectations of society, while our bodies decay in time. The "they" make the unsophisticated and gullible "toe the line" while the more sophisticated and cynical "play their game." The "they" do a good job in keeping our focus on the unimportant, mundane, and the superficial aspects of life.

We develop an artificial interest in knowing who wins *America's Got Talent*, and we follow the latest gossip concerning Prince Harry and Meghan Markle. Not that we might have a passing interest in these things, but we feel the peer pressure to do so by the "in group." These preoccupations, though they seem important in the group-think of the "they," lead us to live, as Heidegger says, an inauthentic existence.

"Isn't this a good thing?" you may ask. Why be preoccupied with thoughts of our own death that we have no control over? It's a melancholy thought that we will wind up six-feet-under (or in an urn on someone's mantle). Can't we have the *carpe diem* without thinking that tomorrow we will die?

What Brian May implies in the song is that there is a difference between living an authentic vs. an inauthentic life. Contemplation of death forces us to face and confront what is important. The urgency of the event kicks us in the ass to the realization that we don't have much time left.

Our actions need to count in the here and now. Stop wasting your precious time looking at a picture of what your "friend" on Facebook had for lunch. Living a meaningful life defeats the thoughts that life is futile.

Heidegger's hyphenated phrase "being-towards-death" is a stance we take that is essential to our nature. It lifts us out of our immersion in the inauthentic life of the everyday world. The "they"—and society in general—at the same time tries to pull us down into the mire.

As we rise from the mire, deep down inside ourselves, we want to realize our possibilities and fulfill our potential. "We don't waste no time at all" once we realize death comes to us all. Time spent worrying about the lives of celebrities and idle gossip can be better used on worthwhile purposes and goals we wish to accomplish before the hammer falls.

Sartre and Nuclear War

The second half of the song shifts attention away from the individual and transitions to global concerns. It brings to light the ultimate "being-toward-death": the potential destruction of humanity. May and his bandmates grew up at a time when they practiced hiding under school tables in case of nuclear bombs overhead.

The fear of nuclear war and total annihilation is symbolized in the mushroom cloud. Nuclear destruction is the ultimate way we face our finitude on a massive scale. It seems in the song that Freddie beseeches us to resign ourselves to succumb to it, because of its inevitability. Perhaps it's the voice of the "they" telling us not to take personal responsibility for our actions?

This part of the song strikes a chord with us: both on a conscious and subconscious level. In the year the song came out (1984), most of us thought that nuclear war with the Soviet Union was imminent.

We were fresh off watching the made-for-tv movie *The Day After*. That movie scared the shit out of me for several weeks. Nuclear war felt like a very tangible possibility. The presence of death loomed like a shadow over us. The song's focus on this both forces us to embrace our finitude, but also points to our moral and political responsibilities.

Enter Jean-Paul Sartre, the best-known existentialist philosopher of the twentieth century. For Sartre, Lady Mercy wouldn't be home to shield us from the fallout: because she's a fairy tale. Unlike Heidegger (who defended his views as theistic), Sartre thought there was no God. But, much like Heidegger, Sartre believed in living an authentic life.

What separated Sartre from Heidegger was his idea of radical responsibility. With no god (and no God) watching over us, responsibility for our actions rests on *our* shoulders. He thought that we could change the world through politics. Even if we are "convinced our voices can't be heard," they will be if we get involved.

This is an important responsibility on our part. Unfortunately, there's no guarantee of anything good happening. History won't care if we destroy each other or unite as one in peace. It only records what happened (if there is anyone left to record anything).

Sartre wrote a play called *The Condemned of Altona* where (ten centuries from now) humans no longer exist due to nuclear war. The only thing left to judge us will be the crabs walking in our footsteps (couldn't resist the Police allusion). With the tensions brewing between the United States and Soviet Union at the time, this reality seemed likely—and the urgency to stop it acute.

It Isn't Us versus Them

Sartre advocated peace for humankind. He saw war firsthand as a soldier in World War II. He saw mass destruction and served time as a POW. He saw the inhumanity of it all. After the war, President Truman introduced a new kind of ongoing conflict with the Soviet Union—called the Cold War.

This created an "us versus them" polarity: with nuclear holocaust the likely outcome. Rather than seeing each other across this political divide as sharing the same hopes and fears, it made us stand "tall and proud" for our country—where we must win at all costs. The guy in the Trans Am shares this false vision of how the world should be, manufactured by our political leaders. Not the "One Vision" Queen substitutes as world peace.

Sartre thought that Cold War politics offered us nuclear blackmail. Governments (another form the "they" takes) feed us a line of shit that peace is only possible if we have nuclear superiority. If we align with either side, it will only lead to the opposite of peace: destruction. It conditions us to think we can't trust the other side. Mutual suspicion and antagonism reigns. Ironically (they tell us), an unsteady peace is possible only if we prepare for war.

Now I'm Gonna Tell Ya . . .

This black-and-white thinking, according to Sartre, created a war of "Good versus Evil." Ronald Reagan fanned the flames of this view when he called the Soviet Union an "evil empire" as well as "the focus of evil in the modern world." A mistranslation of Nikita Krushchev's famous line "We will bury you," from the Soviets a few decades earlier didn't help either, when these tensions escalated.

We need to redirect our focus, Sartre says. See war as the evil and the way of peace the good. When we look at "the Other" as a demon, we are more likely to want to destroy it. Like Sting in his song "Russians," we hope they love their children too. If we see them as people and not as their government, we will know they want peace and security like us. We will know they do once we make this "paradigm shift."

Political neutrality for Sartre is an impossibility. We need to take a stand politically and march in the streets—and scream louder and louder until everyone realizes mutually assured destruction will be our fate if we stay the course. Sartre was no armchair talking head either. He marched with the students in the streets for peace.

Like in the song, if we "just surrender" to the masses who want peace, it "won't hurt at all." We need to get real and reject the bullshit that governments feed us. Once we see what joins us—rather than what separates us—we will see that the prospect of war is idiotic.

What we don't want to be is the guy in the Trans Am in Highlander. He seems to think a nuclear war is winnable. The shirt he wears reads something like "take this Moscow!" with what I assume is a nuclear bomb. He desires the hammer to fall on *them* before the Soviet "hammer" descends on *us*—without comprehending the consequences of these actions.

Dropping bombs on an imagined enemy far away seems like a good idea. Just dead commies stripped of their humanity. The millions of lives lost in the process is a mere statistic, as Stalin quipped, when we try to comprehend massive loss of life.

This inauthentic stance toward death is what May wants us to discard in "Hammer to Fall." Don't listen to the "they" and their pressure to keep us preoccupied with bullshit. Be critical of what the government tells us about nuclear superiority guaranteeing peace. Take responsibility for our actions to have a meaningful life and make our voices heard if we don't agree politically.

Once we see the song from the existential view of both Heidegger and Sartre, our transition to an authentic relation with death will provide meaning in our lives. And in the chaotic world around us.

18
We Want to Love Forever, Forever Is Ours Today

JOHN SHOOK

The movie *Highlander* made its theatrical debut on March 7th 1986, starring Christopher Lambert as the immortal Scotsman Connor MacLeod. That movie soundtrack was the first opportunity to hear Queen's new song "Who Wants to Live Forever?"—to be promptly followed by the arrival of Queen's album *A Kind of Magic* in June and the song's release as a seven-inch single.

European concert-goers could also attend The Magic Tour during the summer of 1986, which turned out to be Freddie Mercury and the band's last tour. The appearance of the music video on MTV, after its filming in September, got attention from a vast American audience, but the song only climbed the UK music charts, peaking at No. 24.

Four versions of the song resulted from these releases: a two-minute song during the movie sung by Mercury, followed by two and a half minutes of piano arrangement; the 5:15 minute song on the album played by the band and sung by Mercury; a 4:01 minute version on the song's seven-inch single; and the single version backed by an orchestra with the opening stanza sung by Brian May and mostly Mercury singing the rest.

Instrumental arrangements also appeared later: a 2:30 minute orchestral arrangement on the *Highlander, The Original Scores* CD (1995); a 3:20 minute version by May on piano entitled "Forever" as a bonus track for the album's CD reissue (2011); and three tracks of variations on guitar and piano brought together with the album version for the *Highlander Soundtrack Expanded 25th Anniversary Edition* CD (2011).

Spiritual Performance

"Who Wants to Live Forever?" was composed by May with support from Michael Kamen, who provided the movie's orchestral score (that surrounds Queen's six songs on the soundtrack). The music video version is backed by a full philharmonic orchestra and forty choirboys, conducted by Kamen. Perhaps that video of Mercury's sternly dramatic rendition (surrounded by a candle-lit cathedral-like staging), more so than the studio recording, guaranteed its enshrinement among the band's most powerful and heartfelt songs. This song has certainly endured among those cherished by Queen fans. In 2014 *Rolling Stone* magazine asked its readers to rank their favorite Queen songs—number five was "Who Wants to Live Forever?"

For a rock band, "Who Wants to Live Forever?" has to surely be Queen's most spiritual performance. This is quite something to consider given that "Bohemian Rhapsody" has metaphysical overtones, "Somebody to Love" is a faith-seeking gospel song, and a track titled "Jesus" was on Queen's debut album. "Love of My Life" offers a lyric paean to love gained and love lost. Yet "Who Wants to Live Forever?" is a somber elegy that transports the listener to a transcendental place, through life to death and beyond. A life's span isn't enough—not even the life of an immortal—to measure the duration of love.

In the *Highlander* movie, the song begins as Connor MacLeod brings his new love Heather to his isolated Highland home. As Mercury sings about building dreams, we view the domestic scene transpire as the years go by. Their boundless love is visible as they enjoy their passing days, which flow together to seem like one sweet moment. This thing that binds their dream is love: love of the highest and purest degree. Mercury reaches the phrase "who dares to love forever," and then we see Heather's aged face with tired eyes reaching his, to hear "when love must die." The instrumental track sweeps on to echo the soaring challenge of that terrible question. Heather dies of old age in his arms, and then we see her grave scene marked by the raised cross of Connor's ground-impaled sword, as the homestead burns down in flames.

May was as emotionally moved by that cinematic sequence of their domestic existence as any movie watcher could be. His later recollection of the band's viewing at a screening of unedited footage revolved around that scene of Heather's aging and demise under the youthful eyes of her ageless lover. His own life was in emotional turmoil, with family and marriage troubles during those years:

> We went to see the Highlander rushes with Russell Mulcahy, and that was our first experience in any way with Highlander—I hadn't read the script, I don't think any of us had—and it was very moving. [It's] about a man who becomes conscious that he's immortal, and he's reluctant to accept that fact, but he's told that if he falls in love he's in big trouble, but of course he falls in love anyway. And the girl that he falls in love with eventually grows old and dies in his arms, and that kind of opened up a floodgate in me. I was dealing with a lot of tragedies in my life, the death of my father, the death of my marriage, and so forth. I could immediately hear this "Who Wants to Live Forever?" in my head, and it was almost complete in the car going home . . . (Brian May, Greatest Video Hits 2 DVD commentary)

As lines assembled in his thoughts, the tune settled into the key of E minor. This key's Aeolian mode is well-known among music devotees for expressing prolonged regret and unending sorrow.

Haydn bestowed the nickname of 'Trauer' (mourning) upon his Symphony No. 44 in E Minor. Chopin's Prelude in E Minor (Op. 28 No. 4) played at his own funeral. Mozart's famous Mass in C Minor and Requiem in D Minor deliver the somber tonality of humble piety, but he only ever dared to compose a single work in E minor, his Sonata for Piano and Violin No. 21 in E Minor (K 304)—as his mother was dying. None of Beethoven's major works in minor keys, not even his Fifth and Ninth symphonies, called for that notorious E minor key. To easily hear what this mode is capable of doing to the ear and the heart, recall the perennial holiday hit by Trans Siberian Orchestra, "Christmas Eve/Sarajevo 12/24" that medleys together "God Rest Ye Merry Gentlemen" and "Carol of the Bells" in that gloomily restless key of E minor.

Besides their unsettling forcefulness, classical or contemporary works in that distinctive Aeolian mode share the strange way that they sound even better the louder they are played. There is no loudness too great to reach when performing a massively musical and choral hymn of that magnitude, letting it fill any secular space, and well beyond. Awesome and dreadful all at once, this resounding key unlocks that dark door from roomy mundane comfort for a judgmental confrontation with the fearsome almighty. Only in E minor does humanly-tuned musicality accord with that soul-shrinking finality of eternality. Eternity awaits no matter what we do, and we the living can already dimly hear its hollowed voice like the resounding emptiness of the cold tomb.

Love Is Eternal

In that E minor key, the cumulative import of "Who Wants to Live Forever?" pushes beyond the genres of rock anthem or rock opera. Swelling with a momentous sound like a cathedral organ's bone-shaking thunder, Mercury's vocals flash with lightning across the dark to raise a brave face up against the doom of fate.

The beating heart of May's poetry keeps us alive despite the pulse-stopping cold we have to eventually endure. The question must be asked, and it can be answered. *Who dares to love forever?* The true lover never stops loving, and never has to. Whether one is mortal or immortal, love is eternal. Death is a parting, but it neither prevents the blossoming of love nor does it represent the end of love.

How could the *Highlander* episode for Heather and Connor be a tragedy? Love consummated for a lifetime could never be tragic. Do you feel sorry for Connor? You shouldn't. Do you save more pity for Heather? There's no good reason for that, either. Is living a life in love ever tragic? Impossible. Suffering during this mortal life may come with love and loss, to be sure. But that's no proper criterion for a tragic narrative. As Heather ages and eventually reaches her end, there is no regret ever shown on her face (to join the understandable bewilderment at Connor's ever-youthful visage). There should be no regret over the path of her life—not when she feels no regrets at all.

One might be able to guess correctly that Heather's puzzlement at his vigor is innocent of any doubts about loving him completely. Lingering doubts about the wisdom of love are for Connor, not Heather. Heather always knows that she loves him, fully and faithfully.

On her deathbed she has only two questions. She never really knew why he stayed. His answer, that he loves her now as much as their first day, is the right answer about what true love is like. She then says that she wants to stay with him forever. He vows to never forget her, which is also the genuine answer. She collapses gently with her last question, "Where are we?"

He recounts their typical scene of an ordinary day, as he can always remember perfectly, which is again the best reassurance of faithful love. May's third stanza captures this truth. Touch my tears, touch my world—the bond of connection, of unification, makes you and I into a "we" that transcends anything. When can we have forever? On any day, that one sweet moment, that is when we can love forever, for forever is ours today.

Poetry and theater beckon us to visit a higher philosophical and theological plane. We should not refuse that invitation, especially when accompanied by the grim hand of E minor's grip upon us. Like tremulous Dante led on by the somber Virgil, we must take our glimpse into the abyss.

Philosophers, ever since the ancients, have easily linked life and love with laughter and joy. Must the end of one union determine the end of the other? Perhaps not. The time-honored traditions tell us that the gods are happy because they are immortal. To be happy ourselves, we must be like the gods—or at least join the gods wherever a final rest in peace can be reached. Religions from time immemorial have said that some sort of immortality is essential for finally attaining life's purpose. That death-defying act is only possible if God surely awaits on the other side of death. Count no one happy until they are dead to stand before the deity everlasting.

God is necessary for immortality, according to the sage hierophants and high priests. How else could love ever be victorious? Philosophers of religion have (almost) all agreed: believe in God by faith or prove God's reality by reason, but by whatever holy road, stay on it without straying from devout conviction. If God is real, then immortal life is real, and then love's power is real, and the full meaning of a life (long or short) is thereby ensured. Religion first, love second, in order of life and logic. The joys of immortality depend ultimately on

God, so you'd better love God or else life's long labors will all be lost and death will win.

Down into That Abyss

This priestly doctrine, repeated theologically and philosophically down the ages, has heard little dissent, except from the merry little band of atheists closing their ears against any pious echoes of eternity. Oh, and one other oft-neglected group (well, they hardly form a coherent troop, separated by centuries and civilizations): the scattered existentialists among the more-mystical minded that can appear from time to time in most any religion. Hindu and Buddhist, Daoist and Zen, and Jewish, Islamic, and Christian orientations are represented among them, this mysterious and practically heretical chorus of contrary voices. Love doesn't depend on immortality or God, they can each affirm. Rather, the eternal and divine are revealed to be nothing other than Love in essence and omnipotence.

A powerful Christian writer entirely on the side of love and life during the twentieth century was Christian existentialist Gabriel Marcel (1889–1973). In this modern line of thought (going back to Søren Kierkegaard), a phenomenology and philosophy of love proceeds ahead of reason in order to approach with due fear and trembling such a tremendous subject as God.

As subjects ourselves—lonely souls longing to know ourselves and other people around us as much as a distant God—the only bridge between the infinite and the finite has to be already built for us to cross. Or else the bottomless chasm between the created and the Creator cracks open wider and wider. Do not look down into that Abyss as you take the first steps. Your mind can now only deceive you, for no charts of concepts and inferences are trustworthy. What guides one's steps over the threshold through a door that opens but once for each of us? Marcel gives all the credit and glory to Love.

Marcel tells us about what is really real and what is not. Fear not that bridge, or what lies on the other side. If you build a bridge to another, just one other person, and create it in love, then love will see everything through:

> Love, in so far as distinct from desire or as opposed to desire, love treated as the subordination of the self to a superior reality, a reality at my deepest level more truly me than I am myself—love as the breaking of the tension between the self and the other, appears to me to be what one might call the essential ontological datum. I think, and will say so by the way, that the science of ontology will not get out of the scholastic rut until it takes full cognisance of the fact that love comes first. (*Being and Having*, p. 167)

Love is essential. Love has ontological priority. Love is undeniable and irrefutable, like nothing else in this world or out of this world. In philosophical terms, there is no higher praise to bestow. Marcel's existentialist claim here is so radical that it is difficult to even hear properly. Tune yourself to a strange new key, as disturbing as it may be. Here is the answer: loving one other person is as good as understanding how to love God and having God love you.

Love Works Miracles

Thinking about how God loves you indeed seems comforting, like a watchful eye over you all the time. Childhood is like that, and so is our fond recollection of childhood now as adults, and the myth makes the magic seem real. It's all been already done for us, for us all, from the beginning, just as the scriptures say. Marcel is warning us that childish tales are for childish ways. Adulthood is a time of responsibility. Our lives are just what we can make of them. If there is any providential plan, we are co-creators. For Marcel, we are even responsible for creating our own souls—at least any sort of soul worth the rewards of immortality. Spirit is not made to be solitary, or subsidiary. Each of us must create the love we seek, and that is why we innately seek another. Love, for Marcel, is:

> a certain spiritual interconnection at the heart of which my existence can preserve its meaning and its value. We are not dealing here with an abstraction, an impersonal order: if I inspire another being with love which I value and to which I respond, that will be enough to create this spiritual interconnection. The fact of the reciprocal love, the communion, will be enough to bring about a deep transformation in the nature of the bond which unites me to myself. (Homo Viator, p. 49)

The transforming power of love is the only opportunity for soulful immortality. That's good news. Even better news comes next: the lover is already immortal! It could not matter that one is still alive, for nothing about love depends on death. And it cannot matter that one's beloved is no longer among the living, for love's eternal bond has already been forged and the bridge has been safely crossed. Loving fidelity, Marcel says, is "the only means we have of effectively vanquishing time" (p. 152). Forever is ours today.

It is too often repeated, without comprehension, that we must respect the power of love. Love works miracles. Marcel heartily agrees. Love must be the highest power, for it makes eternality and divinity possible in its irreplaceable creativity. What else could transform the transient into the permanent? Mere desire for each other as mortal lovers in flesh and blood is a start, but not the end goal. Death terminates desire. Death cannot terminate love. There is one qualification alone for realizing this supreme truth: love must be experienced for it to fulfill our greatest hope, or else it amounts to nothing at all.

Imagine Them Happy

> Even if it is agreed that the act by which beings who love one another are united by a common bond implies within itself the inherent need for eternity (*Ewigkeitsforderung*), what enables us to say that this need is met in some substratum of reality which eludes our sight? . . . what we have to deal with here is in reality the metaphysical status of hope, of hope taken in its specific character, as opposed to desire. (*The Mystery of Being*, pp. 154–55)

The only way to make love real is to realize love for one's self. Do you hope for a forever ever after? Hope is always paired with love. However, not even God could guarantee that for you. If there is to be a God, that God needs us, in the true love of lovers bound together.

The good news is that anything living in creation has this loving experience accessible and available during the course of life. Waiting for God to show up, now or later, is pointless and profitless. One's soul is at stake now, not later at the end of days. Arrive at the end of mortal time without love in your past and present, and there is no God who could save your future.

Connor MacLeod is no tragic hero. What has he ever lost, that must be lost forever? He hopes he is worthy of the vast powers, and the vaster responsibilities, that come with being a Prince of the Universe. We hold out hope for him by the movie ending, not because he has endured, but because he has loved. Immortality is godlike, but only love is divine.

Mortality as such is not a tragedy. Neither need be immortality. Where the greatest good abides, nothing tragic can win. However long a life, there is nothing guaranteed about loving another, but there could only be tragedy if you never love. It's not about your final destination in due time, but instead it's really about your destiny to abide in true love. Destiny did arrive in full for Heather and Connor. Pity only the living not in love. Do not pity the lovers in death. They have forever, for ever and ever. When you think of Heather and Connor, imagine them happy.

Let the album version's final word of wisdom be heard at the end: Who waits forever anyway?

VIII

My Fairy Kings

19
Master Stroke of a Fairy Feller

JARED KEMLING

Like all great artists, Freddie Mercury is a tantalizing, scintillating figure. His music, like his life, is complex and dynamic. You want to know what's hiding behind that gaze, behind that toothy smile, that wit.

Freddie is a contradiction of confession and mystery—slippery truths and mesmerizing falsehoods. He seems to oscillate between profound wisdom and puerile hedonism. Everyone has their own favorite Freddie—what he means to them, how they like to see him. Maybe someday you can tell me yours. What follows is mine. An attempt to wrap my head around Freddie as a person and as a musician.

So who is my Freddie? He's young. We're still a long way from the Freddie at his final press conference, announcing his illness to the world but a moment before leaving it (so shockingly quickly). And he's not rocking Wembley, or hosting a bacchanalian party. It's not even the Freddie sitting alone at the piano, writing his songs. No, this Freddie is standing in a museum (he was an art major once upon a time, lest you forget). He's looking at a very peculiar painting. And he's caught between two worlds. Between two people. He sees his future—his shiny rock dream—sees it clearly. But he's also haunted by the life he's leaving behind, the person who doesn't fit into those rock dreams.

It's 1973, and Queen are writing and preparing to record their second album—the one that will give them their first hit single, and really launch their careers. But this Freddie doesn't know that yet. I love *Queen II* for its progressive songs and fantastical lyricism. But as anyone who has listened to the album will know, those aspects are really only featured on Side Black of the album: Freddie's side. So it shouldn't be a surprise that Side Black is my favorite part of the record (and what really makes it, in my opinion).

When Queen were writing their early albums (1972–1974), concept albums and rock operas were all the rage, and they've since been inextricably linked with the more progressive flavors of rock. I've always been a sucker for that kind of stuff—I mean, mixing epic music with fantasy mysticism and sci-fi grandiosity? It's a no-brainer. It's clear that Freddie was drinking at least a bit of the concept album kool-aid (so at least I'm not the only one). Side Black functions as a miniature progressive concept album: a series of fairy-tale vignettes set (potentially) in the fictional land of Rhye.

And while "March of the Black Queen" is the most epic song on the album (and in their whole catalog, in my opinion), nothing epitomizes the Victorian fairy-tale concept of Side Black better than the song "The Fairy Feller's Master-Stroke." Casual listeners will be forgiven for misunderstanding the opening line as "He's a fairy fella" (fellers not exactly being a common occupation nowadays), and thinking that the song might have something to do with gay symbolism (and perhaps it does, on some level).

But those who do their best to parse the barrage of esoteric lyrics will have a number of questions, the most pressing of which being: 'What the hell is this song about?' In short: it's the key to unlocking *my* favorite version of Freddie.

The Fairy Feller's Master Stroke

So to answer the first question: a "feller," at least in this case, is an old-timey word for someone who cuts down (or fells) trees. It's also a term used in sewing, but that's neither here nor there. And the particular feller named in the song is, indeed, a literal fairy. The characters in the song—from more recognizable names such as Mab, Titania, or Oberon, to smaller characters such as the Ploughman, the Tatterdemalion, or the pervy satyr—are based on an artwork entitled "The Fairy Feller's Master-Stroke," painted by a man named Richard Dadd between 1855 and 1864. Dadd himself will be a very important element, and we'll get to him momentarily. For now, let's think about the painting itself.

The painting, which can be found in the Tate Britain art museum in London (at least, when not touring) is relatively small: a roughly two-foot rectangle, but packed with intricate detail. It's also unfinished, with portions of the bottom sketched in but not fully painted. The painting depicts a traveling party of fairies, sprites, and tiny animals (a dragonfly, gnats, tiny centaurs) that have come to a stop in a grassy field.

Queen Mab's tiny carriage has broken down (just to the left of the magician's crown), leaving the tiny crowned figure in a flowing white robe stranded. The host of fairies have gathered to watch the feller as he prepares to chop a hazelnut in half with one blow of his ax (the "master-stroke")—so that the queen's carriage can be repaired or built anew. The reference to Mab comes from Shakespeare. In *Romeo and Juliet*, Mercutio has a monologue where he describes the tiny Queen Mab riding in a hazelnut carriage as she brings dreams into sleeping minds.

One can easily get lost tracing the intricate, miniaturized shapes of the painting with their eyes, trying to interpret the various figures. I'm imagining the young Freddie standing in front of the painting, doing just that. Dadd wrote a long (and somewhat unclear) 1865 poem about the painting (titled "Elimination of a Picture and Its Subject") which helps to give some context to the characters, but they are still open to interpretation. Some see the magician-like figure in the center of the painting as a representation of the Pope. Others argue that the apothecary in the upper right is a depiction of Dadd's own father (more on that in a second), who was himself a chemist.

In a BBC Radio One interview (December 24th 1977) Freddie explains that he was "terribly inspired" by the painting and "did a lot of research." This was unusual for him, he says, as he was normally less methodical in writing his lyrics. According to legend, Freddie not only visited the painting at the Tate often—he even dragged the other band members along with him. But Freddie was not alone in this: a number of great artists have also been inspired by the painting (including Terry Pratchett, Neil Gaiman, Alan Moore, and Octavio Paz).

So, then. Why was Freddie so obsessed with this painting? Why *this* Freddie? I'm certainly curious—aren't you? It's not surprising that he was interested in art generally; after all, he graduated with a degree in graphic design from Ealing Art College (skills which he put to use designing the Queen Crest). But as he admits in that 1977 interview, Freddie didn't usually take inspiration from artwork when writing his lyrics . . . With the exception of "The Fairy Feller's Master-Stroke." So why this painting in particular?

He seems (especially at that time) to have had an interest in Victorian literature, fairy-tales, and so on. Perhaps it was merely the fantastical imagery and subject that drew him to the painting? This is speculation on my part, but I like to think that there was more to it than that—that Freddie was drawn to that painting for deeper reasons. In order to unpack those reasons, we need to talk a bit more about the man behind the painting: Richard Dadd (1817–1886).

Dadd: I'm Going Slightly Mad

In some ways, Dadd himself is even more interesting than his painting. He showed promise as an artist from an early age, and was admitted to the Royal Academy of Arts at the young age of twenty. He founded an artist group with other promising young artists known as "the Clique." Although the rest of the Clique would go on to become established painters (and themselves be admitted to the Royal Academy), they are mostly remembered today for their criticism of the Pre-Raphaelite Brotherhood, a later artistic group which would go on to become more famous and more influential.

In 1842, Dadd was invited to go on an expedition (as a draftsman) by Sir Thomas Phillips. The ten-month tour wound through Europe into Greece, Turkey, then through Syria and into Egypt. First in Syria, and then in Egypt, Dadd began to experience violent and delusional thoughts, claiming to be under the influence of the Egyptian God Osiris. Upon his return to England in the spring of 1843, he was pronounced of unsound mind by his doctors, but was not institutionalized . . .

In August, he invited his father for a walk in the park, then stabbed him to death with a knife. He seems to have believed that his father had been possessed by the devil, and that his murder was commanded by Osiris (potentially to set the God free in some way). Mama, just killed a man . . .

Dadd fled to France, where he attempted to kill a stranger before being captured and placed in the French Asylum at Clermont for several months. He was returned to England, where he spent the rest of his life in two mental institutions: first at Bethlem Hospital (colloquially known as "Bedlam") from 1844 to 1866, and then transferring to the newly opened Broadmoor Hospital (from 1866 till his death in 1886). In total, he spent forty-two years in mental institutions.

Today he would likely have been diagnosed with violent schizophrenia, but at the time he was labeled merely as "insane"—stone cold crazy, you know? As a side note, several of his siblings also reportedly suffered from mental illness, and his brother George was later committed to Bethlem as well.

While his career as a public artist had ended, he still continued to paint. The doctors at Bethlem and Broadmoor encouraged his painting: perhaps trying to understand the man through his art, or simply appreciating his talent. He was given art supplies, and his caretakers functioned almost as "patrons," some even privately collecting many of his paintings. "The Fairy Feller's Master-Stroke" in particular was commissioned by George Henry Haydon, who was head steward at Bethlem. Dadd worked on it from 1855 to 1964. When he was scheduled to be transferred to Broadmoor, he was forced to present it to Haydon unfinished.

Dadd's murder of his father become a well-publicized event: the newspapers were quick to position him as a tragic, artistic "genius," overcome and overwhelmed by his over-active imagination. The link between artistic genius and insanity is an ancient one: Seneca the Younger attributed to Aristotle the claim that "there is no great genius without a touch of madness." Certainly the association between insanity and artistic genius was still alive and well in the middle of the nineteenth century (no doubt aided by the Romantics). Regardless, . . . for most of Dadd's lifetime, he was remembered more as an insane murderer than an artist.

It wasn't until the second half of the twentieth century that Dadd's work as an artist began to be rediscovered and newly appreciated. The sparking event for this resurgence is perhaps an unlikely one: the war.

Julian Dadd and his two brothers (Dadd's great-nephews) served in World War I: the two brothers were killed, and Julian himself was severely wounded. As a result, Julian would experience his own mental health issues, ultimately committing suicide in 1937.

During the war, the three brothers befriended the poet Siegfried Sassoon. Years later, Sassoon acquired Richard Dadd's "The Fairy Feller's Master-Stroke" as a wedding gift from his mother-in-law (his wife's grandfather being the private collector who had originally acquired it). Sassoon decided to donate it to the Tate in 1963, in memory of Julian and his brothers.

And here's a bit of trivia that's guaranteed to blow your mind . . . There was another poet who served in the Royal Welch Fusiliers along with Siegfried Sassoon and Julian Dadd—Robert Graves (whom we'll come to know in the next and final chapter)! Graves and Sassoon became close friends during the war, and often read and commented on each other's works later in life. Like Sassoon, Graves also befriended Dadd's great-nephews during the war.

It's a rather fascinating coincidence that around the same time that Brian was being inspired by Graves's *The White Goddess*, Freddie was being inspired by Dadd's "The Fairy Feller's Master-Stroke." Yet these two seemingly disparate sources of inspiration actually share this hidden connection, forged in the blood and gunpowder of World War I. Divine inspiration and poetic madness—Side White and Side Black. It's all rather fitting, I think.

With his work now housed in a prominent museum (thanks to Siegfried Sassoon), Richard Dadd began to gain popularity. The 1960s was a time in which moods were changing about mental health: the trend was toward deinstitutionalization, and the Victorian asylum system was seen as regressive (hello Foucault). Dadd was cast as a bit of a tragic symbol: a figure suffering under the repressive older system, someone the Victorian sensibility had wrongly tried to lock away and forget.

Today there are plays and biographies about his life, his work is prominently featured in major museums, and he has inspired numerous artists (most importantly for us: Freddie). How did the artwork of an insane man, painted in a mental hospital, get so popular? And what does this have to do with Freddie?

Outsider Art

In philosophy of art, works like Dadd's might nowadays be described as "outsider art," and his popularity relied in some part on a growing twentieth-century fascination with outsider art. The concept of outsider art is very fluid, and can signify different things to different people. It also holds a complex and fluid relationship to other similar "genre" designations such as: naive art, folk art, primitivism, and intuitive or visionary art. But we don't need to dive into all of that right now. For our purposes, let's say that outsider art encompasses any artistic endeavor that is disconnected from, or on the margins of (outside), mainstream culture.

In a limited sense, a work might be considered "outsider" if it's created outside of the established art community (an amorphous structure of galleries, critics, auctions, magazines, art colleges, and so on). It's in this sense that outsider art overlaps with naive art and folk art—it's not created for commercial purposes, seeking fame, or in reaction to (or consciousness of) trends or movements in the art community.

But there's a broader level here, as well—the outsider art that many find most interesting is not merely outside the artistic community, it's *outside of mainstream culture as a whole*. Art that is so original, so individual, so alien, that it doesn't seem to have a connection to the culture that it emerges from. This could include artwork by prison inmates, hermits living on the edge of society, child-made art, and possibly even animal-made art (what's more outsider than an elephant, after all). But many find that the most influential and fascinating examples of outsider art come from the art of the mentally ill.

If the artist is secluded and lives most of their life in a mental institution (as Dadd did) they are already cut off from mainstream culture in a very literal, physical sense. But as a result of their mental illness, some would argue that they are also on the margins of culture in a mental or emotional sense. Hypothetically, their unique perspective may allow them to create art that no one else is capable of.

I should note that there are some interesting ethical issues around the concept of art of the mentally ill—is a fascination with it somehow paternalistic, voyeuristic, or dehumanizing? Or is it a positive—an attempt to personalize and valorize a marginalized group that are often seen as dangerous or worthy of pity (or disgust, or fear)? I'm not gonna talk about that stuff right now, but maybe you can bring it up at your next dinner party? I dunno.

Interest in outsider art was already burgeoning at the beginning of the twentieth century. But I suspect that it was the war—with the millions of soldiers coming home injured in body, mind, and spirit—that really prompted the movement. In 1922, the German psychologist and art historian Hans Prinzhorn wrote his *Artistry of the Mentally Ill (Bildnerei der Geisteskranken)*, which is a seminal work in the philosophy of outsider art.

As we saw with Dadd, nineteenth-century psychologists had already sought to understand and diagnose their mentally ill patients by analyzing the art that they created. But Prinzhorn was one of the first to treat the art of the mentally ill as something aesthetically valuable in its own right, rather than a tool for diagnosis. The book would prove influential for a number of art movements at the time.

In particular, the French artist Jean Debuffet was inspired by Prinzhorn's work, and in 1948 he founded "*La Compagnie de l'art brut*" or "The Company of Raw Art" with a number of other artists and thinkers. By the way, while the term "outsider art" is more common in English-speaking countries today, Debuffet's term *art brut* ("raw art") is still frequently used. So now you know. The goal of Debuffet's "company" was to discover, promote, and preserve the works of outsider artists. Debuffet's own personal collection is now housed in Switzerland as the "*Collection de l'art brut,*" a museum dedicated to outsider art.

With all that said, when Sassoon donated "The Fairy Feller's Master-Stroke" to the Tate in 1963, it didn't take long for it to gain attention and popularity as a significant example of the *nouveau* trend of Outsider Art. The painting (and the tragic story of its creator) spoke to the times.

Freddie—the Master-Stroke

So that's all of the necessary context. You understand the painting, the painter, and the Zeitgeist that brought this particular painting to this particular museum. Good work making it here! Now we can return to a young musician, standing in front of a peculiar fairy painting at a museum in London. What draws him to this painting in particular? What inspires him to write a song about it?

I've already said that a general fascination with Victorian fairytale symbolism doesn't seem like the whole picture (in my opinion). Now that we know a bit more about Dadd, and the history of outsider art, perhaps we can go a bit deeper. Could it be that Freddie recognizes something in Dadd? Is there a sense of kinship there, from one outsider to another?

Let's consider the facts. Ethnically Iranian (or: Persian), Freddie was an immigrant, growing up in Zanzibar and India before moving to England. His family was Parsi, so they practiced Zoroastrianism—meaning that in addition to being an immigrant, he was from a small religious minority not well understood (and an object of anti-Persian or anti-Iranian bigotry).

He was born with hyperdontia, having four supernumerary incisors—while not extremely disfiguring, these certainly altered his facial appearance and pronunciation, giving him a slight lisp. He was known to be self-conscious about his extra teeth (covering them with his hand when he smiled), although he refused to surgically remove them out of the belief that they contributed to his vocal range and resonance.

And then, of course, he was also gay (or bisexual, depending on whom you ask) in a country that only "legalized" homosexuality in 1967, three years after he first arrived.

Certainly a gay immigrant from a religious minority with an unusual facial structure and a lisp has every right to feel like an outsider, if anyone does. And yet, it's not that simple, is it? Because whatever Freddie may have *felt* (and of course we can only speculate), he *wasn't* an outsider, at least not in the sense of outsider art.

Despite being almost painfully shy in his private life, to the public he was a star—flamboyant and vibrant, witty and charming, raunchy and exciting. This young man, seemingly destined for outsider status, had instead risen to the top of British (and in many ways: international) culture. The outsider had penetrated to the very center of his culture, and was being celebrated.

And it's this contradiction, this tension, that I find very interesting about Freddie. We could debate the contributing factors that led to this unique circumstance. Certainly some of it was luck, and some of it was innate talent. But it seems to me that a lot of it was sheer determination. Even while growing up in Zanzibar and India, Freddie was fascinated with Western music. As a school boy, he formed a rock group (The Hectics), playing piano and consciously striving to imitate the likes of Elvis, Little Richard, and Fats Domino. He made the decision to start going by "Freddie" rather than "Farrokh," although that probably had as much to do with being bullied as it did with a desire to fit into Western culture.

Regardless, when his family moved to England (which Freddie was greatly excited by), he made a concerted effort to anglicize himself—seeking a clean break from his earlier life. After graduating from art college, he decided not to pursue life as an illustrator. Instead, he threw himself fully into the possibility of a music career. He was fastidious about his style and appearance, working endlessly to imitate his musical icons, especially Jimi Hendrix.

In short, his appearance, clothing, stage presence, and rock icon attitude were things that he carefully constructed. This is not to say that he was inauthentic; merely to point out that much of Freddie's life was a carefully executed project of self-curation, built around an ideal image of himself as a rockstar—an image that he had held since childhood.

To me, that history is part of what may have drawn Freddie to Dadd's "The Fairy Feller's Master-Stroke." Dadd, the outsider, whose painting is now being improbably celebrated, hung in a premier art gallery. I think that contradiction speaks to Freddie's own life, to his struggles with his outsider aspects (and his own growing cultural recognition). Freddie was not an outsider, on the surface. And maybe he didn't even feel like an outsider, then or ever (although his shyness and lifelong privacy might signal otherwise).

But I think that he was, at the very least, *haunted* by the ghost of an outsider Freddie. A Freddie who wasn't able to "crack the nut"—to penetrate into the heart of British culture, to leave behind the shell of his previous life. A Freddie (or Farrokh) whose music remains unheard, unsung. The dying rock dreams of a Persian boy in India, singing Elvis to himself at night—until he gives up the music, gives up the pain of what might have been . . .

Was Freddie Mercury ever haunted by Farrokh Bulsara? Did he reminisce on what he had to leave behind: the cost of becoming an "insider"? I'm sure it was no "bed of roses," despite all of the fame and fortune it brought him. Did he empathize with Dadd? It wouldn't take more than a slight twist of history to put Freddie in a mental institution himself—after all, homosexuality was still being treated as a mental illness into the 1970s (and even today, in some quarters).

He could have been locked up, "treated" with electrical shocks or drugs intended to make him throw up at the thought of sexual relationships with another man—so-called 'aversion therapy'. Of course, we might wish to more accurately replace the terms 'treatment' or 'therapy' with another "T" word here. But that's not where Freddie ended up, thankfully.

So that's my favorite Freddie. Standing in front of a painting as a young man—a ghost hanging over his shoulder, and visions of success and stardom burning in his eyes. With all of the determination and intensity of that little figure in the painting, preparing to crack open the nut, Farrokh forged for himself a new 'carriage of dreams'.

The Master-Stroke of this particular fairy fella (Farrokh Bulsara) wasn't any particular melody, song lyric, or bit of showmanship—it was the creation of "Freddie Mercury." The single decisive swing that cracked open a culture, creating a place for this gay Zoroastrian immigrant boy: this "quare fellow." A vehicle that allowed Freddie to reach into the mindless sleep of people everywhere and plant a spark of dream, as the Queen of Fairies herself had done (a fellow Queen).

A rock dream. A dream of belonging—like a shooting star, leaping through the sky. Thanks for the dreams, Freddie. Thanks for the music.

20
Worshiping the White Queen (As It Began)

JARED KEMLING

Could you believe me if I told you that the members of Queen were the secret prophets and priests of an ancient goddess from before the dawn of history? That they were another entry in a long line of British poets (including Shakespeare and Keats) who got their artistic and symbolic powers through a mystical connection to a pan-European, bronze-age moon goddess?

In full disclosure: even as I write it, I'm not absolutely certain of it. But it would be cool, right? And I'm a big fan of the rule of cool.

And . . . isn't there *something* a bit pagan and wild about Queen? Doesn't just a *tiny* part of you want to believe? Just enough that you'll read through to the end of this chapter . . . right? Good. So we're all agreed.

As It Began

But before we get to moon goddesses: some preliminaries. Just to set the stage. When you're a child (at least in my experience), you absorb songs out of the cultural aether years before you become conscious of the names, labels, and bands that go along with them. In my case, the only early musical passion to take concrete form was Buddy Holly, whom I loved from a young age. And I suspect the clarity of my interest had a great deal to do with *The Buddy Holly Story* (the biopic with Gary Busey) that I would watch obsessively. The movie gave a shape and a face to the music. The rest of my musical taste was an inchoate mix of oldies (which in my day meant the music of the Fifties and Sixties) and whatever was available on the radio.

It wasn't until I was a bit older (maybe ten to thirteen) that I began to interest myself in not just songs, but *bands*: I started wanting to know who was behind the music. I would ask: who sings that song? And that song? And I remember distinctly—there were two names that came up time and time again. The Beatles . . . and Queen (incidentally, two groups who were big fans of Buddy Holly). It's an odd feeling to find out after the fact that many of your favorite songs come from the same band. So that sparked my curiosity. As I got old enough to start buying my own CD's I picked up a greatest hits album (if memory serves: the *Platinum Collection*, which came out in 2000, when I was thirteen).

My love for Queen was cemented by a high school belting "Killer Queen" on late night car rides, "Good Old-Fashioned Lover Boy" around bonfires, and "Bicycle Race" at the Drama cast party (from the jukebox at the local Denny's). Ever since, Queen has been my easy answer to that dreadful question of "favorite band" (even if the real answer is more complicated than that).

Procession/Progressive

Once I moved beyond the greatest hits and into their actual albums, *Queen II* quickly became my favorite. I have a special fondness for all of their early, more progressive (and eclectic) albums; but the imagery and themes of *Queen II* spoke to me (a life-long lover of all things fantasy and mythology). It expanded on the prog-rock promise of tracks from their debut like "Great King Rat" and "My Fairy King," as well as providing the most epic Queen song of all time, "The March of the Black Queen" (sorry "Bohemian Rhapsody").

Queen II was also a step up, production-wise: the band's eponymous debut album had been recorded in bits and pieces at Trident Studies over the entirety of 1972 (during late-night studio downtime when Trident artists such as Elton John, David Bowie, and Paul McCartney weren't in the studio). While the debut album was ambitious in many aspects, the band had been dissatisfied with the production on it; many fans still find the original mixes muddied (especially compared to the 2011 remasters, which are now the standard versions).

In contrast, *Queen II* was recorded in a month (August 1973), featuring many songs that had been written during the sessions for the first album (or even stretching back to the members pre-Queen groups). With *Queen II*, the band now had the freedom and the resources to push their technical studio ambitions to the next level. The result was the birth of the textured studio sound (overdubs, complex vocal harmonies, and ambitious song structures) that the band came to be known for. "The March of the Black Queen" in particular was so overdubbed that the tape went transparent and (supposedly) even snapped. *Queen II* was also the first album to feature Brian May playing his handmade "Red Special" guitar through John Deacon's handmade "Deacy Amp"—a combo which would create the uniquely versatile and glowing guitar tones that May is now famous for.

Rather than the more traditional 'A' and 'B', the band labeled the sides of *Queen II* "Side White" (mostly Brian May's songs, plus Roger Taylor's "The Loser in the End") and "Side Black" (entirely Freddie Mercury's compositions). The iconic album cover featured the

Mick Rock photograph of the band's heads floating in a diamond formation on a black backdrop (an image later immortalized in the Bohemian Rhapsody music video). Meanwhile, the album interior continues the Black/White theme with a photo of the band dressed all in white against a white backdrop. *Queen II* advanced the band's ambitions in almost every way: songwriting, production, and imagery. Speaking of, let's take a moment to consider the imagery of the band, shall we? By imagery, I mean: how they presented themselves, styled themselves, what kind of aura and mythology they created.

Queen/Mother

It doesn't take a close examination of Queen's catalog to see that the band is drawn to the theme (and symbolism) of strong female figures. The name of the band itself is obviously evocative here. It was Freddie who had suggested the name Queen, and while he was aware of the gay overtones, he found the imagery to be universal, immediate, and open to many interpretations. Ultimately, he was hoping to convey that the band was a regal British rock band in line with the glam rock and progressive spirit of the times—although he admitted to worrying the name would make them seem like more of a pop group than they were (at the time, anyway).

However, the focus on feminine imagery goes far beyond the band's name. A number of songs famously make use of mother figures: from the "Mama" that the mournful killer in Bohemian Rhapsody cries out to, to Roger Taylor's ode to mothers everywhere in Side White's "The Loser in the End." We see this theme throughout their career, from the character "Mother Mercury" mentioned in "My Fairy King" on the debut album, all the way through the track "Mother Love" on their final studio album *Made in Heaven*.

In addition to mother figures, they also wrote a number of songs centered on characters described as Queens, such as the tantalyzing *femme fatale* featured in "Killer Queen." However, in my opinion, the most interesting use of Queenly characters are the opposed pair featured on *Queen II*. We have the White Queen from Side White's "White Queen (As It Began)," and the Black Queen from Side Black's "The March of the Black Queen." These tracks anchor their respective sides, and are the foundation for the mythological and narrative structure of the album.

Black/White

"The March of the Black Queen" is a glorious panoply of excess, glam, and dark Victorian fairy tales. It features obscure lyrical references to water babies, blue powder monkeys, and tattooed pies (incidentally, if anyone knows the meaning of that last one, please let me know). The Black Queen reigns with her left hand, rules with her right, and is queen of the night. Freddie's lyrics are certainly open to interpretation, but seem (to me at least) to draw from sources such as the legends of the Pied Piper, Sweeney Todd, and Jack and the Beanstalk (specifically the giant's attempt to bake bread out of Jack's bones). The Black Queen is a powerful chthonic figure: with the ability to mesmerize and control, she roams the land leaving terror and death in her wake.

"My Fairy King" from the first album also features a direct quotation from Robert Browning's *The Pied Piper of Hamelin*. In many ways "My Fairy King" is a thematic precursor to, and narrative partner of, "The March of the Black Queen." Fans speculate that both songs (as well as several others) describe characters and events taking place in the fictional land of Rhye: a fantasy world Freddie created with his sister Kashmira as children (which may have been inspired by his childhood in Zanzibar, as well as his Zoroastrian heritage). This world is most famous for its appearance in Queen's first hit single "Seven Seas of Rhye," the final track of *Queen II,* which trails out with a rendition of "I Do Like to Be Beside the Seaside" (taken by some as further evidence tying Rhye back to tropical Zanzibar).

However, as interesting as the Black Queen is—it's the White Queen side of the pair that I'm most interested in discussing here. May's "White Queen (As it Began)" was written before (and likely inspired) Freddie's darker take. May wrote the song during studio sessions for the first album (summer of 1972); however, the song ended up being held for the second album. On a personal level, he wrote the song about a girl at Imperial College London that he admired from afar for years, but never spoke with.

However, another, more *interesting* (from a philosophical standpoint) influence on the song was a book May was reading at the time: *The White Goddess* by Robert Graves. May, thinking about this student that he worshiped from afar, put two and two together, and wrote a song inspired by Graves's work. It was a bonus that the mythical feminine imagery would fit perfectly with the band's recently decided upon name. Little did he know that fifty years later, his songwriting choice would inspire a philosopher to think way too much about something simple and straightforward (as philosophers are wont to do).

The White Goddess

Remember all that talk of mystical moon goddesses and whatnot that I promised you at the beginning? This is that bit. Alright, here we go. Robert von Ranke Graves (1895–1985) was a British poet, novelist, and mythologist. His most influential work is the 1948 *The White*

Goddess, the basic premise of which is that bronze age Europeans originally worshiped a primordial goddess that he refers to as the "White Goddess." He believes the central homeland of these bronze age peoples was once the Aegean coast (roughly modern Greece and Turkey).

In the second millennium B.C.E., these early peoples were displaced by a group of Indo-Europeans from the east, who worshiped a trinity of masculine deities (which he speculates were Mitra, Varuna, and Indra). Today we refer to this culture as the Indo-Iranians, but they have historically been called the "Aryan" people. The Indo-Iranian religion is seen by modern scholars as the basis for both Iranian Zoroastrianism (Freddie's familial religion!) and Indian Hinduism. The two traditions, as a result, share many Gods, names, and concepts. So basically, this Aegean tribe of goddess worshipers were kicked out of their home by the Indo-Iranians.

Graves argues that this displaced tribe, these "People of the Sea," eventually settled all over Europe, even as far as Britain and Ireland. And they brought their religion with them. According to Graves, the matriarchal religion of these people is at the heart of the myths of the Hebrews (and hence all of the Abrahamic traditions), the Ancient Greeks, and the Celts. For example, he sees traces of this older matriarchal tradition in the enduring British love for their Queens (how interesting!). So perhaps being a fan of Queen (the band) means that I too am an inheritor of this great tradition?

Graves only spends a short chapter outlining his account of the history and religion of these people. The majority of the book is a swirling analysis of poetry, mythology, and linguistics—he spends several chapters hypothesizing about the origins of the Greek and Irish (or: Ogham) alphabets, for example.

The feeling that the reader gets, at least in my opinion, is that the goal of the book is to argue that British (especially Irish and Welsh) culture is tied in a fundamental way to Greek (and to a lesser extent, Hebrew) culture. He tries to demonstrate parallels and ties between Greek and British mythology, language, culture, and religion—arguing that the British versions of the myths and stories are just as ancient as the Greek (and in many cases may represent an older, more "pure" form of the original bronze-age traditions).

Graves's theory of the White Goddess seems to be just one aspect of this larger project. In mentioning various myths, he will point out instances of matriarchal religion, but it is not quite the overarching theme of the book the way the title might suggest to a first-time reader. It's worth repeating at this point that Graves is primarily a *poet*, not an archeologist, anthropologist, or ancient historian. And he approaches the subject *as* a poet, arguing that the language of ancient poems and mythologies (and even the alphabets which comprise those poems) can tell us something important about ancient cultures. I suspect it is this poetic sentiment which drew Brian May (certainly a poet himself, amongst other things) to the work.

Graves's view of poetry is itself quite interesting. He believed that the insight poetry supplies seems to be an almost semi-mystical intuition that derives (in part) from the poet's degree of authentic understanding of the White Goddess. In other words: the White Goddess is the muse of all true poets. Only in connection to her can poetry blossom. He discusses Shakespeare, Keats, and Coleridge, for example, displaying how each (in his opinion) demonstrates a deep understanding and appreciation for the White Goddess. He finds evidence for this all over Shakespeare, but especially in the use of the witches in *Macbeth* and the depiction of Titania in *A Midsummer Night's Dream*. He also sees Keats's *Belle Dame Sans Merci* as evidence of sensitivity to the White Goddess.

Graves sees poets as the modern priests to the White Goddess. In fact, he argues that priests and poets used to be one and the same—he sees the development of a historical schism between the poetic and the sacerdotal to be a grave mistake. It is through poetry—through language, and song, and dance—that we connect to the spiritual, the mystical, and to Nature. The poet (shaman, magician, gleeman) speaks words of power and imbues meaning and power into the everyday—dividing the sacred from the profane. Perhaps Graves would be happy to know that one of the greatest rock bands of all time (and British to boot) also had an appreciation for the White Goddess? I like to think so.

The Matriarchal Religion Tradition

It might not come as a shock (based on the wishy-washy nature of his scholarship, as described above), but Graves's work was not well-received among the academic community—seen by many as overly imaginative and without substantial evidence to back up his broad claims. *Also* not surprising, perhaps, was that the book proved to be quite successful (at least as far as these things go). It was (and continues to be) very influential on the various "modern paganism" groups that were becoming increasingly popular at the time ("peace and love, man"). In other words, hippies were really into Graves and his ideas—historically accurate or not.

Whether Brian May was reading the book as an academic (remember that he has his PhD in astrophysics) or a counter-cultural enthusiast, I have no idea. However, while Graves himself might be a bit fast-and-loose with the actual historical evidence, his work is just a small part of a broader scholarly tradition arguing for the existence (and influence) of a prehistoric "matriarchal religion." This tradition still has its critics, but includes a number of thinkers more concerned with scholarly rigor (and therefore more accepted) than Graves.

The first modern thinker to argue for the importance of matriarchal religion was Johann Jakob Bachofen (1815–1887), a Swiss anthropologist and historian who, in 1861, published the (horribly titled) *Mother Right: An Investigation of the Religious and Juridical Character of Matriarchy in the Ancient World.* In *Mother Right "Das Mutterrecht,"* he argued that modern patriarchal cultures had replaced earlier matriarchal societies that emphasized the role of women (especially mothers) and worshiped primarily goddesses.

These matriarchal societies are associated with the rise of agriculture in the Neolithic, and the central goddess oversaw the most important cultural spheres of the times (such as fertility, family, and agriculture). An important example of the remnants of this earlier matriarchal heritage are the Eleusinian mystery cults of Ancient Greece, centered on the worship of Demeter (and her daughter Persephone). This cult is thought by a number of scholars to trace back at least to the Bronze Age (3300–1200 B.C.E.), pre-dating the rise of the Olympian pantheon in Greece. This parallels Graves's account of the patriarchal religions displacing (but also blending with) an earlier matriarchal tradition. Graves speculated that Zeus, Poseidon, and Hades developed out of Mitra, Varuna, and Indra.

A second figure who needs to be mentioned here is Sir James George Frazer (1854–1941). Frazer didn't believe in an early matriarchal religion—instead, he thought proto-religions were largely based around fertility cults featuring ritual kingly sacrifice (generally representing a dying-and-reviving solar god). However, his emphasis on comparing mythology (and magic) with the development of religion was hugely influential on anthropology (as well as many other fields). His classic *The Golden Bough* (first published in 1890, republished in many forms since then, and never out of print) was a large influence on Graves, and is mentioned throughout *The White Goddess*.

Another predecessor of Graves (also cited a number of times in *The White Goddess*) was the British classicist (and all-around badass, guaranteed to blow your mind) Jane Ellen Harrison (1850–1928), who lived a very interesting life. She's described by contemporary historian Mary Beard as the first woman in England to become a fully professional academic. Harrison was a founding member of the Cambridge Ritualists, a group that took inspiration from Frazer, but emphasized the primacy of ritual—they believed that we should use rituals to explain myths (not the other way around).

Lastly, a thinker who follows Graves in arguing for the matriarchal religion is renowned Lithuanian archeologist and anthropologist Marija Gimbutas (1921–1994). She was widely acclaimed early in her career for her "Kurgan Hypothesis" which argued that the homeland of the Proto-Indo-European culture (which is the linguistic and cultural ancestor of much of Europe, Iran, and India) originated from the Pontic Steppe north of the Black Sea. This hypothesis has been substantiated (although not proven definitively) by some modern genetic studies.

And yes, in case you were wondering—these Kurgan people (named after the Russian term for the barrow-hills they left behind) are the linguistic inspiration for the *Highlander* character of the same name (another Queen connection)! A much more badass name (I think we can all agree) than "The Knight," which is what the character was called in the original screenplay.

So perhaps we should understand *Highlander* as playing out a version of Graves's ancient tale: a battle between the patriarchal Kurgan, who invades the homeland of the matriarchal Connor MacLeod (a Scotsman, after all). Okay, so maybe he wasn't quite "matriarchal"—but there's *something* there in his ultimate fate as a magical conduit of love, understanding, and empathy (and he does seem to *worship* Heather, we might say). And of course, his fellow Scots *do* argue that witchcraft is the source of his immortal powers.

In her later career, Gimbutas wrote several books making an argument very similar to Graves's: that this Kurgan culture brought a patriarchal religion and culture into Europe, supplanting what she considered to be an earlier matriarchal tradition. She certainly has more scholarly credit to her name than Graves, and she provided archeological findings that she felt supported her case—nevertheless, many scholars find her matriarchal interpretations problematic (especially to the degree that they hypothesize a universal, pan-European religion).

The Triple Goddess—White, Red, Black

The goddess that both Graves and Gimbutas argue is at the center of this pan-European Ur-religion is a "Triple Goddess." A Triple Goddess is something of a feminine alternative to the Christian Trinity or the Hindu Trimurti (and to a certain extent the Greek Zeus, Poseidon, and Hades). She represents a unity of three phases or figures of the feminine—traditionally described as the Maiden (Virgin), Mother, and Crone.

In modern Neopaganism (influenced by Graves and Gimbutas), these figures may be associated with phases of the moon, as well as the territory they govern (heavens, earth, and underworld). For example, Graves says that he calls her the White Goddess because that's the first color of her "moon-trinity," but that she is equally the *white* goddess of birth and rebirth (the new, or waxing, moon), the *red* goddess of love and battle (the full moon), and the *black* goddess of death and divination (the old, or waning, moon).

Earlier, I noted that Queen made frequent references to strong feminine figures and imagery. And I mentioned how Robert Graves believed that all true poets are priests and heralds of the White Goddess. Now consider that Brian May has stated that he was reading *The White Goddess* around the time that he wrote “White Queen (As it Began),” which would be around the summer of 1972, as the band was in the studio for their first album—so the very beginning of their career.

So the question here is: what influence did Graves’s book have on Brian May’s musical philosophy (or that of the band as a whole, through May)? He remembered reading it enough to cite it as an influence for the song—but more than that, I really don’t know. Maybe he hated the book. Maybe it profoundly influenced his understanding of what it means to be a poet and an artist. Only he knows (and if you’re reading this Brian, I’d really like to know the answer).

What I *can* say is this: if we exclude the instrumental rendition of the British anthem “God Save the Queen,” the band wrote exactly three songs titled after a Queen. We have “White Queen (As It Began)”—a song about the beginnings of love for a pure young maiden, as the night grows pale, with stars of lovingness in her hair. We have “Killer Queen,”—about a self-confident, mature woman who is just as ready to drive you wild with passion as she is to bathe red with blood in explosions of dynamite and gunpowder. And finally, we have “The March of the Black Queen,” about a grim figure coming in the dead of night to cut men down to size and make them march to her tune.

If that isn’t exactly Graves’s white goddess of birth and rebirth, red goddess of love and battle, and black goddess of death and divination—then I don’t know what is. So, were Queen prophets and priests of Graves’s moon goddess all along? Were they (intentionally or unintentionally) channeling their connection to this pagan deity into their music?

Maybe it's just a coincidence, if you believe in coincidences. But I think that (following the rule of cool) we could say that Queen is carrying on a British tradition that Robert Graves claims stretches back for millennia. They are poets and priests of a primordial sort, inviting us to worship with song and dance, connecting us modern listeners to these ancient triune figures—keeping them vital in a new age, and in a new way. And that's some *Mutterrecht* I can get behind.

Bibliography (I Want It All)

Adorno. Theodor W., and Max Horkheimer. 1997. *Dialectic of Enlightenment*. Verso.

Aquinas, Thomas. 2022. *The Summa Theologica: Treatise on the Angels*. John Laney.

Aristotle. 1935. *Aristotle, From Natural Science, Psychology, The Nicomachean Ethics.* Odyssey Press.

——. 2002. *The Nicomachean Ethics*. Oxford University Press.

Augustine. 2003. *Concerning the City of God against the Pagans*. Penguin.

Babbitt, Irving. 1979 [1924]. *Democracy and Leadership*. Liberty Fund.

———. 1991 [1919]. *Rousseau and Romanticism*. Routledge.

Balashov, Yuri. 2011. Persistence. In Callender 2011.

Bengtsson, Jan Olof. 2006. *The Worldview of Personalism: Origins and Early Development*. Oxford University Press.

Blake, Mark. 2012 [2010]. Is This the Real Life? The Inside Story of Queen. Da Capo.

———. 2016. *Freddie Mercury: A Kind of Magic*. Backbeat.

———. 2022. *Magnifico! The A to Z of Queen*. Permuted Press.

Bortolotti, Lisa. 2013. Rationality and Sanity: The Role of Rationality Judgements in Understanding Psychiatric Disorders. In Fulford et al. 2013.

Bourne, Craig. 2011. Fatalism and the Future. In Callender 2011.

Callender, Craig, ed. 2011. *The Oxford Handbook of Philosophy of Time*. Oxford University Press.

Chusid, Irwin. 2000. *Songs in the Key of Z: The Curious Universe of Outsider Music*. A Capella.

Diogenes Laertius. 1991. *Lives of Eminent Philosophers*. Volume II. Harvard University Press.

Dainton, Barry. 2010. *Time and Space.* McGill-Queens University Press.

Doll, Darci. 2020. *A Eudaimonistic Critique of Heteronormativity*. PhD dissertation. Michigan State University.

Eiss, Harry. 2012. *The Fairy Feller's Master-Stroke*. Cambridge Scholars.

Emerson, Ralph Waldo. 2021 [1841]. *Self-Reliance: The Original 1841 Essay.* Thames and Hudson.

Everley, Dave. 2020. How Prog Were Queen? *Prog* (July 18th).

Faeelin. 2004. Pythagoras in Persia. <www.alternatehistory.com/forum/threads/pythagoras-in-persia.3381>.

Fulford, K.W.M., Martin Davies, Richard G.T. Gipps, George Graham, John Z. Sadker, Giovanni Stanghellini, and Tim Thornton, eds. 2013. *The Oxford Handbook of Philosophy and Psychiatry*. Oxford University Press. <https://doi.org/10.1093/oxfordhb/9780199579563.013.0030>.

Fraassen, Bas van. 1970. *An Introduction to the Philosophy of Time and Space*. Random House.

Graves, Robert. 1966. *The White Goddess: A Historical Grammar of Poetic Myth*. Farrar, Straus, and Giroux.

Grünbaum, Adolf. 1974. *Philosophical Problems of Space and Time*. Reidel.

Huggett, Nick, Carl Hoefer, and James Read. Absolute and Relational Space and Motion: Post-Newtonian Theories. *The Stanford Encyclopedia of Philosophy* (Fall 2021). <https://plato.stanford.edu/archives/fall2021/entries/spacetime-theories>.

Hume, David. 1742/2011. Of the Delicacy of Taste and Passion. In *Essays* <https://www.gutenberg.org/files/36120/36120-h/36120-h.htm>.

——. 1760. Of the Standard of Taste. In Modern History Sourcebook: David Hume <https://sourcebooks.fordham.edu/mod/1760hume-taste.asp>.

Inglis, Ian. 2013. *Popular Music and Television in Britain*. Ashgate.

Jones, Leslie-Ann. 2011. *Freddie Mercury: The Definitive Biography*. London: Hodder and Stoughton.

MacGregor, John M. 1989. *The Discovery of the Art of the Insane*. Princeton University Press.

Marcel, Gabriel. 1949. *Being and Having*. Dacre Press.
———. 1951. *The Mystery of Being, vol. 2, Faith and Reality*. Translated by G. S. Fraser. The Harvill Press.
———. 1962. *Homo Viator: Introduction to a Metaphysic of Hope*. Regnery.
Marchetti, Sarin, ed., 2022. *The Jamesian Mind*. Routledge.
Martin, Bill. 1996. *Music of Yes: Structure and Vision in Progressive Rock*. Open Court.
Maudlin, Tim. 2015. *Philosophy of Physics: Space and Time*. New Jersey: Princeton University Press.
May, Brian, and Simon Bradley. 2014. *Brian May's Red Special: The Story of the Home-made Guitar that Rocked Queen and the World*. Hal Leonard.
Mozersky, Joshua. 2011. Presentism. In Craig Callender, ed. *The Oxford Handbook of Philosophy of Time*. Oxford University Press.
Nussbaum, Martha, and Juha Sihvola, eds. 2002. *The Sleep of Reason: Erotic Experience and Sexual Ethics in Ancient Greece and Rome*. University of Chicago Press.
Pattison, Robert. 1987. *The Triumph of Vulgarity: Rock Music in the Mirror of Romanticism*. Oxford University Press.
Plato. 1954. *The Last Days of Socrates*. Penguin.
———. 1989. *Plato: The Collected Dialogues*. Princeton University Press.
Power, Ed. 2016. There Can Only Be One: Why *Highlander* Will Live Forever. *Telegraph*, June 16th <www.telegraph.co.uk/films/2016/06/16/there-can-only-be-one-why-highlander-will-live-forever>.
Purvis, Georg. 2011 [2007]. *Queen: Complete Works*. Titan.
Queen Official YouTube Channel. 2016. Queen—A Kind of Magic Interviews. YouTube Video, 12:24, January 4th <https://youtu.be/wKTyBWDX4aQ>.
Queen. Save Me. Live from Hammersmith <https://www.youtube.com/watch?v=yWULxtWCShk>.
Richards, Matt, and Mark Langthorne. 2018 [2016]. *Somebody to Love: The Life, Death, and Legacy of Freddie Mercury*. Weldon Owen.
Ryn, Claes G. 1997 [1986]. *Will, Imagination, and Reason: Babbitt, Croce, and the Problem of Reality.* Transaction.
Savitt, Steven. 2011. Time in the Special Theory of Relativity. In Callender 2011.
Scruton, Roger. 1998. *An Intelligent Person's Guide to Modern Culture.* Duckworth.

Seneca. 1989. *Ad Lucilium Epistulae Morale*s *Volume III*. Translated by Richard Gummere. Harvard University Press.

———. 1994. *Moral Essays Volume I*. Harvard University Press.

Shook, John R. 2022. The Will to Believe in One's True Being: Love and God for William James and Gabriel Marcel. In Sarin Marchetti, ed., *The Jamesian Mind*. Routledge.

Sklar, Lawrence. 1988. *Space, Time, and Spacetime*. University of California Press.

Smeenk, Chris, and Christian Wüthrich. 2011. Time Travel and Time Machines. In Callender 2011.

Tekin, Serife. 2011. Self-Concept through the Diagnostic Looking Glass: Narratives and Mental Disorder. *Philosophical Psychology* 24:3 (June) <https://doi.org/10.1080/09515089.2011.559622>.

Tromans, Nicholas. 2012. Richard Dadd's Master-Stroke. March 14th <https://publicdomainreview.org/essay/richard-dadds-master-stroke>.

Vailati, Ezio. 1997. *Leibniz and Clarke: A Study of Their Correspondence*. Oxford University Press.

Weinberg, Steven. 1972. *Gravitation and Cosmology*. Wiley.

Bohemian Biographies

Editors

JARED KEMLING is just old enough to have had a cd collection as a teenager—and ever since he first got his hands on Queen's *Platinum Collection,* he's had a go-to answer for that paralyzing question: "What is your favorite band?" After a year or two playing rock music in clubs as a high-schooler, he decided that the academy would be more comfortable than a sweaty tour bus, and he became a philosopher—so that was probably the right choice . . . right? He has served as editor for a variety of academic journals, and his first edited volume—*The Cultural Power of Personal Objects*—was released in December 2021. He is a longtime fan of the Pop Culture and Philosophy series, and is excited to be a part of it.

RANDALL E. AUXIER is old enough to be Jared Kemling's daddy, but happens not to have had any such children (that he knows about). There was an advantage here, however, in that he first fell in love to the strains of "Bohemian Rhapsody" and got broken up with by a girl singing "You're My Best Friend" to him at the park, when he thought they would be doing something else. There is something quite tantalizing about Queen's music for those who watched it unfold. They had their own rules. What would they do next? Auxier wrote *Metaphysical Graffiti: Deep Cuts in the Philosophy of Rock* (2017), and *As Deep as It Gets: Movies and Metaphysics* (2021); he co-edited books on Bruce Springsteen, Tom Petty, and The Wizard of Oz, and actually has a long list of scholarly books and articles as well, and some textbooks on logic, persuasion, and communication, because that pays better than writing academic or pop culture books.

Chapter Authors

Snita Ahir-Knight has been a visiting scholar in philosophy and a teaching fellow in ethics at Te Herenga Waka—Victoria University of Wellington, Aotearoa, New Zealand. Her main research interests include mental disorder and health care. She also has a current and established career as a social worker and child and adolescent therapist, which informs her philosophical research. Her clinical background includes working with children, youth and their families in the United Kingdom and Aotearoa New Zealand. She says the song "Don't Stop Me Now" helps her to push through trail runs, and she's justified in feeling sadness about never seeing the classic line-up of Queen perform live.

Jan Olof Bengtsson is the author of *The Worldview of Personalism: Origins and Early Development* (2006). A special issue of *The Pluralist* was devoted to the book in 2008. Bengtsson has taught the history of ideas at Lund University in Sweden.

Living in the shadow of the Old Main tower of Kutztown University in Pennsylvania, **Robert DeVall** lives with his wife Louise, four children, and four active cats. When not occupied with his duties as a shipping manager, he enjoys reading philosophy, running 5ks, and practicing two systems of aikido in nearby Allentown.

Darci Doll practices a certain kind of magic as an assistant philosophy professor at Delta College. In addition to pop culture, Darci studies a crazy little thing called love in the context of Aristotelian virtue ethics. She has published in other volumes such as: *The Ultimate Supernatural and Philosophy, The Handmaid's Tale and Philosophy, Black Mirror and Philosophy,* and *Better Call Saul and Philosophy.*

Steven Gimbel is Professor of Philosophy at Gettysburg College where he held the Edwin T. and Cynthia Shearer Johnson Chair for Distinguished Teaching in the Humanities. He is author of *Einstein's Jewish Science: Physics at the Intersection of Politics and Religion*; *Einstein: His Space and Times*; and *Isn't that Clever: A Philosophy of Humor and Comedy*.

Christopher M. Innes teaches philosophy at Boise State University in Idaho. Music is understood in philosophy, and Innes uses a lot of music in his teaching. The fundamentals are still perplexing, but this does not stop him from revising his textbook (published in early 2021) that he uses in his undergraduate philosophy classes. His specialty is in social and political philosophy, where the questions about the mysteries of government and who should be in charge go unanswered.

Bohemian Biographies

Andrew Kaplan has been pondering the relationship of philosophy to other interests for several years now. Currently based out of Philadelphia (the City of Brotherly Love no less), he is currently taking a pandemic-induced break from academia, working at Lehigh University in their admissions department, although a return to the fold is likely in the near future. His first exposure to philosophy as an academic was in his first undergraduate year, and although his former advisor still reminds him he didn't understand a word of the first reading, pondering large, abstract ideas has become a constant feature of his life.

Julie Kuhlken is a recovering philosophy professor who keeps falling off the wagon and writing yet another unpaid essay. This compulsive behavior has killed innumerable trees in the service of aesthetics, practical philosophy, and political philosophy. Her day job is to 'taste' wine at Pedernales Cellars, the winery she owns in the Texas Hill Country, but she reminisces not too fondly of her days as a professor, having taught at Misericordia University, Concordia University, and Goldsmiths College in the UK. She indulges in her habit with the lowlifes of the Southwestern Philosophical Society who enable her by sending her articles to review and comment upon.

In the spirit of Neil Young and the Scorpions, **Michael F. Patton** has been rocking people like a hurricane for a long time. He is the author (with illustrator Kevin Cannon) of *The Cartoon Introduction to* Philosophy (2015). After teaching at the university level since 1990, in places as varied as Lodi, NJ and Hilo, HI, he is now Emeritus Professor of Philosophy at the University of Montevallo in Montevallo, Alabama. He rocks people at conferences and the occasional adjunct teaching gig while living and loving with his wife, Cheryl, and their four misanthropic cats.

Douglas Rasmussen earned his Master of Arts degree in English Literature from the University of Saskatchewan where he wrote on the TV series *Breaking Bad* and continues to contribute essays on various aspects of film and popular culture. His subjects have ranged from *Star Trek*, to *Judge Dredd, Scream,* action films, Quentin Tarantino, and Japanese cult cinema. He has been a fan of the band Queen ever since his youth, even if the robot on the cover of *News of the World* always did creep him out.

Kristina Šekrst is a researcher who turns speculation into reality, and a philosopher who does the opposite. She teaches courses in Philosophy and Linguistics at the University of Zagreb. Her main philosophical interests include logic, philosophy of science, philosophy of language and philosophy of film. She first listened to

Queen on a record player, as a twelve-year-old anti-social nerd. Mumbling the middle part of "Bohemian Rhapsody" all the time did not, surprisingly, help her social life.

JOHN R. SHOOK teaches philosophy in the Washington DC area. He has also been a philosopher at Oklahoma State University and the University of Buffalo. His areas of interest include American pragmatism, philosophy of science, ethics, and philosophy of religion. If you ask him about his favorite philosopher, he would give John Dewey. You can find his books about philosophy, science, and religion easily enough, but *The God Debates* is particularly recommended. If you haven't seen the movie *Highlander* yet, watch it immediately. If you have, watch it again. It's a kind of magic. As for John, Queen has been rocking him since the bygone days of AM radio, and their timeless artistry is endlessly inspiring.

KEVIN C. TAYLOR is an Instructor of Philosophy and Director of Religious Studies at the University of Memphis. He specializes in Japanese Buddhist philosophy, especially Zen Master Hakuin Ekaku, and has been training in Japanese swordsmanship since 1999. In addition to teaching Religion and Asian Philosophy, Taylor also teaches Data Ethics and Applied Ethics. His katana is named Thoth for the Egyptian god of wisdom.

MEGAN VOLPERT is author or editor of over a dozen books on popular culture, including two Lambda Literary Award finalists and an American Library Association honoree. She won Georgia Author of the Year for her newest work, *Boss Broad* (2019). Volpert is a part-time Assistant Professor of Interdisciplinary Studies at Kennesaw State University, has been teaching public high school English in Atlanta for over a decade and was 2014 Teacher of the Year. She writes for *PopMatters* and has edited anthologies of philosophical essays on the music of Tom Petty and the television series *RuPaul's Drag Race*.

ROBERT S. VUCKOVICH is headstrong, writing philosophical pieces is his goal, and he's been doing it for so long, taking its toll, but he's doing something constructive about it. He used to be a man with academic plans. He gave up on Kierkegaard and Dostoevsky for a more cynical view of man. Reading up on the stoics might make most people gag; yet, his discovery of Marcus Aurelius and Cleanthes is really no drag. With several ideas and projects that are way too groovy, he aims to put together a collection of papers on a classic sci-fi horror movie. And, there's nothing you can do about it at all.

Index

absolute space and time, 149, 150, 153, 260
abstraction, 12, 95, 108, 166, 225, 265
Adidas, 119, 129
Adorno, Theodor, 80–82, 84, 109
Aegean (coast), 251
Aeolian (musical mode), 220
aesthetic, 105, 113, 114, 136, 166, 184, 185, 239, 265
aether, 151, 152, 245
agriculture, 254
Ahir-Knight, Snita, 29, 30, 32, 34, 36, 38, 264
Ahriman (Angra Mainyu), 58
Ahura Mazda, 58
akousmatikoi (Pythagoreans), 169
alchemy, 64, 92–94, 96, 99
alcohol, 7, 40, 43, 210
alienation, 175
Alighieri, Dante, 113, 222
allegory (of the cave), 44
ambiguity, 80, 88, 106, 107
anesthetic, 210
"Another One Bites the Dust" (song), 130, 167–69, 190, 208
anthem, 29, 36, 38, 49, 69, 89, 108, 118, 174–76, 197, 208, 221, 257
anthropology, 252, 254, 255
anxiety, 23, 34, 37
Aotearoa (New Zealand), 37, 264
Aphrodite, 163
Apollo, 124
Apology (Platonic Dialogue), 174, 177, 180
Appiah, Kwame Anthony, 176
Aquinas, Thomas, 63, 259
Aramis, 54
Archeology, 252, 255, 256
Aristotle, 8, 9, 12, 18, 19, 21, 23, 24, 53, 92, 204, 236, 259, 264
art, 36, 78, 107, 113, 115, 143–45, 159, 161–63, 165, 167, 169, 184–87, 189, 190, 192, 231, 233–36, 238–242, 260, 265
artists, 62, 72, 74, 78, 84, 112, 186, 231, 234–36, 238–240, 247, 257
artistic, 69, 74, 90, 107–09, 113, 115, 117, 136, 143–45, 184, 185, 235, 236, 238, 245

artistry, 119, 136, 143, 239, 266
artwork, 233, 234, 238, 239
Aryans, 251
Asmoday (demon), 60, 62
Assyrians, 58, 59
astrochemist, 93
astrology, 92, 96
astronaut, 149, 154, 155
astronomy, 158
astrophysics, 80, 93, 149, 157, 173, 253
asylum, 235, 237
Athens, 123, 124, 178, 179, 203
atoms, 92, 158
Augustine, 63, 259
Aurelius, Marcus, 266
Austin, Mary, 4–9, 11, 12, 15, 17, 20, 21, 23, 24, 255
authenticity, 17, 21, 108, 109, 211, 213, 215, 252
authoritarianism, 203
Auxier, Randall E., 53, 54, 56, 58, 60, 62, 64, 66, 91, 92, 94, 96, 98, 100, 102, 104, 159, 160, 162, 164, 166, 168, 263
avant-garde, 89, 118

Babbitt, Irving, 105, 110, 112, 114, 261
Bachofen, Johann Jakob, 254
Balashov, Yuri, 259
ballad, 10, 118
Banks, Tony, 115
Baptist church, 60
bass, 95, 97–99, 164–66, 168, 189, 195
Baudrillard, Jean, 129, 130
BBC (Radio One), 153, 188, 234
The Beatles, 55, 98, 136, 246
beats (musical), 97, 98
beauty, 9, 11, 12, 63, 108, 117, 163, 185–87
Beelzebub, 5, 58, 65
Beethoven, Ludwig van, 84, 100, 101, 220
being-toward-death, 211, 212
Bengtsson, Jan Olaf, 105, 106, 108, 110, 112, 114, 116, 118, 120, 259, 264
Berkeley, George, 173
Bethlem (hospital), 235, 236
"Bicycle Race" (song), 59, 86, 88, 90, 246
bisexual, 4, 15, 20, 241
bismillah, 5
Black Sabbath, 109
Blake, Mark, 56, 259
blending (musical), 100, 102, 103, 167–69, 187
blood, 64, 83, 126, 132, 175, 178, 195, 225, 237, 257
bluegrass, 97
blues, 118, 131, 138
"Bohemian Rhapsody" (song), 4, 8, 10, 12, 69, 82, 84–87, 108, 117, 128, 168, 183, 186, 191, 218, 247, 248, 263–66
Bolan, Marc, 39
Bortolotti, Lisa, 31, 259
bourgeois (decadence), 110, 112, 120
Bourne, Craig, 259
Bowie, David, 20, 35, 36, 56, 130, 135, 161, 188, 208, 247
Bradford (England), 183
Bradley, Simon, 261
Brady, Tom, 99
Brenda (*Highlander*), 200
"Brighton Rock" (song), 111, 190
British, 11, 138, 141, 174, 241, 243, 245, 248, 250–53, 255, 257, 258
Broadmoor (hospital), 236
Brown, Clancy, 195
Browning, Robert, 249
Buckingham Palace, 116
Buddhism, 125, 197, 199–202, 223, 266
Bulsara, Farrokh (*see* Freddie Mercury), 3, 61, 65, 243

Bulsara, Kashmira, 49
Busey, Gary, 246
bushido, 196, 197, 205

Cambridge Ritualists, 255
Canaan, 58
capitalism, 109, 110
Celts, 251
chemistry, 91, 93, 94, 234
Chirpin (album), 39
Chomsky, Noam, 127–29
Chopin, Frederic, 220
chorus, 36, 39, 41, 44, 46, 47, 75, 88, 166, 223
Christianity, 58, 60, 63, 70, 106, 114, 223, 256, 262
Chusid, Irwin, 259
closeted (sexuality), 17, 131
Coleridge, Samuel Taylor, 252
Confucianism, 197, 204, 205
creativity, 23, 62, 63, 72, 74, 76, 81, 95, 135, 139, 225
critic (art, music), 16, 56, 94, 98, 101–04, 109, 110, 113, 116, 183, 184, 186, 187, 189, 190, 192, 238, 253
Croce, Benedetto, 112
cynicism (philosophy), 40, 41, 43, 81

Dadd, Julian, 237
Dadd, Richard, 112, 233–243, 262
daemonic, 106, 107, 109
Dainton, Barry, 259
Daoism, 223
Das Mutterrecht (Bachofen), 254, 258
Davies, Martin, 260
Deacon, John, 6, 86, 98, 99, 115, 160, 165, 189, 190, 195, 210, 247
Deacy Amp, 165, 247
Debuffet, Jean, 240
Def Leppard, 130
deity, 58, 123, 222, 251, 258
Delphi (oracle of), 178
Demeter, 254
democracy, 106, 114, 116, 120
demons, 58, 60–62
Devall, Robert, 207, 208, 210, 212, 214, 264
Dick, Luke, 167, 168
Dickinson, Emily, 72
Diogenes (of Sinope), 40, 41, 43, 49, 176
Dionysian, 116, 188
disco, 115, 140, 190
dogma, 63, 75, 76, 169, 177
Doll, Darci, 15, 16, 18, 20, 22, 24, 259, 264
Dostoevsky, Fyodor, 266
drugs, 7, 9, 16, 22, 80, 210, 243
drumming, 40, 50, 97, 126, 133, 137, 160–62, 164, 188, 189, 195
dualism, 60, 106, 112, 157, 166
Dungeons and Dragons, 207
Dylan, Bob, 54, 107

Ealing (art college), 234
Egypt, 58, 59, 63, 196, 235, 266
Einstein, Albert, 150–52, 264
Eiss, Harry, 260
Ekaku, Hakuin, 266
Elektra (records), 4
Eleusinian (mystery cults), 254
Emerson, Ralph Waldo, 70–78, 260
erotic, 10–12, 18, 19, 24, 63, 261
eternity, 156, 209, 220, 221, 223, 225, 226
ethics, 18, 22, 70, 72, 73, 77, 166, 173, 176, 204, 239, 259, 261, 264, 266
eudaimonia, 18, 19, 259
Europe, 57, 63, 217, 235, 251, 255, 256

Everley, Dave, 105, 112, 117, 118, 260
evil, 57, 60, 107–09, 111, 115–17, 166, 197, 214
existentialism, 107, 113, 208, 212, 215, 223, 224
Ezra, 58

Faeelin, 167, 260
Fairmont (club), 80, 88
fairy, 81, 82, 112, 212, 229, 231–37, 239–244, 247–49, 260
fame, 15, 20, 85, 191, 238, 243
family, 19, 37, 40–44, 74, 116, 141, 143, 154, 183, 185, 219, 241, 242, 254, 264
famous, 40, 81, 82, 152, 157, 161, 196, 197, 204, 209, 214, 220, 235, 247, 248, 250
fans, 39, 79, 81, 85, 86, 88, 89, 125–27, 168, 190, 195, 197, 198, 208, 210, 218, 245–47, 249, 251, 263, 265
fantasy, 88, 112, 173, 195, 196, 198, 232, 234, 247, 249
Fasil, Iman (*Highlander*), 203
fatalism, 156, 259
"Fat Bottomed Girls" (song), 86, 88, 90, 96, 119
Faust, 61, 63
Favre, Brett, 99
Fechner, Gustav, 57
feeling, 6, 11, 18, 20, 22, 29, 34, 35, 37, 55, 89, 95, 97–99, 101, 102, 104, 124, 126, 128, 131, 142, 154, 156, 158, 167–69, 189, 211, 221, 241, 242, 246, 251, 264
feminine, 248, 250, 256, 257
femme fatale, 249
fidelity, 22, 24, 225
films, 174, 198, 200, 201, 203, 204, 261, 265
Flash Gordon, 198, 207
Foucault, Michel, 237
Fraassen, Bas van, 260
France, 57, 129, 175, 235, 240
Frazer, Sir James George, 254, 255
frets, 99, 139, 140
Fulford, K.W.M., 259, 260

Gaiman, Neil, 234
gay, 7, 15–17, 19, 20, 22, 23, 54, 108, 109, 131, 232, 241, 243, 248
gender, 16, 17
genius, 37, 131, 236
Gimbel, Steven, 133, 134, 136, 138, 140, 142, 144, 264
Gimbutas, Marija, 255, 256
Gipps, Richard G.T., 260
glam (genre), 20, 39, 188, 189, 208, 248, 249
gleeman, 253
god, 5, 7, 8, 57, 58, 61, 63, 70, 71, 77, 81, 107, 116, 123, 134, 181, 192, 202, 203, 209, 213, 220, 222–24, 226, 235, 254, 257, 259, 262, 266
goddess, 145, 163, 237, 245, 250–57, 260
gods, 65, 108, 166, 167, 178, 222, 251
Goethe, Johann Wolfgang von, 61
"Good Old-Fashioned Lover Boy" (song), 15, 17, 19, 21, 23, 25, 246
Graham, George, 260
Graves, Robert, 237, 250–58, 260
Greece, 8, 10, 18, 124, 145, 163, 203, 235, 251, 252, 254, 256, 261
Grünbaum, Adolf, 260
guitars, 80, 87, 97–101, 110, 111, 116, 117, 120, 126, 127, 133, 137–141, 143–45, 159,

160, 164, 165, 173, 184, 186, 187, 189, 190, 192, 195, 218, 247, 261

Hades, 254, 256
Hagar, Sammy, 126
Hamlet, 54, 82
Hammersmith Odeon (venue), 100, 119, 183, 190, 191, 261
Hanslick, Eduard, 94
harmonics, 164
harmony (musical), 163, 168, 187, 198, 204, 205, 247
Harrison, George, 99
Harrison, Jane Ellen, 255
Hartshorne, Charles, 162
Harvard University, 134, 135
Haydn, Joseph, 220
Haydon, George Henry, 236
Heather (*Highlander*), 199, 202, 219, 221, 227, 256
heaven, 58, 61, 147, 204, 205, 248, 256
Hebrew, 58, 59, 251, 252
Hedonism, 9, 16, 22, 24, 197, 231
Hegelianism, 112
Heidegger, Martin, 208–13, 215
Hendrix, Jimi, 242
Heraclitus, 124, 125, 127, 128
hero, 57, 107–09, 116, 123, 175–77, 179, 196, 199, 226
heteronomous, 84, 85, 90
heterosexuality, 5, 19, 20
Highlander (movie), 195–202, 205, 207, 209, 215, 217–19, 221, 255, 261, 266
Hinduism, 223, 251, 256
history, 39, 54, 57, 58, 70, 72–75, 84, 98, 99, 113–15, 130, 143, 149, 152, 161, 162, 166, 179, 191, 192, 196, 213, 239, 240, 242, 243, 245, 251, 252, 253, 254, 255, 260, 264
Hobbes, Thomas, 128, 129
Hoefer, Carl, 260
Holly, Buddy, 246
holy, 57, 58, 197, 222
homophobia, 20, 65
homosexuality, 20, 241, 243
hubris, 197, 203
Huggett, Nick, 260
humanism, 105, 112
Hume, David, 185–87, 189, 260
Hutton, Jim, 16, 23
hyperdontia, 241
hyperreality, 129, 130

Iblis, 60, 62
ideology, 112, 116
illness, 29, 32, 48, 49, 231, 236, 239, 243
imagery, 20, 85, 88, 234, 242, 246, 248, 250, 257
imagination, 31, 47, 59, 86, 101, 105, 114, 135, 150, 152, 156, 215, 226, 227, 236, 253, 261
immigrant, 63, 241, 244
immortality, 62, 63, 78, 174, 195–204, 207, 209, 217–19, 221–23, 225, 226, 248, 256
Imperial College London, 80, 173, 250
impermanence, 197, 199–202
inauthentic, 211, 215, 242
India, 61, 63, 102, 241–43, 251, 255
Indo-Europeans, 251
Indo-Iranian, 251
Indra, 251, 254
industry (culture), 80, 81, 83, 84, 87–89
influence, 15, 16, 22, 33, 34, 58, 59, 84, 92, 101, 110, 114, 128, 132, 143, 179, 191, 198, 205, 235, 250, 253, 255–57
influential, 235, 239, 240, 250, 253, 254
Inglis, Ian, 101, 260

Innes, Christopher M., 183, 184, 186, 188, 190, 192, 264
"Innuendo" (song), 69, 75–78, 119, 120
insanity, 35, 201, 236, 238, 260
inspiration, 16, 38, 43, 72, 107, 112, 117, 144, 145, 157, 225, 234, 237, 238, 240, 250, 255, 266
instrumentalism, 134–37, 144
instruments, 101, 102, 111, 125, 133, 134, 136–39, 142–45, 160, 162, 164
interpretation, 3, 4, 8, 9, 18, 108, 109, 127, 131, 157, 233, 234, 248, 249, 256
interviews, 15, 19, 101, 129, 130, 153, 198, 199, 201, 234, 261
intimacy, 8, 40, 125
intuition, 72, 95, 104, 120, 136, 157, 158, 238, 252
Ionian, 166
Iran, 241, 251, 255
Ireland, 251, 252
Irrationality, 3, 30–33, 38
Isaiah (Book of), 58
Islam. 58, 59, 61, 223
Isle of Wight Festival, 131
Israel, 59
"I Wanna Testify" (song), 39–41, 45–47, 50

Jack and the Beanstalk, 249
Jackson, Michael, 190
Jagger, Mick, 161
James, Henry, 72
James, William, 261, 262
Japan, 90, 195–97, 265, 266
Jazz (album), 85–90
jazz (music), 97, 99, 160, 161, 184, 189, 190
Jesus (song), 218
Joel, Billy, 101
John, Elton, 101, 130, 161, 247
Jones, JP, 61
Jones, Leslie-Ann, 260
Journey (band), 126, 127
Judaism, 58, 59, 208, 223, 264
Judge Dredd, 265
judgment, 5, 115, 127, 160, 184, 185, 187, 189, 191, 213, 220, 259, 265
justice, 55, 77, 113, 129, 180, 203, 205
justification, 6, 18, 34–36, 43, 48, 179, 264

Kamen, Michael, 218
Kansas (band), 54, 160
Kaplan, Andrew, 3, 4, 6, 8, 10, 12, 265
Kastagir (*Highlander*), 204
Keats, John, 245, 252
Kekulé, August, 92
Kemling, Jared, 231, 232, 234, 236, 238, 240, 242, 244–46, 248, 250, 252, 254, 258, 263
key (music), 164, 220, 224, 259
keyboard, 79, 98, 102
Kierkegaard, Søren, 223, 266
Klosterman, Chuck, 94, 176
Kojiro, Sasaki, 197
Krueger, Freddie, 201
Krushchev, Nikita, 214
Kubrick, Stanley, 57
Kuhlken, Julie, 79, 80, 82, 84, 86, 88, 90, 265
Kurgan (culture), 255, 256
Kurgan (*Highlander*), 196, 197, 200–05, 255

label (records), 81, 83
Laertius, Diogenes, 41, 43
"La Marseillaise" (song), 175
Lambert, Adam, 123, 125, 127–31, 133, 195, 217
Langthorne, Mark, 4, 16, 261
"Lazarus" (song), 56

"Lazing on a Sunday Afternoon" (song), 83
Led Zeppelin, 111, 112, 208
left-handedness, 98, 102
legato, 98
Leibniz, Gottfried, 150, 262
LGBTQ+, 16–18, 22
Lydian (music), 77
"Lily of the Valley" (song), 117
lisp, 241
Lithuania, 255
logic, 31, 84, 130, 152, 157, 222, 263, 265
London, 119, 173, 183, 233, 240, 250, 260
loneliness, 131, 223
longing, 6, 11, 12, 81, 223
lovers, 6, 42, 63, 66, 219, 221, 224–27, 246
loving, 40, 46, 221, 224–26, 265
lyrics, 30, 39, 49, 70, 83, 85, 86, 106, 108, 111, 115, 119, 173, 176, 185, 208, 218, 232, 234, 243, 249

Mab, 233
Macbeth, 252
MacGregor, John M., 260
Mach, Ernst, 150
Macleod, Connor (*Highlander*), 195, 196, 198, 200–02, 204, 205, 217, 219, 226, 255
Madison Square Garden, 88, 124
madness, 29, 48, 75, 117, 236, 237
magic, 57, 92, 96, 103, 151, 152, 162, 196–99, 217, 224, 254, 256, 259, 261, 264, 266
magician, 64, 233, 234, 253
Marcel, Gabriel, 223–25, 260, 262
Marchetti, Sarin, 261, 262
Markle, Meghan, 211
marriage, 41, 42, 53, 196, 219
Mars, 89, 163
Martin, Bill, 261
Martin, Dean, 184, 188
Martin, George, 136
Marx Brothers, 86
Masamune, 196
mathematics, 20, 152, 164, 166, 167, 169
matriarchy, 251–56
Maudlin, Tim, 261
May, Brian, 3, 7, 21, 30, 49, 53, 80, 86, 87, 97, 99–101, 107, 111, 126, 130–34, 136, 138, 139, 141, 143, 144, 149, 155, 157, 158, 160, 165, 173, 184, 186, 187, 189, 190, 192, 195, 197–200, 202, 207, 209, 211, 217, 219, 221, 222, 237, 247, 250, 252, 253, 257, 261
McCartney, Paul, 98, 99, 247
media, 17, 87, 89, 90, 129
melody, 95, 111, 160, 166, 168, 186, 243
Mengele, Josef, 62, 63
Mercury, Freddie, 3–13, 15–17, 19–25, 30, 33, 35, 56, 59–61, 63, 65, 69, 72–80, 82, 86, 87, 89–91, 95, 97, 99–104, 107, 109, 115, 123–34, 136–38, 143, 144, 155, 159, 161, 165, 169, 173, 174, 181, 183, 185–88, 195, 197, 205, 208, 210, 212, 217, 219, 231–34, 237, 238, 240–44, 247–251, 259–261
Mercutio, 233
metaphysics, 9, 77, 125, 134, 135, 173, 218, 226, 260, 263
Michelson, Albert, 152
A Midsummer Night's Dream (play), 252
Minelli, Liza, 130
Minns, David, 4, 6, 7, 11
Mitra, 251, 254
Moët et Chandon (champagne), 64

Montesquieu (Charles Louis de Secondat), 57
moon goddesses, 245, 250, 256, 257
morality, 10, 18, 19, 22, 53, 70, 106, 115
mores, 8, 11, 72, 174
mortality, 62, 200, 210, 221, 225, 226
mothers, 82, 115, 116, 119, 154, 157, 158, 220, 237, 248, 249, 254, 256
Mozart, Wolfgang Amadeus, 57, 220
Mozersky, Joshua, 261
MTV, 119, 217
Mulcahy, Russell, 219
Mulder, Fox, 53
Musashi, Miyamoto, 197
muses, 54, 145, 252
museums, 231, 233, 237, 238, 240
mysticism, 159, 161, 163, 165, 167, 169, 232, 245, 250, 253
mythology, 123, 224, 247–52, 254, 255, 260

Nazism, 200, 208
neglect, 40, 42, 43, 180
Nehemiah, 58
neo-liberalism, 115
New Orleans, 80, 88
Newton, Isaac, 149, 150, 152
New York, 7, 11, 142, 176, 195
New Zealand, 37, 264
Nietzsche, Friedrich, 56–58, 65
A Night at the Opera (album), 49, 83, 86, 89, 117
Nihilism, 57, 106, 107, 112
Nolan, Christopher, 155
Norton Motorcycle, 141
nuclear (bomb), 212–15
Nussbaum, Martha, 261

Oberon, 233
octaves, 15, 139, 140, 165, 187
Ogham (alphabet), 251
"Ogre Battle" (song), 82, 187
The Onion (satire), 60
ontology, 224
Oracle at Delphi, 178, 179
Osiris, 235
Ouroboros, 92
outsider art, 238–43, 259
over-dubbed, 91, 247

paganism, 245, 253, 258, 259
painting, 62, 112, 184, 231, 233–36, 238, 240, 242, 243
pantheism, 106, 107, 110, 112–14
Parliament (band), 39
Parsi, 61, 64, 65, 241
Parsons, Alan, 136
patriarchy, 254–56
Pattison, Robert, 105–07, 109–114, 261
Patton, Michael F., 173, 174, 176, 178, 180, 265
perdurantism, 157
performance, 29, 34, 39, 40, 51, 56, 74, 79–91, 93, 100, 119, 125, 133, 135–38, 140–42, 152, 177, 183, 185, 187, 189, 190, 205, 218, 220, 264
Perry, Steve, 126, 127
Persephone, 254
Persia, 54, 57–59, 61, 63, 165, 166, 169, 241, 243, 260
persona, 82, 85, 89, 142
The Persuasions (band), 39, 41
phenomenology, 223
philautia, 10, 11
philia, 10, 12
Phillips, Sir Thomas, 235
physics, 57, 62, 92, 149–53, 156–59, 165–67, 261, 264
piano, 81, 98, 100–102, 142, 143, 167, 183, 217, 218, 220, 231, 242

Pied Piper, 249
Pineda, Arnel, 126
Pink Floyd, 83, 113, 136
Plato, 8, 18, 20, 44, 84, 203, 260, 261
pleasure, 6, 8, 12, 19, 21, 23, 24, 53–55, 85
poetry, 61, 70, 72, 78, 221, 222, 237, 245, 250–53, 257, 258, 260
politics, 61, 74, 77, 106, 128, 212–15, 264, 265
Pope, the (Christianity), 234
Poseidon, 123, 254, 256
postmodernism, 110, 114, 116
Power, Ed, 201, 261
Pratchett, Terry, 234
Prenter, Paul, 16, 17, 21
Pre-Raphaelite Brotherhood, 235
presentism, 155–57, 261
Presley, Elvis, 110, 131, 242, 243
primitivism, 238
"Princes of the Universe" (song), 163, 195, 197, 203–05
Prinzhorn, Hans, 239, 240
progressive (music), 54, 83, 84, 105, 107, 109–11, 113, 115, 117–120, 160, 208, 232, 246–48, 260, 261
prophecy, 57, 58, 65, 117, 245, 257
psychiatry, 29, 32, 259, 260
psychology, 22, 40, 50, 106, 239, 259, 262
psychosis, 29, 115, 201, 203
Purvis, Georg, 261
Pythagoras, 161, 164, 166, 168, 169, 260
Pythagoreans, 163, 165, 169

qualia, 127
quintessence, 73, 82, 90–93, 95–97, 99, 101, 103, 106, 195

Rachel (*Highlander*), 196, 200
Racism, 31, 75
Radio, 85, 138, 153, 168, 188, 234, 246, 266
Ramirez (*Highlander*), 196, 197, 199, 203
Ramones (band), 106
Rasmussen, Douglas, 69, 70, 72, 74, 76, 78, 95, 265
Ratt (band), 126
Read, James, 260
Reagan, Ronald, 109, 214
realism, 134–37, 141, 145
relativity, 110, 150, 151, 155, 156, 261
religion, 8, 18, 56–61, 65, 70, 71, 75, 76, 84, 106, 107, 112, 166, 169, 222, 223, 241, 251–56, 264, 266
Republic (Plato), 44, 203
Rhodes, Zandra, 119
rhythm, 95, 97, 101, 185, 189
Richards, David, 135–37
Richards, Matt, 4, 16, 261
Richrath, Gary, 160
riffs, 101, 111, 187, 190, 207
ritual, 31, 254, 255
Rogers, Paul, 123, 130
Romanticism, 63, 105–7, 109, 111–17, 119, 261
Rome, 163, 261
Romeo and Juliet, 233
ronin, 196
Roth, David Lee, 126
Rousseau, Jean-Jacques, 109, 114
Royal Welch Fusiliers, 237
RuPaul, 266
Russell, Bertrand, 176
Russell, Leon, 101
Ryn, Claes G., 112, 261

Sade, Marquis de (Donatien Alphonse François), 62
Sadker, John Z., 260

samurai, 196, 197, 199, 203–05
Sartre, Jean-Paul, 212–15
Sassoon, Siegfried, 237, 240
Savitt, Steven, 261
schizophrenia, 37, 236
Scotland, 185, 195, 196, 200, 202, 217, 255, 256
Scruton, Roger, 111, 113, 261
Šekrst, Kristina, 149, 150, 152, 154, 156, 158, 265
Selfhood, 72, 108
"Self-Reliance" (Emerson), 70, 72, 73, 75–77, 260
Seneca, Lucius Annaeus, 40, 45, 47–49, 51, 236, 261
sex, 7, 8, 9, 11, 12, 16, 20, 22, 23, 65, 73, 80, 88, 89
Shakespeare, William, 233, 245, 252
Shakiko (*Highlander*), 196
Sheffield, Norman, 83
Shook, John, 217, 218, 220, 222, 224, 226, 256, 262, 266
Sihvola, Juha, 261
Sinatra, Frank, 184, 188
singing, 5, 30, 33, 36, 49, 50, 73, 75–77, 82, 85, 87, 89–91, 100, 109, 111, 119, 123, 126, 128, 129, 137, 162, 168, 174–76, 183, 184, 188, 195, 205, 217, 219, 243, 246, 263
Sklar, Lawrence, 262
Smeenk, Chris, 262
Socrates, 156, 174–181, 185, 203, 261
songwriting, 55, 86, 100, 161, 167, 174, 191, 248, 250
Soviet Union, 176, 212–15
spacetime, 92, 149, 151–53, 155–57, 260, 262
Spinoza, Baruch, 176
spirituality, 59, 70, 71, 77, 112, 128, 166, 169, 218, 225, 253
Springsteen, Bruce, 127, 263
Stanghellini, Giovanni, 260
Steinman, Jim, 101
stoicism, 40, 47, 202, 266
Stradivari, Antonio, 141–43
Strauss, Richard, 57
Styx (band), 54, 160
Sweeney Todd, 249
Swigger, Jocelyn, 142, 144, 145
Switzerland, 240
swords, 34, 35, 195–97, 204, 207, 209, 219, 266
Syria, 235

talent, 54, 55, 62, 136, 142, 183–85, 187, 188, 191, 192, 211, 236, 242
Tarantino, Quentin, 265
Taylor, Kevin, 195, 196, 198, 200, 202, 204, 266
Taylor, Roger, 3, 23, 39–51, 97, 115, 125, 133, 137, 144, 161, 164, 187–89, 247, 248
Tekin, Serife, 34, 35, 262
"Tenement Funster" (song), 48
"Teo Torriatte" (song), 109, 165, 166, 169
testifying, 40, 42–44, 47, 48, 51
"The Fairy Feller's Master-Stroke" (song), 82, 112, 232–34, 236, 237, 240, 242, 243, 260, 262
"The Loser in the End" (song), 247, 248
therapy, 29, 36, 37, 243, 264
Theseus (ship of), 123, 124
Thin Lizzy, 126
Thornton, Tim, 260
Thrasymachus, 203
Three Musketeers, 54, 55, 66
thrownness (Heidegger), 209
"Tie Your Mother Down" (song), 115, 119
Titania, 233, 252
tragedy, 120, 192, 198–200, 202, 219, 221, 226, 227, 236, 237, 240

transcendence, 3, 24, 106, 112, 128, 218, 222
transformation, 4, 11, 42, 43, 58, 65, 87, 93, 96, 208, 225
Trans-Siberian Orchestra, 220
Trauer Symphony (Haydn), 220
tremolo, 139, 141
Trident Studios, 83, 247
Trimurti, 256
Tromans, Nicholas, 262
Truman, Harry S, 213
Turkey, 235, 251

utility, 6, 23, 24, 53, 114

vacuum, 151
Vailati, Ezio, 262
Van Gogh, Vincent, 95
Van Halen, 126
Varuna, 251, 254
Venus, 163
Victorian, 112, 232, 234, 237, 238, 240, 249
video (music), 5, 10, 15, 17, 30, 35, 36, 48, 87, 99, 102, 119, 205, 217, 218, 248
Virgil, 222
Vocal, 6, 15, 117, 126, 127, 129, 161, 187, 221, 241, 247
Volpert, Megan, 123, 124, 126, 128, 130, 132, 266
Vuckovich, Robert S., 39, 40, 42, 44, 46, 48, 50, 266
vulgarity, 105–7, 109–20, 261

Wakeman, Rick, 101
Wayne's World, 80, 128, 174, 181
"We Are the Champions" (song), 49, 79, 86, 108, 109, 174–77, 180
Weinberg, Steven, 262
Wembley Stadium, 79, 87, 90, 124, 130, 231
Whitman, Walt, 106
"Who Wants to Live Forever?" (song), 156, 197–201, 217–223, 225–27
wisdom, 18, 19, 53, 55, 70, 177, 179, 221, 227, 231, 266
worship, 71, 124, 245, 247, 249–251, 253–58
Wüthrich, Christian, 262

Yasna, 55
Young, Neil, 265

Zanzibar, 54, 61, 102, 161, 241, 242, 250
Zappa, Frank, 173
Zarathustra, 54, 57, 58
Zeitgeist, 240
Zellis, Brian "Jobby," 141, 142
Zen Buddhism, 125, 223, 266
Zend Avesta (Zoroastrianism), 57
Zeus, 254, 256
Zoroaster, 57–59, 61, 62, 169
Zoroastrianism, 20, 55–57, 59–61, 161, 166, 241, 243, 250, 251